FSC
www.fsc.org
MIX
Papier aus verantwortungsvollen Quellen
Paper from responsible sources
FSC® C105338

If you have any concerns about our products,
you can contact us on
ProductSafety@springernature.com

In case Publisher is established outside the EU,
the EU authorized representative is:
Springer Nature Customer Service Center GmbH
Europaplatz 3, 69115 Heidelberg, Germany

Printed by Libri Plureos GmbH
in Hamburg, Germany

CHALLENGES FOR ECONOMIC POLICY COORDINATION WITHIN EUROPEAN MONETARY UNION

Challenges for Economic Policy Coordination within European Monetary Union

Edited by

Andrew Hughes Hallett

University of Strathclyde

Peter Mooslechner

Oesterreichische Nationalbank

and

Martin Schuerz

Oesterreichische Nationalbank

SPRINGER-SCIENCE+BUSINESS MEDIA, B.V.

Library of Congress Cataloging-in-Publication data is available.

ISBN 978-1-4419-4889-2 ISBN 978-1-4757-4738-6 (eBook)
DOI 10.1007/978-1-4757-4738-6

Printed on acid-free paper

Table of Contents

Editorial

The establishment of European Monetary Union (EMU) has been a great success on a technical, legal and procedural level. Its launch marked the beginning of a new era; policymakers are now confronted with new challenges. After all, EMU accelerates economic integration in the European Union and ties the economies of the Member States closer together. However the performance of the Euro, uneven growth in output and investment, and the lack of structural reform, have raised questions about the performance of EMU in practice.

There is a general consensus on the rationale for economic policy coordination. Economic textbooks explain that the objective of macroeconomic coordination in an interdependent world is to take into account spill-over effects and avoid free riding. Taking a broad-based and pragmatic approach, we see coordination as a mix of information exchange, discussions, policy dialogue, formal agreements and jointly determined actions between policy institutions.

The existing literature on economic policy coordination, however, seems far from able to provide robust conclusions about how the necessary interaction of institutions and policies should be organized. To some extent, this may stem from the fact that the conditions under which we gained our knowledge on economic policy coordination differ greatly. The experience of some will have been shaped by a regime shift from a system of fixed exchange rates to a world of flexible exchange rates, that of others by substantial demand or supply side shocks across the system. This is why there seems to be a case for putting renewed emphasis on the subject under the new framework set by EMU.

During the 1990s, the process of creating a European Monetary Union triggered a substantial amount of theoretical and empirical research devoted to a better understanding of the consequences of this development for Europe. One central aspect of this literature is that economic policy coordination may well be a prerequisite for successfully combining the single monetary policy with the economic policies that have been left to be determined at the national level.

At the Community level a large number of coordination instruments – ranging from the "Broad Guidelines" to several "Dialogues" – already exist. This, by itself, underlines the widespread need for coordination from a political perspective. But, at the same time, important gaps have developed between different perspectives on policy coordination – the most obvious one between the rhetoric on policy coordination on the one hand and the actual results on the other hand. The situation is further complicated by the fact that, in those processes, different degrees of coordination are being targeted.

The contributions to this publication comprise mainly papers presented at a workshop on *"Challenges for Economic Policy Coordination within EMU"* organized by the Oesterreichische Nationalbank in Vienna on January 22, 1999. Furthermore, a few essays that focus on more general issues have been added to the volume. The sequence of the papers is intended to reflect a move from these rather general issues on coordination to more specific questions related to EMU.

The first paper, by *Bryant*, focuses on the topic of macroeconomic stabilization policies. He examines the institutional contexts in which cooperation takes place and reviews the historical experience from the early postwar years. Bryant considers analytical uncertainty about the functioning of the world economy as the greatest impediment to international macroeconomic cooperation. Thus, policy analysis should focus more on feasibility than desirability. A prerequisite for progress is an improved analytical understanding of macroeconomic interactions.

The policy coordination literature deals a lot with international policy spill-over effects that operate through the exchange rate. *Persson* and *Tabellini* discuss a simple static two-country model with a focus on international spill-overs via the real exchange rate. Each country has a prospective credibility problem in monetary policy. As it has an incentive to engage in competitive devaluations this implies a conflict over real exchange rates. Without any mechanisms of international coordination, two suboptimal results will emerge. Inflation will be too high and too variable, and there will be suboptimal fluctuations in real macroeconomic variables.

One crucial issue in the field of policy coordination is the role that institutions play in supporting desirable policies. In this respect, a pending question is how institutions can fulfil their surveillance tasks in practice. *Barry Eichengreen* considers the shortcomings in the area of multilateral surveillance and offers some suggestions of how to make the International Monetary Fund (IMF) a more effective crisis manager. He discusses the prospects for expanding private-sector burden sharing when a crisis strikes.

The policy lessons of the abundant literature on coordination for the unique project of Economic and Monetary Union are controversial. *Mooslechner* and *Schuerz* provide a selective review of different strands of coordination literature with a focus on their implications for EMU. Policy optimization approaches to regime analysis are juxtaposed with institutional approaches, and some general policy lessons are discussed. Specific strategic interaction problems within EMU are identified. The authors conclude that coordination within EMU will be necessary and should even gain importance in the near future.

Next, *Italianer* takes an institutional perspective on the coordination issue and describes a number of policy instruments within the European Union that have been prepared to deal with the challenge to combine a single currency for an area that is shaped by asymmetric structures with a number of national policy-making functions that have remained within national jurisdiction.

The rules of the Stability and Growth Pact are discussed rather critically by a number of authors. Firstly, *Demertzis – Hughes Hallett – Viegi* stress the point that this Pact may become a liability. They simulate different scenarios of the interaction between monetary and fiscal policy, which lead them to make the practical suggestion of an "inflation and growth targeting contract" and to argue in favor of a stronger version of accountability. Secondly, *Canzoneri* and *Diba* consider the constraints on national deficits agreed in the Stability and Growth Pact. They examine the merits of the Pact from the point of view of ensuring monetary stability and conclude that the case for such fiscal constraints is in fact weaker in the EU than in the USA.

Hughes Hallett and *McAdam* find evidence that the choice of monetary rules and the fiscal restrictions inherent in EMU do interact and affect the policy outcome. As the Stability Pact is likely to restrict the size of any fiscal interventions, a more expansionary form of monetary rule would be desirable.

In an essay on unemployment, wage developments and the policy mix in EMU, *Collignon* argues in favor of expanding the policies to be coordinated. To achieve an optimal policy mix, the role of wage bargaining has to be strengthened.

Bayer reviews the role of social partners in the coordination process, mainly from an institutional angle, and *Durand* discusses whether the new institutional arrangements influence financial markets and also tackles the issue of systemic risk.

Winkler explains – from a central bank point of view – why the European central bank, which conducts a single monetary policy aiming primarily at the objective of price stability, must in its own interest be critical of any attempt to establish a system of coordination that might restrain the options available to the central bank.

To sum it up, coordination of economic policies is happening at different institutional levels and to different degrees within EMU. Such coordination will be strengthend in the future. However, the views on the adequate policies differ enormously, as this book shows. What is necessary is to develop further our understanding what kind of coordination and which institutional setting of policy coordination can be expected to be more favorable than others. We hope that this book provides an intellectually stimulating contribution to the ongoing debate.

Andrew Hughes Hallett
Peter Mooslechner
Martin Schuerz

1. The Coordination of National Stabilization Policies: Evolution of National Policies and International Institutions*

RALPH C. BRYANT
Brookings Institution

Nations experiencing a progressive integration of their economies confront a central issue: when should their governments cooperate in making decisions about their macroeconomic stabilization policies and, if they do so, how ambitious should that cooperation be?[1]

Virtually all forms of intergovernmental cooperation entail consultations and exchanges of information. In most circumstances, such consultations and exchanges are widely thought to be beneficial. More ambitious forms of cooperation involve *coordination* of national monetary and fiscal policies. This essay is concerned with such coordination, not merely with the milder and less controversial forms of cooperation.

Three different analytical perspectives have been brought to bear on the problems of intergovernmental cooperation and coordination. Economists have most often favored a traditional policy-optimization analysis. Another strand in the literature focuses on the rule analysis of international regime environments. An institutionalist analysis has been developed by scholars in international relations and political science.[2]

From each of these perspectives, a fundamental rationale supports the case for coordinating national stabilization policies. Because economic integration across national borders has generated a growing variety and intensity of collective-action problems with international dimensions, the force of that rationale has been increasing during recent decades.

The essence of the rationale is straightforward. Decentralized national decisions that fail to take into account the cross-border spillovers from policy actions can produce outcomes that are inferior to more efficient outcomes attainable through informed collective action. The inferior outcomes are examples of situations in which negative externalities lead to "market failures". If governments consult and bargain with one another intelligently and cooperatively, they may be able to identify mutually beneficial adjustments of their policy instruments that offset the market failures and thereby permit their nations to reach higher levels of welfare.

Governmental efforts to coordinate policies will not invariably be successful. In

*The views in this study are those of the author and should not be attributed to the trustees, officers, or other staff members of the Brookings Institution.

A. H. Hallett et al. (eds), Challenges for Economic Policy Coordination with European Monetary Union, 1–25.

international coordination, as in all other areas of economics and politics, government intervention intended to remedy a market failure can be counterproductive. In some circumstances, coordination efforts can lead to "government failures" and thereby lower rather than raise welfare.

My personal eclecticism leads me to give more weight to the potential benefits of attempted coordination than to the potential risks. On the whole, international cooperation among governments can reasonably be expected – in many, though admittedly not all, circumstances – to advance the common interests of their citizens.

One reason for my bias in this direction stems from my belief in subsidiarity as a principle for governance. Subsidiarity is the presumption that decentralized allocations and exercises of political authority are to be preferred in the absence of compelling reasons for centralization. In other words, lower-level, local jurisdictions should make decisions unless convincing reasons exist for assigning them to higher-level, more central authorities, with the burden of proof always resting on the proponents of centralization.[3]

A presumption for subsidiarity is a safeguard inhibiting government officials from trying to coordinate stabilization policies with excessive zeal. When national governments respect subsidiarity as a guideline, actual coordination will be attempted only when strong evidence is accumulated suggesting that spillover externalities are causing major difficulties and that a feasible adjustment of national policies seems likely to improve the macroeconomic outlook significantly.

Can coordination of macroeconomic policies yield large gains in welfare? The existing theoretical and empirical evidence is, unfortunately, inconclusive. Estimates of the potential gains are sensitively dependent on the specific analytical model and the ancillary assumptions used in a researcher's analysis. A majority of researchers tend to the view that the incremental gains from coordination are significant but modest. Further research is required to produce a reliable consensus.[4]

Coordination of stabilization policies can be activist. That is, policymakers can exercise discretionary flexibility to alter their instrument settings and to try to identify bargains with other nations' policymakers. Alternatively, coordination can focus on rule-based national operating regimes. In that case, international cooperation comes into play mainly to establish the presumptive guidelines, agreed to internationally, that condition the rule-like constraints followed by each national government.

Some proponents of rules rather than discretion regard rules as a first-best approach to policy. Other proponents believe that activist full coordination is not feasible and that rule-based coordination, as a second best, can emulate some of the favorable consequences that would be achieved if full coordination were feasible. I see merit in both analytical approaches to coordination issues and do not rank rules as preferable to discretion, or vice versa. Much more research needs to be done on both activist and rule-based approaches. Indeed, differences of view about rules and discretion – with the associated themes of commitment, credibility, and time consistency – are among the most salient and controversial issues about all aspects of the conduct of macroeconomic stabilization policies. The debate about the domestic and international aspects is certain to continue well into the 21st century.

A major insight of institutionalist analysis is that intergovernmental cooperation, when most manifest, can be explained as regime maintenance and satisficing stabilization, and especially as the management of actual or latent crises. The presumption of diffuse reciprocity means that governments agree to cooperate because they plausibly expect to benefit over many periods on many issues, but not necessarily every period on every issue. Institutionalist analysis also calls attention to multiple-agent interactions within national governments that are ignored when national governments are assumed to make decisions as unitary actors. The institutionalist perspective is a complement to, rather than a substitute for, the policy-optimization analysis and rule analysis favored by economists. Insights about cooperation and coordination derived from all three analytical perspectives can be combined to generate a balanced and more thoughtful understanding.

Analytical uncertainty about the functioning of the world economy is, in my view, the single greatest impediment to international macroeconomic cooperation. Hence I have stressed – controversially – that the *feasibility* of cooperation and coordination, not their desirability, should be the primary focus of attention in policy analysis. Policymakers considering coordination should use all the information available to them about cross-border interactions. But they should not try to suppress differences in view attributable to different analytical models. It makes sense for policymakers engaged in international consultations to try to identify mutual adjustments in national policies that promise potential gains, as judged by any of the analytical models preferred by individual participating governments. The greater the consensus among differing models about the potential gains, the more seriously should policymakers consider implementing the mutual policy adjustments. Because of model uncertainty, however, there can be no assurance that such policy adjustments will exist in any particular circumstances.

An improved analytical understanding of macroeconomic interactions among national economies is a prerequisite for making progress on virtually every significant macroeconomic issue, positive or normative, confronting national policymakers. This improved understanding is inescapably necessary for more successful international coordination of stabilization policies, whether activist or rule based.[5]

The analytical points I have just summarized are a sound foundation for examining real-life manifestations of intergovernmental consultations and cooperation. In the remainder of this essay, I focus on the institutional contexts in which efforts at cooperation and coordination have occurred. I begin with generalizations about historical experience. I conclude with normative recommendations for facilitating progress over the medium and longer runs.[6]

Historical Experience

In the 1990s, a variety of institutional forums existed for international (as opposed to merely regional) consultations about macroeconomic policies. The most prominent were the annual summit meetings of G-7 heads of state and the periodic meetings of G-7 finance ministers and central bank governors, supplemented by contacts and meetings among the G-7 sherpas or finance ministry deputies. Other influential forums included the regular meetings of central bank governors at the Bank for International Settlements; the periodic meetings of the Interim Committee of the International Monetary Fund (IMF),[7] backed up by regular meetings of the IMF Executive Board; and meetings of ministers and of the Economic Policy Committee and its Working Parties (especially Working Party 3) at the OECD. These forums were ongoing activities. If a perceived crisis with implications for macroeconomic policies arose, the forums were sometimes also called into play for discussion and management of the crisis.

During the decades since World War II, intergovernmental consultations and cooperation about macroeconomic policies have been episodic. Periods characterized by considerable, sometimes even intense, activity alternated with times in which efforts flagged noticeably. Several of the episodes of greatest activity were initiated by periods of crisis. The effective performance and the prestige of the institutional forums tended to fluctuate up and down with the episodic cooperative efforts.

The early postwar years witnessed a flurry of activity, including the successful conclusion of top-level negotiations establishing the Bretton Woods institutions (the IMF and the World Bank) and the General Agreement on Tariffs and Trade (GATT). The Marshall Plan contributed to the rebuilding of Europe. This period in some respects was a high-water mark for economic cooperation among the largest industrial nations. It was also a period, however, in which political and economic power was unusually asymmetric. If the theory of a hegemonic power inducing "hegemonic stability" has empirical validity, the dominant position of the United States in the early postwar years probably provides the strongest evidence.

The United States did not permit the IMF to be an effective central forum for cooperation in the 1950s. European governments, led by France, began to challenge the dominance of U.S. views on international monetary issues in the 1960s. Nonetheless, the Bretton Woods era in the 1950s and 1960s maintained a fairly high degree of intergovernmental consultation. Working Party 3 of the OECD functioned quite effectively as a key forum for these discussions. The creation of special drawing rights (SDRs) in the second half of the 1960s is a noteworthy illustration of successful international macroeconomic cooperation.[8]

By the end of the 1960s, an increasingly integrated world economy and linked financial markets were experiencing greater cross-border pressures. Intergovernmental tensions about economic matters were growing. The breakdown of the Bretton Woods exchange-rate arrangements in 1971–73 and the first major increase by OPEC countries in their oil prices in 1973–74 severely strained the international institutions and the political impulses to cooperation. In response to these turbulent events, to be sure, a sustained effort was made to reconfigure the international regime environment (to "reform the international monetary system") through the negotiations of the Committee of Twenty. But in the end, only a minimalist rewriting of the IMF Articles of Agreement proved possible.[9]

The 1973–74 increases in oil prices gave rise to extensive intergovernmental discussions designed to preclude mutually defeating efforts to avoid surges in current-account deficits or competitive currency appreciations. Special oil-adjustment facilities were created within the IMF. An International Energy Agency was established. With the wisdom of hindsight, we now know that the supply-shock aspects of the increases in oil prices were not well understood at the time. Some aspects of macroeconomic policies were designed less than satisfactorily. Not all the cooperative understandings embodied in the International Energy Agency may have been wise. Even so, extensive international consultations focused on the problems. It was well recognized, and acknowledged in intergovernmental communiques, that decentralized national policies could have systemic effects that were counterproductive. I personally doubt that international cooperation focused on the oil-price increases itself created adverse consequences. My inclination is to judge international cooperation in that period as modestly successful on balance.

The annual economic summit meetings, initially including only the five largest industrial countries (G-5) but subsequently expanded to the seven largest (G-7), were initiated at Rambouillet in 1975. The 1977 London and 1978 Bonn summits, sometimes praised and even more often criticized, were the most ambitious of postwar efforts to actually *coordinate* economic policies. The second major increase in world oil prices, catalyzed by revolutionary developments and the fall of the shah in Iran, followed shortly after the 1978 summit. That dramatic, unforeseen change in world economic conditions, which is not always analyzed correctly and put into appropriate perspective in accounts of that period, accounts for much of the contentious appraisal of the Bonn 1978 summit agreement. In my view, the 1977–78 economic summit consultations are examples of modestly successful international economic cooperation.[10]

Subsequent years were characterized by continued economic turbulence. With the election of Ronald Reagan as U.S. president, a significant change in economic ideology occurred in the United States in the early 1980s – including attitudes about the benefits and costs of international cooperation. The early 1980s thus witnessed an ebbing of commitment to international discussions and cooperation, especially to consideration of the coordination of national macroeconomic policies.

By 1985 dissatisfaction with the experience of the early 1980s was high. The U.S. dollar had greatly appreciated against other major currencies. Even the U.S. government, helped greatly by the appointment in early 1985 of a differently minded Treasury secretary, had reached the conclusion that cooperative efforts to intervene in exchange markets could be beneficial. Another major international economic event in the 1980s was the inability or unwillingness of many developing nations to fully service their external debts. The resulting crises severely shook their economies and stimulated cooperative efforts to ease their debt-servicing problems.

The latter half of the 1980s thus was a time when international consultations and cooperation were again more in favor. Unlike at the Plaza Hotel meeting in September 1985, however, at which all the governments agreed on concerted exchange-market intervention that would be appropriate, the postures of the governments were frequently in conflict. Proposals for "coordination", as often in the past, were little more than hopes that *other* nations would take policy actions that would prove beneficial for the proposing nation.

Cooperation in October 1987 represents another example of successful intergovernmental consultations and coordinated crisis management. Many national stock markets fell sharply together in a period of a few days during that month. A coordinated, temporary easing of monetary policies in several of the G-7 countries (an expansion of liquidity that was subsequently reversed after confidence returned) helped to assuage worries that the market crashes would persist. Concerns that any one central bank might have had that its own currency would depreciate unduly in response to a unilateral lowering of its interest rates were dissipated when the central banks promptly acted together.[11]

In the final decade of the 20th century, the world economy was again buffeted by disruptions of global consequence. The Persian Gulf War, the reunification of West and East Germany, the collapse of the Soviet Union, and the associated repercussions in Eastern Europe caused disorder in the early 1990s. The Tequila crisis pummeled Latin America in 1995 after the devaluation of the Mexican peso. In the final years of the decade, financial turbulence reappeared in a virulent form. The epidemic of Asian financial flu that began in Thailand in July 1997 spread contagiously to many other Asian nations, notably Indonesia, Korea, Malaysia, Philippines, Hong Kong, Taiwan, and Singapore. In August 1998, the debt default in Russia and the devaluation of its currency triggered a reevaluation of credit risks throughout the world's financial markets. Even domestically within the United States and Europe, most investors ran for cover in the fall of 1998. Brazil suffered a financial crisis in January 1999. Millions of people in emerging-market nations lost their jobs, endured severe recessions, and suffered sharp declines in wealth. Many residents of wealthy nations experienced losses.[12]

Prior to the mid-1990s, consultations among major governments about cooperative changes in standards and institutions influencing cross-border finance proceeded sluggishly. The Tequila crisis of 1995 caught the governments' attention and brought more focus on financial-stability issues. Concern and cooperation subsided somewhat in 1996 and the first half of 1997. The Asian financial crises and the credit-spread turbulence that followed the Russian devaluation in 1998 created a new sense of urgency and again galvanized the momentum for international cooperation.

In old-fashioned times, one spoke of the international monetary system or the international financial system. In 1998, to suggest that there can be something new under the sun, participants in intergovernmental discussions agreed to use the term "architecture" instead of "system". Much popular discussion was thereafter devoted to "reforming the international financial architecture". And some significant progress did in fact occur.[13] With the world economy looking more robust in 1999–2000 and the world financial system showing fewer manifestations of fragility, however, there also seemed some risk of the major governments once again slowing the pace of cooperative reforms.

Generalizations from Historical Experience

My perspective on the episodic postwar experience with international macroeconomic cooperation suggests several generalizations. As with all generalizations, exceptions and details have to be suppressed.

First, recent history has been characterized by substantial variation in the types and intensities of shocks hitting the global economy and individual national economies. During periods in which shocks have been large and created major changes in macroeconomic conditions, government officials have been confronted with augmented uncertainty about appropriate adjustments in their stabilization policies. The net implications of the augmented uncertainty for intergovernmental cooperation are ambiguous. Uncertainty in general makes cooperation more difficult. Yet if the shocks have pronounced cross-border consequences and seem to threaten crisis conditions, governments also have sharply increased incentives to try to manage the crisis.

Some periods have certainly been characterized by a crisis atmosphere and have triggered intergovernmental efforts to manage the crises.[14] Variations in underlying shocks and economic conditions have thus been an important factor explaining the episodic nature of governments' efforts to consult and cooperate. Unexpected large shocks occurring after particular coordinating actions have been implemented have also been a major reason why the international coordination of macroeconomic policies is a contentious subject for debate.[15]

Second, the postwar period has been characterized by up-and-down variation in the political inputs to international macroeconomic cooperation. These fluctuations – in political awareness of the potential benefits and in the willingness to exert leadership to explore opportunities for cooperation – have been an additional factor explaining the episodic nature of cooperative activities. On the whole, I do not detect a discernible secular increase in the political willingness to cooperate. And most observers would assign the political factors a less important role than that owed to fluctuations in the nature and severity of underlying shocks.

From one perspective, it may seem surprising that the political propensity of national governments to cooperate has not gradually increased over recent decades.[16] Many types of cross-border spillovers, after all, have gradually increased in intensity. In turn these increases in interdependence have reduced the effects of an individual nation's policy instruments on national variables relative to the effects on variables in other countries. With this diminution in the relative potency of national policies, it may seem natural to expect that governments would wish to cooperate to help offset the decreased autonomy of national policies. Whether this expectation is in fact natural, or whether instead one might infer that intergovernmental cooperation is less important because policy instruments are less effective, is a difficult unresolved issue that cannot be tackled carefully here.

My third generalization is that the episodic nature of international macroeconomic cooperation cannot be attributed, at least not in a major way, to unevenness in the pace of evolution of the international institutions and forums. Although the existing institutional forums could have been strengthened somewhat, the forums themselves do not seem to me to have been a major impediment to improved consultations or to more effective efforts to coordinate policies.

Fourth, the episodic ups and downs in international macroeconomic cooperation cannot be readily explained by changes over time in the basic analytical difficulties that inhibit cooperation. (Note that I am distinguishing between institutional structures themselves, the subject of the preceding generalization, versus the analytical knowledge and resources available to them.) Owing to limited improvements in knowledge and modeling capabilities, the analytical difficulties were a bit less severe in the 1990s than in the 1950s and 1960s. Modest progress was made in the macroeconomic analysis of domestic economies. Limited but not dramatic progress was made in the analysis of cross-border macroeconomic interactions. Even so, model uncertainty remained severe throughout all the postwar decades. The small improvements in analytical understanding of the global economy are not promising candidates for explaining why some eras witnessed greater cooperative activity than others.

The preceding generalizations refer broadly to the world economic system as a whole and worldwide cooperation. If one instead focuses only on macroeconomic cooperation within regions, the generalizations have to be amended. The picture looks especially different if one concentrates on Western Europe alone. Like the global economy, regions have also experienced heterogeneous variation in the types and intensities of shocks. The basic analytical difficulties that inhibit macroeconomic cooperation are highly relevant within regions as well as among regions. But the episodic variation in *political* inputs to cooperation tend to be somewhat less pronounced within regions. The evolution of the European Community, now European Union, has been associated with a gradual, persistent increase in macroeconomic cooperation – much of it triggered by the constraints of the European Monetary System and desires for eventual European monetary union, but some of it attributable to other pressures from European regional integration. Moreover, consultative processes and institutions of the European Union have also been gradually strengthened.[17]

To add perspective, the four preceding generalizations about macroeconomic cooperation should also be seen in the light of developments in intergovernmental cooperation outside the area of macroeconomic policies. Analytical difficulties in certain regulatory or microeconomic areas, though notable, are often less an obstacle than for macroeconomic policies. Political impediments to cooperation are also sometimes less severe. Consider three examples. Problems associated with cross-border collective goods have become gradually more important in the area of the regulation and supervision of financial institutions. Quite substantial progress in dealing with these problems has occurred in the past two and one half decades, illustrated by the Concordats on supervision of banks' foreign establishments and by the capital-adequacy guidelines developed by the Committee on Banking Regulations and Supervisory Practices at the Bank for International Settlements. Bank fraud and bank failures with cross-border spillovers, such as the notorious cases of Bank of Commerce and Credit International in 1991 and Baring Brothers in early 1995, appear to have been well handled by international cooperation among bank supervisory authorities.[18] Nascent cooperative efforts in the environmental area, such as the Montreal protocol to reduce emission of chlorofluorocarbons to mitigate stratospheric ozone depletion, have borne significant fruit. Despite the agenda of accumulating problems, progress on issues pertaining to natural resources and the environment has probably outpaced progress in international macroeconomic cooperation.[19] The microeconomic area of product standards, contentious though it is, has also witnessed significant developments in international cooperation.[20] The limited but noteworthy progress in these other areas cautions against holding a pessimistic view about the long-run prospects for international cooperation about macroeconomic stabilization policies.

Given the historical experience of the postwar decades and the preceding generalizations, should one conclude that international macroeconomic cooperation has been deficient, that too little effort has been put into international consultations and too little support given to international institutions? Or given the difficulties and the domestic political constraints, should one instead be surprised that so much effort has been put into cooperative activities and that international institutions play as prominent a role as they do? Both perspectives have some validity, in my judgment, though the undramatic truth lies somewhere in between.

A verdict that macroeconomic cooperation has been deficient seems especially appropriate for a few periods, for example the early and mid-1980s, when political will flagged and the efforts of key governments to cooperate were unusually timid. In those episodes, the rhetoric in favor of enhanced cooperation, and much more so the substance, fell well short of what would probably have been feasible and desirable. Even in more auspicious periods, moreover, governments have had a propensity to be shortsighted. Typically, an individual government has favored consultations and coordination when, in effect, its own participation might induce favorable behavior by other governments, but not when the process would uncomfortably constrain its own options. Just as superstition is some other person's religion and protectionism is some other nation's commercial policy, stubborn attachment to outmoded ideas of national sovereignty inhibits *other* nations from participating in mutually beneficial efforts at international cooperation.

Nonetheless, the opposite verdict – that cooperation has been surprisingly vigorous – also contains important elements of truth. Much of political and institutionalist analysis, for example, reminds us of the domestic political structures and attitudes that constrain government officials from ambitious efforts to cooperate. All things considered, political leadership has sometimes been able to catalyze intergovernmental cooperation even when the odds would have led analysts to conclude it could not be done.

Between the two extreme verdicts, my own views are closer to the latter perspective than to the assertion that cooperation has been uniformly deficient. I would disagree sharply with an assertion that political timidity and shortsightedness have been the overriding impediments to international consultations and coordination. The lack of convergence in analytical views about how national economies interact with one another has often been an equally severe impediment.

As historical studies in other areas have shown – for example, Richard Cooper's analysis of international efforts during the nineteenth and early twentieth centuries to control the spread of contagious diseases, or Peter Haas's account of recent international agreements to ban chlorofluorocarbons to protect stratospheric ozone – governments are likely to forge an agreement for dealing with a problem only after they, or the "epistemic community" of relevant professional analysts, have reached consensus in diagnosing the problem and identifying measures that will alleviate it.[21] Consensus on an appropriate analytical framework, as well as on the objective to be pursued, is a necessary – though, again, not a sufficient – condition for successful international cooperation.[22]

Because of this last point, I reserve my harshest criticisms of the historical experience for the failure of governments to place greater emphasis on improving analytical knowledge about the functioning of the world economy. One can, it is true, point to some examples of government officials encouraging and catalyzing relevant research. OECD staff members in the 1960s and 1970s were encouraged to develop a capacity for systemic analysis of the world economy (though government support waned in the 1980s). Parts of the IMF staff in the 1980s became active in research that tried to model the world economy (though not with notable support from national governments). The Federal Reserve system in the United States continued a long tradition of supporting macroeconomic modeling. Examples can be found in several other central banks or government agencies. The study of official intervention in exchange markets resulting in the Jurgensen report and its associated staff papers is a rare illustration of background research sponsored collectively by governments.[23] By and large, however, research has not received priority attention from government officials.

Likely Evolution in the Short Run

How may cooperative efforts focused on macroeconomic policies proceed in the next few years? The best guess is that national governments will continue with roughly the same patterns of behavior they followed on average in the 1990s. If and when new shocks or new crises occur, international consultations are likely to be modestly enhanced. Possibly, some additional cooperative undertakings may be tried. But substantially increased attempts to foster an activist international coordination of policies among the large industrial countries seem unlikely, with the possible exception of strengthened regional attempts in the European Community.

The various existing institutions and forums do serve, and are perceived by national governments as serving, important communicative goals. They are the primary venues for intergovernmental consultations. Indeed, they constitute the core of the existing weak international regime environment for macroeconomic stabilization policies. I see little evidence that consultations and information exchanges through these forums became significantly more intense on average in the 1980s and 1990s.

To be sure, during times of perceived crisis – most recently and notably following the financial turbulence in Asia and Russia – consultations became more intense. That observation applies with equal force, however, to the more distant past. Speaking loosely, the regime environment has been firmly established but subject to only modest adaptations and enhancements. For the near-term future, in the absence of continued crisis situations this business-as-usual climate might well continue.

The existing procedures for international exchanges of forecasts and current economic information are an important subset of these consultations. Some of this activity occurs through the OECD and has an influence on the OECD staff's analysis in the *OECD Economic Outlook*. In recent years, as part of the G-7 consultation process and the preparation of the IMF's *World Economic Outlook*, the IMF staff has participated at least as actively as the OECD staff in such consultations. The substantive content of the G-7 consultations has been marginally improved as a result of the IMF participation. Informally, with less detail, and without public release of the analysis, an analogous exchange of views among central banks takes place at the monthly meetings of the Bank for International Settlements. As discussed below, over the longer run this type of consultation procedure can be greatly improved. For the shorter run, it seems unlikely that major changes are feasible (because governments do not appear to want them).

Beginning in the latter part of the 1980s, consultations among the G-7 nations have deemphasized exchange-rate, monetary, and budgetary policies of the G-7 nations themselves and the possible cross-border coordination of these policies. Other subjects of mutual interest have increased in relative importance. Conditions in the former Soviet Union and Eastern Europe and possible financial and technical assistance from the G-7 nations to those regions have featured prominently. Collective measures to ease the debt crisis in developing countries occupied center stage in the 1980s. Issues of financial stability and the supervision and regulation of financial institutions gained prominence after the Asian financial turbulence. Other topics have included trade policies (especially the Uruguay round of trade negotiations prior to their conclusion in 1994), energy and energy security issues, and "structural" reforms within domestic economies. For the near-term future, the tendency to concentrate on subjects other than macroeconomic policy coordination is likely to continue.[24]

The sharp depreciation of the Mexican peso after December 1994 and subsequent fears about defaults on Mexican government debt illustrate how a new crisis, especially one judged to have possible systemic implications, can catalyze reevaluation of existing procedures and institutions. In early 1995 the IMF established a very large standby lending arrangement for Mexico. Precedents and normal presumptions about the amount that an individual nation can borrow from the IMF were set aside because the circumstances were deemed exceptional. Moreover, the G-7 consultations in spring 1995 cautiously considered possible new cooperative actions – for example, the creation of an international "emergency fund" to mitigate disruptive capital flows and some form of a special "work-out facility" to smooth government-debt problems of the types associated with the Mexican crisis.

In the summer of 1995, it seemed unlikely that any of the more ambitious new proposals would command general acceptance by the G-7 or the Interim Committee. Yet the Mexican crisis, combined with sharp appreciations in the early months of 1995 of the Japanese yen and European currencies against the U.S. dollar, had at a minimum reignited old concerns and caused some governments to marginally rethink their views on international macroeconomic cooperation.

In the event, the onset in 1997 of multiple Asian financial crises, beginning with the devaluation of the Thai baht in July, occasioned still further rethinking. Large stabilization packages were negotiated for Thailand, Korea, and Indonesia. And intensified intergovernmental discussions were launched to consider major changes in the international financial architecture, including more ambitious efforts to establish international financial standards and heightened efforts to foster cooperation in the prudential oversight of financial activity.

By the fall of 1998, at the height of the uncertainty following the Russian default and ruble devaluation, the central banks of the major industrial nations all took steps to provide additional liquidity to financial markets. These expansionary actions for monetary policy were taken separately, but with considerable international consultation. As after the stock-market crashes in October 1987, the close timing and mutual supportiveness of these policy actions represented a *de facto* coordination of national monetary policies.

Desirable Changes for the Medium Run: Enhanced Analytical Support

I have stressed that an improved analytical understanding of macroeconomic interactions among national economies is a prerequisite for the development of enhanced cooperation through presumptive guidelines for rule-based national operating regimes or for more successful efforts at activist coordination. When I formulate normative recommendations for the longer-run future, therefore, my primary emphasis is on ways that governments might more actively encourage the development of analytical support for their efforts to promote strengthened "multilateral surveillance".[25]

In the past, the governments of the major countries have taken little direct interest in promoting an improvement in analytical understanding. Nor have they put pressure on the international organizations to make this objective a high priority for staff work. Such efforts as have been made have been sponsored by individual central banks, or individual groups within international organizations, or research or academic institutions.

The paucity of analytical support for international consultations has been more pronounced than can be explained by the inadequacies of existing knowledge. The series of annual summits and G-7 ministers' meetings has had even less continuity and institutional infrastructure than consultations conducted through the IMF, the OECD, or the BIS. G-7 meetings have not been backstopped by consistent staff support. The G-7 governments have not wanted to establish a new secretariat to support the G-7 process and at the same time have been unwilling to allow existing international organizations such as the IMF or OECD to become actively enough involved to play that role.[26]

This aspect of international economic cooperation is also unlikely to change in the short run. But it could – and should – be strengthened over the medium and long runs. Several years ago, I sketched a vision of how the institutional evolution of international macroeconomic cooperation might proceed.[27] In that sketch I failed to emphasize enough the importance of establishing a staff group at an international institution charged with the collective task of improving analytical knowledge about international macroeconomic interactions and diffusing that knowledge more widely. Staff support of that type, backed up by an international epistemic community, is a necessary precondition for progress of other sorts.

The IMF, or perhaps a combination of the IMF, OECD, and the World Bank, is the most logical institutional locus for this staff support for strengthened multilateral surveillance. An inferior alternative would be to establish an explicit secretariat for the G-7 and to locate the analytical staff support as part of that secretariat.[28] Several keen observers of international consultations argue for more active use of the IMF and its staff rather than creation of a competing G-7 secretariat.[29] I share that judgment, both about general staff support for the backstopping and monitoring of G-7 consultations and in particular for the location of a special support staff charged with emphasizing the analytical foundations for international cooperation about macroeconomic stabilization policies. The support staff, both general and special, could be incorporated into the IMF Research Department or lodged in a newly created IMF department.

Analytical foundations are not a sexy subject for policymakers. But over the longer run, building more solid analytical foundations is the only reliable way to improve policy debate and render policy decisions more robust to error. Progress in model evaluation and model improvement is the ultimate answer to the problem of competing models.[30]

By tradition and comparative advantage, society looks to the academic community for new knowledge to be created and analytical foundations to be rebuilt. For the area of international cooperation about macroeconomic stabilization policies, as in general, the academic community can and should play an important role in improving analytical foundations. But policymakers cannot count solely on the academic community to make sufficient progress. Most academic researchers have limited knowledge of the ways in which unresolved analytical issues surface in policy discussions. Without sustained contact with the policy community, therefore, researchers are much less likely to condition their research in ways helpful to policymakers. Even more important, the structure of incentives and rewards for advancement in the academic community inhibit academics from giving priority attention to the analytical needs of policymakers. Fellow academics accord much higher praise, and give much greater weight in decisions about university appointments, to new theoretical wrinkles published in prestigious academic journals than to thoughtful efforts to refine empirical models by better application of existing analytical knowledge. Even the small group of academic economists who develop forecasting and simulation models usable for policy analysis are reluctant to devote their limited resources to model validation and model evaluation. Few academics hand out kudos to researchers who do the hard work of identifying the deficiencies in existing analytical frameworks or who carefully try to remedy inadequacies in existing data sources. To complement and supplement academic research, policymakers thus have a strong interest in making adequate resources available for officially commissioned research in support of strengthened multilateral surveillance.

Two types of research might be commissioned from support staff lodged in the IMF. One type, the responsibility mainly of the general support staff, would focus on topics figuring prominently in discussions about current policy or policy in the immediate future. Analyses of controversial aspects of the current economic outlook, for individual economies or the world system, would typically dominate the work. The second type, the responsibility of the special support staff, would have a longer horizon. Projects would be chosen because of their potential importance as building blocks for improved analytical foundations, not because they could be expected to have an immediate pay-off.

Consider two examples of the longer-horizon type. First, the special support staff might be charged with careful evaluation of alternative rule-based national operating regimes and with alternative specifications of presumptive international guidelines for the regimes.[31] The research would have to begin with quite simplified specifications of regimes and guidelines (for both monetary and fiscal policies) before more complex and realistic alternatives could be examined. Model evaluations and comparisons would inevitably be at the core of this work.

Second, the special support staff might be tasked with defining and estimating alternative concepts of equilibrium exchange rates and of equilibrium interest rates (national and global). What normative and modeling assumptions have to be specified to identify an exchange rate deemed to be in "equilibrium"? Essentially the same analytical issues are at stake if policymakers wish to identify when a nation's exchange rate is "misaligned" or "overvalued" or "undervalued". How can policymakers tell when a nation's real interest rate (or "the global" real interest rate) is too high or too low? Under what circumstances might a policymaker conclude that an exchange rate or an interest rate should be judged "excessively variable"?

Analysts have great difficulty in supplying helpful, nontautological answers to these questions. A carefully defined equilibrium rate must be characterized as a dynamic time path rather than a single value. Any specific calculation of an equilibrium path necessarily makes use of normative assumptions and therefore cannot be "neutral" about policymakers' goals. Moreover, estimates of equilibrium paths, for exchange rates or interest rates, are inescapably contingent on the particular theoretical or empirical model(s) in the context of which the estimates are made. Because estimates are both goal contingent and model contingent, in principle a multiplicity of useful calculations of equilibrium paths may exist. Analysts and policymakers have only begun to clarify the relevant concepts and empirical procedures, despite their clear importance for national policy decisions and international cooperation.[32]

My major emphasis is on analytical research by a strengthened IMF staff, which would facilitate more effective international consultations. But there is also substantial scope for improving the public release of macroeconomic analysis already conducted by the IMF, OECD, BIS, and World Bank. For example, copious macroeconomic analysis by the IMF staff of developments within particular countries can usefully be shared with a wider public. Greater outside scrutiny can improve the analysis itself and could raise the quality of domestic policy debate. Confidentiality for certain aspects of reports and discussions of course needs to be maintained. There is a minor risk that the quality and frankness of some analysis can decline when it is made publicly available. But more transparency would, on balance, strengthen rather than weaken the IMF. Analogous points apply to many parts of the macroeconomic analyses at the OECD, BIS, and World Bank that are not currently placed in the public domain.

Happily, in very recent times substantial progress has been made along these lines. The IMF now regularly releases so-called Public Information Notices (PINs) after the annual Article IV consultations with individual countries. In 1999 and early 2000, four fifths of all completed Article IV consultations resulted in publication of PINs.[33] Still more significant, the IMF has been experimenting with publication of staff reports associated with Article IV consultations. In a pilot program initiated in 1999, individual countries could voluntarily approve release of the staff report prepared during their consultation. By the spring of 2000, 58 member nations had volunteered to participate and some 40 staff reports had been published.[34] The IMF now makes a wide range of additional staff reports and working papers available through its internet web site. The BIS, the World Bank, and the OECD have also significantly enlarged the amount of formerly-confidential material that is now released to the general public.

Collection and publication of statistical data, for national economies and for the global economy, is another collective good now supplied in some degree by international institutions but which will always require improvement and rethinking. Even within countries the quality and availability of data leave much to be desired. As regional economies and the world economy become still more integrated, the demand for reliable and consistently compiled data will increase further. International institutions must play a catalytic role in meeting this need.

The flow data available for the capital accounts of balances of payments and the corresponding stock data for nations' external-asset and external-liability positions are a salient but little emphasized example. For studying a variety of analytical questions in macroeconomics and finance for open economies, analysts require much better data on these cross-border relationships. In principle, one requires a breakdown of the balance sheets of financial institutions in all the important national jurisdictions, cross-classified by currency of denomination, residence of customer, and type of customer. Better data are certainly needed for cross-border security transactions and the corresponding stock asset and liability positions. Because off-balance sheet items such as futures, swaps, and other derivatives have become increasingly important, one needs substantial information on them as well. Ideally, over time international institutions would compile better quality and more comprehensive aggregates – national, regional, and global – for these data. Progress would gradually be made toward the ultimate objective of compiling a flow-of-funds accounts, consistent with national income accounts, for the world as a whole. The actual availability of such financial data falls very short of what is desirable in principle. Only a handful of countries have well-developed flow-of-funds accounts; and for them, the cross-border aspects are weakest. Although some potential building blocks are assembled at the BIS, the IMF, the OECD, and the World Bank, policymakers have so far given little thought to these data issues at the world systemic level.[35]

The primary impetus for enhanced analytical support for multilateral surveillance will have to come from policymakers and their advisers. But in a modest way there exists an epistemic community of individuals outside of governments and international organizations – for example, in academic institutions – who also try to advance theoretical and empirical knowledge about cross-border macroeconomic interactions. Members of this community also hope to, for example, evaluate alternative rule-based national operating regimes and alternative specifications of presumptive international guidelines. They too aspire to estimate equilibrium paths for exchange rates and interest rates. Far-sighted policymakers have a clear interest in nurturing this epistemic community, encouraging it to play an active role in developing analytical knowledge and applying that knowledge to international consultations.

A Longer-Run Vision

For the still longer run, how might international cooperation for macroeconomic policies be improved if national policymakers were to have the benefit of enhanced analytical support, both within national governments and from a secretariat located within the IMF? With the precondition of improved analytical knowledge satisfied, considerably more ambitious consultations and attempts at policy coordination would become possibilities. The evolutionary vision having the greatest appeal to me would have the following elements.[36]

One strand in the vision would extend, and deepen, the research of the IMF special support staff on analytical foundations. I have already stressed the need for and potential benefits of this activity. Like the refinement of statistical data, this activity must be a continuing obligation of the staffs of international institutions as far into the future as our imaginations can extend.

A second strand would entail gradual intensification of ongoing (lower-level) international cooperation about macroeconomic stabilization policies. Intergovernmental consultations about the current world economic outlook, backstopped by the international secretariat responsible for administrative and analytical support (the IMF general support staff), would be augmented. As a result, governments would be helped much more than at present to identify potentially fruitful opportunities for activist coordination.

Each national government participating in ongoing consultations about the current world economic situation would submit periodic projections of a "baseline outlook" to the international staff secretariat. The frequency of the projection "rounds" and meetings associated with them could vary but might presumptively be twice or three times a year.

At a minimum, each of the G-7 governments and each of the G-7 central banks would be involved. The nature of the consultations and cooperation *within* each country, involving the fiscal authority, the central bank, and other government agencies, would of course vary across the participating countries. Delicate, controversial issues of central-bank independence and the allocation of responsibilities for economic policy within governments have inhibited a deeper involvement of central banks in G-7 consultations. But more extensive involvement by the central banks would greatly improve the quality and relevance of the consultations. A key place for improving within-nation coordination is to develop strengthened interactions between the fiscal authority and the central bank in the preparation of the baseline outlook. Possibly, although not preferably, a nation's fiscal authority and central bank could submit separately prepared versions of the baseline outlook.[37]

The baseline outlook prepared by each national government would either assume "no change" in the nation's macroeconomic policies (no departures from policies presently in force) or alternatively could incorporate policy changes already decided upon or very likely to be made. Each national projection would be derived with the aid of one or more analytical frameworks (models) that try to be internally consistent. Each government, moreover, would be willing to – and would – exchange information about its models and projection methods. An individual government would concentrate most on projecting the key macroeconomic variables pertaining to its own economy. But each government would also be free to submit projections for other economies if it chose to do so.

The supporting international secretariat would also provide its own baseline projection of the outlook for each major country or region. The analytical support staff in the secretariat would make its own models and projection methods transparent to national governments. And it would function as a clearinghouse for the exchange of models and projections among governments.[38]

A wide range of quantity and price macroeconomic variables – for domestic real sectors, domestic financial sectors, balances of payments, and international markets – would be projected and reported in each baseline outlook. Some projections would be made for higher-frequency (monthly) data as well as for quarterly and annual data. Those preparing the projections would employ best-practice analytical techniques to make the projections for each frequency internally consistent. The actual instruments of each nation's monetary and fiscal policies and, of course, the ultimate-target variables of national policies, would feature most prominently. But key intermediate, indicator variables would also be included.

Treatment of exchange rates in these projections would be, no less so than now, a delicate and controversial issue. A politically safe approach would be to have all participants assume that real effective exchange rates (or, within arrangements such as the European Monetary System, nominal exchange rates) would remain unchanged from the values prevailing in a period just prior to preparation of the projections. If mutual trust were high enough and confidentiality could be maintained during the projection process, it would be analytically preferable to follow a second approach as well; in the second approach, the paths of key exchange rates would be projected endogenously.

The international secretariat would play, and would be strongly encouraged to play, a key analytical role in the evaluation of the different versions of the baseline outlook. For example, the secretariat would prepare a systematic comparison of the new baselines prepared for the current round, pointing out inconsistencies among the different nations' and the secretariat's versions. The secretariat would also systematically compare the ex ante outlooks submitted in the preceding round with updated information about ex post outcomes. An integral element of the staff support associated with this process would be the identification of analytical puzzles and gaps in knowledge that warrant further clarification and research.

Another vital component of the evolutionary process of international consultations would be "what-if simulations". Such simulations, judiciously chosen to shed light on issues of current relevance, would examine the consequences of changing this or that policy instrument. Similarly, simulations would be prepared asking: What if such and such a nonpolicy shock were to occur? Changes in macroeconomic variables resulting from these hypothetical policy and nonpolicy alterations would be measured relative to the baseline outlook. Such what-if scenarios would be prepared, at a minimum, by the international secretariat. Ideally, national governments would also prepare them, especially for changes in their own policy instruments, but even for changes in other governments' policy instruments and for various nonpolicy shocks. Differences in models would of course lead to differences in the answers to the what-if questions. No attempt would be made to suppress differences attributable to model uncertainty. On the contrary, the range of differences would be the subject of attention in the consultations and would be important grist for the mill of the analytical support group, suggesting problems with the differing models or properties needing clarification.

Periodic meetings of the national policymakers, and preparatory meetings of their deputies, would typically examine the baseline-outlook projections, some of the most relevant what-if scenarios, and the associated evaluations prepared by the secretariat. No less important, the discussions would involve frank exchanges of information about the individual governments' goals. Efforts would be made to classify differences in the baseline projections and what-if scenarios according to whether they were due to differences in identification of initial conditions (current positions of the national economies), differences in national goals, differences in preferred models, or differences in assumptions about expected future nonpolicy shocks.

The cooperative exercise envisaged here could sometimes give rise to an activist coordination of policies. Examination of the what-if scenarios would in any event keep the participating governments alert to possibilities for mutually beneficial coordination at the same time as they focused on differences among models and the risks of making errors because of model uncertainty. If the process worked well, a creative tension would be maintained and participants would continually try to balance beneficial opportunities against the possibilities for counterproductive consequences. In effect, lookouts would be posted to watch for market failures and government failures alike.

A plausible by-product of this strengthened process for ongoing consultations could be some convergence in the analytical understanding brought by policymakers to the consultations. Preferred models for describing national economies and cross-border spillovers could become less diverse. Preferences for specific rule-based national operating regimes might converge somewhat. One can even imagine that some convergence could eventually take place in the way government officials articulate national goals and identify goals that are commonly shared.

A rudimentary variant of the long-run vision outlined here could conceivably be tried in the medium run. In limited respects, it is even possible to interpret G-7 discussions in the 1990s as hesitantly groping in this direction. The most important ingredient missing from actual experience, however, has been the supporting role of a proactive international secretariat charged with catalyzing the process. Putting greater muscle into such a process will of course be contingent on continuing advances in the underlying analytical knowledge.

If we try to peer into the very distant future, we can imagine international economic cooperation on a scale not discussed in this book. The possible creation of worldwide federalist supranational institutions could become a subject for debate. The explicit harmonization of some national economic policies might be politically feasible and hence would require evaluation of the associated costs and benefits.

Coordination of national monetary policies might evolve toward a "world monetary policy" in an increasingly integrated world financial system. Issues of whether to have a common currency (or a few common regional currencies), and how to manage exchange rates among the separate currencies still in existence, would of course become paramount. Fascinating institutional issues would gain salience: for example, the possible evolution of the IMF (or an entirely new institution?) toward a world central bank and the political independence of that bank from supranational federalist institutions and from national governments.

"Fiscal policies" in that far-distant time would be even more complex and multilayered than in the world of the 1990s. One would still find national governments deciding upon and implementing national budgets. Even in such conditions, we would not speak of the explicit harmonization of national (and local) budgetary policies but rather of their coordination. Many layers of the fiscal policies would still be subject to the presumption in favor of subsidiarity, accommodating diversity in preferences, and tying governance and the provision of public goods to different political jurisdictions in which the differing preferences were manifested. But of course analysis and debate would also have to focus on the budgets of the regional and supranational institutions and their interdependence with lower-level fiscal policies and with world monetary policy.

Even to allude to these longer-run issues is to underscore the fact that they will arise only in the distant rather than the near future. For the topic of macroeconomic stabilization policies, therefore, it seems prudent for the time being not to speculate in detail about what lies ahead that far down the road. It is more productive to focus aspirations on what might be accomplished during the short and medium runs (the next decade or two). Within that time frame, the key goal should be for major governments to perceive more clearly their collective interest in establishing adequate analytical support for international macroeconomic cooperation and to give supporting groups sufficient resources and authority to foster that collective interest.

Notes

1. This essay is adapted from chapters 9 and 10 of my book, *International Coordination of National Stabilization Policies*, Washington DC: Brookings Institution, 1995. That book is part of the Brookings series of studies on Integrating National Economies, for which I was a co-organizer and editor.
2. These differing analytical perspectives are identified and reviewed in chapters 3, 4, and 5 of Bryant (1995).
3. The origins of the concept of subsidiarity lie in Catholic theology and governance practices for the Catholic church. The term has of course been widely used in Europe in recent years to discuss alternative allocations of powers within the European Union.
4. Bryant (1995, chap. 3).
5. Bryant (1995, chap. 7).
6. The focus in this essay is on macroeconomic stabilization policies. In a forthcoming book, Bryant (2000), I cast a wider net and discuss intergovernmental cooperation for all types of economic and financial policies, including potential structural reforms of the "international financial architecture".
7. In September 1999, the Interim Committee was renamed the International Monetary and Financial Committee and transformed into a "permanent" institution to meet twice annually, to be preceded by preparatory meetings at the Deputy level.
8. For the top-level negotiations and the immediate postwar period, see Gardner (1969). Solomon (1982) provides a perspective on the Bretton Woods era as a whole. Horsefield, de Vries, and others (1969), de Vries (1976, 1985) and Boughton (1999) provide more detail, including essential documents, about the IMF.
9. Solomon (1982); Williamson (1977); de Vries (1976, 1985); Fischer (1988); and Boughton (1999).
10. Putnam and Bayne (1984); Putnam and Henning (1989); and Holtham (1989a) analyze the 1977–78 summit meetings in detail.
11. For discussion of developments in the later 1970s and the 1980s, see among others Horne and Masson (1988); Putnam and Bayne (1984); Fischer (1988, 1994); Artis and Ostry (1986); Dobson (1991, 1994); Solomon (1991, 1994); and Ghosh and Masson (1994).
12. References include Goldstein (1998); Furman and Stiglitz (1998); Corsetti, Pesenti, and Roubini (1998); Radelet and Sachs (1998); Eichengreen (1999); Baig and Goldfajn (1999); Lane, Ghosh, and others (1999); and Balino, Enoch, and others (1999).
13. See, for example, IMF (1999a, 1999b, 1999c) and Camdessus (2000).
14. Several examples were already given in the preceding section. The most prominent include the sharp oil-price increases of 1973–74 and 1979–80, the developing-nation debt crises of the 1980s, the stock-market collapses of October 1987, the Tequila crisis of 1995, and the Asian and Russian financial crises of 1997–98.
15. The second oil-price shock following on the heels of the Bonn 1978 summit is the archetypal example.
16. Detecting a secular trend in the political propensity to cooperate is of course not straightforward. Empirical measures do not exist. My generalization rests on personal observation and reading over the past four decades.
17. For references about cross-border cooperation within Europe and the evolutionary adaptation of European regional institutions, see, for example, Wallace (1994); Eichengreen (1993, 1996,

1997); Kenen (1992, 1995, 1996); Giavazzi and Giovannini (1988); Sbragia (1992); Gros and Thygesen (1992); Centre for Economic Policy Research/Begg and others (1993); Møller (1995); Bakker (1996); Masson (1996); Newhouse (1997); Begg, von Hagen, and others (1998); Ungerer (1997); Masson, Krueger, and Turtelboom (1997); Buiter, Corsetti, and Pesenti (1998); and Obstfeld (1998).

18. See Bryant (1987, chap. 8), the Integrating National Economies book by Herring and Litan (1995), and Bryant (forthcoming) for discussion of international cooperation among bank regulatory and supervisory authorities.
19. For discussion of international cooperation on natural resources and the environment, see the Integrating National Economies book by Cooper (1994).
20. This area is reviewed in the Integrating National Economies book by Sykes (1995).
21. Cooper (1989); Haas (1992).
22. Dobson (1994), when discussing reasons for "divergences between normative preconditions for successful coordination and realities of G-7 experience in the 1980s", emphasizes the same point: "We learned that we do not have very good analytical tools; not enough is known about how economies actually work and how policies are transmitted across borders. In the 1990s, continuing structural change has exacerbated this situation" (p. C-145). For definition of an epistemic community and the role of such communities in international relations, see P. Haas (1992a, 1992b; also 1990) and Sebenius (1992).
23. Working Group on Exchange Market Intervention (Jurgensen and others) (1983).
24. Observers who are skeptical about the usefulness of efforts to coordinate macroeconomic policies under any circumstances, for example Polak (1981, 1991), tend to applaud the recent focus of international consultations on topics other than exchange-rate, monetary, and fiscal policies. Others with a less skeptical view, for example Dobson (1993), Bergsten and Williamson (1994), and Goldstein (1995), regret the lesser emphasis. The evolution of macroeconomic consultations and coordination in a regional context, particularly within western Europe, is again a partial exception to the trend identified in the text; see Wallace (1994); Eichengreen (1992, 1993, 1997); and Eichengreen and Wyplosz (1993, 1998).
25. The phrase "multilateral surveillance" is the most often encountered term for cooperative systemic oversight of nations' macroeconomic policies. The term surveillance stems in part from Article IV, section 3 of the IMF's Articles of Agreement, which requires the Fund to "oversee the international monetary system in order to ensure its effective operation" and, to fulfill that function, to "exercise firm surveillance over the exchange rate policies of members". Because domestic macroeconomic policies are a fundamental determinant of exchange rates, effective surveillance requires consideration of the whole range of domestic macroeconomic policies.
26. The extent to which the managing director and staff of the IMF are involved in preparatory analysis for G-7 meetings, and in the meetings themselves, is discussed in Crockett (1989); Solomon (1991); Dobson (1991, 1994); Fischer (1994); and Goldstein (1995).
27. Bryant (1990a).
28. Ikenberry (1993) advocates this option.
29. See Dobson (1991, 1994); Solomon (1991); Fischer (1994); and Goldstein (1995).
30. Dobson, speaking about the multicountry macroeconomic models available for assessing the linkages among economies in an internally consistent manner, observes that "few ministers or deputies are enthusiastic about this kind of work. They tend to distrust quantitative sophistication of this kind, even as an aid to judgment, preferring to rely on their accumulated experience and back-of-the-envelope knowledge about linkages. But this kind of work is needed to build a better shared technical understanding of the connections across economies, which eventually will feed upward into the deputies' briefings" (1991, p. 146). Solomon also points to the need for more explicit government support of "an ongoing research program on some of the unresolved analytical problems concerning coordination" (1991, pp. 110). Fischer (1994, p. C-164) emphasizes the need for the IMF "to ensure that the analytic quality of its staff remains very high, and is indeed enhanced".

31. This research would be, in effect, an intensification of the rule analysis discussed in Bryant (1995, chap. 4).
32. Preferably, the general concept of equilibrium paths for exchange rates and interest rates should not by definition exclude certain types of policy action nor embody certain policy goals to the exclusion of others. The current status of analytical understanding about equilibrium exchange rates can be reviewed in the volume edited by John Williamson (1994); see especially the essay by Stanley Black, "On the Concept and Usefulness of the Equilibrium Rate of Exchange", the essay by a group of IMF staff on "The Robustness of Equilibrium Exchange Rate Calculations to Alternative Assumptions and Methodologies", and Williamson's own contributions.
33. The use of PINs was also extended during 1999 to some IMF policy papers.
34. Prior to 1994, virtually all of the background reports, papers, and staff appraisals associated with Article IV consultations with individual countries were treated as confidential. In the fall of 1994, the IMF helpfully began to make publicly available some of the less sensitive documents associated with Article IV consultations, for example the staff reviews known as *Recent Economic Developments.* See Fischer (1994) and Goldstein (1995). The recent progress is summarized in International Monetary Fund, *Report of the Acting Managing Director ... on Progress in Reforming the IMF and Strengthening the Architecture of the International Financial System* (April 2000).
35. Bryant (1991b); Lane and Milesi-Ferretti (1999).
36. Several studies already referenced, including Dobson (1991, 1994), Solomon (1991), and Goldstein (1995), have made recommendations for strengthening international macroeconomic cooperation. See also Artis and Ostry (1986) and Bretton Woods Commission (1994). Crockett (1989) reviews the roles of international institutions in supporting and monitoring international macroeconomic cooperation. My aspirations here are more ambitious than the recommendations in those other studies because I refer to a more distant period in the future and because I make the optimistic working assumption that cooperative efforts can rest on a stronger analytical foundation.
37. Note that this focus on interactions within each national government suggests the likely inappropriateness of analyzing each government as a unitary actor (see Bryant, 1995, chap. 5).
38. The IMF's *World Economic Outlook* and the *OECD Economic Outlook* as published in the 1990s are prototypes for the baseline outlooks of the international secretariat. Similarly, the monitoring surveillance in G-7 consultations in the 1990s contains the seeds of the plant I envisage here.

References

Artis, Michael and Sylvia Ostry (1986) *International Economic Policy Coordination*, Chatham House Papers No. 30, Royal Institute of International Affairs, London, Routledge & Kegan Paul, 1986.

Baig, Taimur and Llan Goldfajn (1999) 'Financial Market Contagion in the Asian Crises', *IMF Staff Papers*, 46 (June 1999), 167–95.

Bakker, Age F.P. (1996). *The Liberalization of Capital Movements in Europe: The Monetary Committee and Financial Integration, 1958–94.* Financial and Monetary Policy Studies No. 29. Dordrecht: Kluwer Academic Publishers, 1996.

Begg, David K., Jurgen von Hagen, Charles Wyplosz and Klaus Zimmermann, eds. (1998) *EMU: Prospects and Challenges for the Euro.* Oxford: Blackwell Publishers, April 1998.

Bergsten, C. Fred and John Williamson (1994) 'Is the Time Ripe for Target Zones or the Blueprint?' In Bretton Woods Commission, *Bretton Woods: Looking to the Future (Commission Report, Staff Review and Background Papers).* Washington, DC: Bretton Woods Commission, July 1994.

Boughton, James M. (1999) *Silent Revolution: The International Monetary Fund, 1979–89.* Washington, DC: International Monetary Fund, 1999.

Bretton Woods Commission (1994) *Bretton Woods: Looking to the Future (Commission Report, Staff Review and Background Papers)*. Washington, DC: Bretton Woods Commission, July 1994.

Bryant, Ralph C. (1987) *International Financial Intermediation*. Washington, DC: Brookings Institution, 1987.

Bryant, Ralph C. (1990) 'Comment' on Jeffrey Frankel, 'Obstacles to Coordination and a Consideration of Two Proposals to Overcome Them: International Nominal Targeting (INT) and the Hosomi Fund', in William Branson and others, eds., *International Policy Coordination and Exchange Rate Fluctuations*, Chicago, University of Chicago Press, 1990, pp. 145–53.

Bryant, Ralph C. (1991) 'Concluding Observations'. In Peter Hooper and J. David Richardson, eds., *International Economic Transactions: Issues in Measurement and Empirical Research*, Studies in Income and Wealth, Volume 55. Chicago: University of Chicago Press for the National Bureau of Economic Research, 1991, pp. 476–83.

Bryant, Ralph C. (1995) *International Coordination of National Stabilization Policies*. Integrating National Economies series. Washington, DC: Brookings Institution, 1995.

Bryant, Ralph C. (2000). *Turbulent Waters: Cross-Border Finance and International Governance in the 21st Century*. Washington, DC: Brookings Institution, forthcoming 2000 (or 2001).

Buiter, Willem H., Giancarlo Corsetti and Paolo Pesenti (1998) *Financial Markets and European Monetary Cooperation: the Lessons of the 1992–93 ERM Crisis*. Cambridge: Cambridge University Press, 1998.

Camdessus, Michel (2000). 'An Agenda for the IMF at the Start of the 21st Century'. Speech in New York City before the Council on Foreign Relations. Washington, DC: International Monetary Fund, February 2000.

Cooper, Richard N. (1984) 'A Monetary System for the Future'. *Foreign Affairs*, 63 (Fall), pp. 166–84.

Cooper, Richard N. (1989) 'International Cooperation in Public Health as a Prologue to Macroeconomic Cooperation', in Cooper, Eichengreen and others, *Can Nations Agree? Issues in International Economic Cooperation*, Washington, D.C., The Brookings Institution, 1989.

Cooper, Richard N. (1990) 'What Future for the International Monetary System?' In *The Evolution of the International Monetary System*, edited by Yoshio Suzuki, Junichi Miyake and Mitsuake Okabe. Tokyo: University of Tokyo Press, 1990, pp. 277–300.

Cooper, Richard N. (1994) *Environment and Resource Policies for the World Economy*. Integrating National Economies series. Washington, DC: Brookings Institution, 1994.

Corsetti, Giancarlo, Paolo Pesenti and Nouriel Roubini (1998) 'What Caused the Asian Currency And Financial Crisis? Part I: A Macroeconomic Overview. Part II: The Policy Debate'. NBER Working Papers 6833 and 6834. Cambridge, MA: National Bureau of Economic Research, December 1998.

Crockett, Andrew (1989) 'The Role of International Institutions in Surveillance and Policy Coordination', in Ralph C. Bryant and others, eds., *Macroeconomic Policies in an Interdependent World*, Washington, D.C., International Monetary Fund, 1989, pp. 343–64.

De Vries, Margaret Garritsen (1976) *The International Monetary Fund, 1966–1971: The System Under Stress*, Washington, DC: International Monetary Fund, 1976. Two volumes: I: Narrative; II: Documents.

De Vries, Margaret Garritsen (1985) *The International Monetary Fund 1972–1978: Cooperation on Trial*. Washington, DC: International Monetary Fund, 1985.

Dobson, Wendy (1991) *Economic Policy Coordination: Requiem or Prologue?*, Policy Analyses in International Economics No. 30, Washington, D.C., Institute for International Economics, April 1991.

Dobson, Wendy (1993) 'Should G-7 Cooperation be Buried?' *International Economic Insights*, vol. 4 (May/June 1993), pp. 35–37.

Dobson, Wendy (1994) 'Economic Policy Coordination Institutionalized? The G-7 and the Future of the Bretton Woods Institution'. In Bretton Woods Commission, *Bretton Woods: Looking to the Future (Commission Report, Staff Review and Background Papers)*. Washington, DC: Bretton Woods Commission, July 1994.

Eichengreen, Barry and Charles Wyplosz (1993) 'The Unstable EMS', *Brookings Papers on Economic Activity* (No. 1, 1993), pp. 51–143.

Eichengreen, Barry and Charles Wyplosz (1998) 'The Stability Pact: More than a Minor Nuisance?' *Economic Policy*, 26 (April 1998), 65–114.

Eichengreen, Barry (1992) 'Should the Maastricht Treaty Be Saved?' *Princeton Studies in International Finance* No. 74, International Finance Section, Princeton University, December 1992.

Eichengreen, Barry (1993) 'European Monetary Unification, ' *Journal of Economic Literature*, vol. 31 (September 1993), pp. 1321–57.

Eichengreen, Barry (1994) *International Monetary Arrangements for the 21st Century* (Integrating National Economies series.) Washington, DC: Brookings, 1994.

Eichengreen, Barry (1996) 'A More Perfect Union? The Logic of Economic Integration'. *Princeton Essays in International Finance*, No. 198. Princeton, NJ: International Finance Section, Princeton University, June 1996.

Eichengreen, Barry (1997) 'Saving Europe's Automatic Stabilisers', *National Institute Economic Review*, 1/97, No. 159 (January 1997), pp. 92–98.

Eichengreen, Barry (1999) *Toward a New International Financial Architecture: A Practical Post-Asia Agenda*. Washington, DC: Institute for International Economics, 1999.

Fischer, Stanley (1988) 'International Macroeconomic Policy Coordination', in Martin Feldstein, ed., *International Economic Cooperation*, Chicago, University of Chicago Press, 1988, pp. 11–43.

Fischer, Stanley (1994) 'The Mission of the Fund'. In Bretton Woods Commission, *Bretton Woods: Looking to the Future (Commission Report, Staff Review and Background Papers)*. Washington, DC: Bretton Woods Commission, July 1994.

Fischer, Stanley (1999) 'Reforming the International Monetary System'. *Economic Journal*, 109 (November 1999), F557-F576. (Revised and updated David Finch Lecture at University of Melbourne in 1998.)

Furman, Jason and Joseph E. Stiglitz (1998) 'Economic Crises: Evidence and Insights from East Asia'. *Brookings Papers on Economic Activity*, 1998:2, 1–136.

Gardner, Richard N. (1969) *Sterling-Dollar Diplomacy: The Origins and the Prospects of Our International Economic Order*, Expanded Edition, New York: McGraw Hill, 1969 (original edition published in 1956).

Ghosh, Atish R. and Paul R. Masson (1994) *Economic Cooperation in an Uncertain World*, Oxford, Basil Blackwell, 1994.

Giavazzi, Francesco and Alberto Giovannini (1988) *Limiting Exchange Rate Flexibility*. Cambridge, MA: MIT Press, 1988.

Goldstein, Morris (1995) *The Exchange Rate System and the IMF: A Modest Agenda*. Washington, DC: Institute for International Economics, forthcoming 1995.

Goldstein, Morris (1998) *The Asian Financial Crisis: Causes, Cures and Systemic Implications*. Policy Analyses in International Economics 55, Institute for International Economics, June 1998.

Gros, Daniel and Niels Thygesen (1992) *European Monetary Integration*. New York: St. Martin's Press.

Haas, Peter M. (1990) *Saving the Mediterranean: The Politics of International Environmental Cooperation*. New York: Columbia University Press, 1990.

Haas, Peter M. (1992) 'Banning Chlorofluorocarbons: Epistemic Community Efforts to Protect Stratospheric Ozone', *International Organization*, vol. 46 (Winter 1992 special issue on *Knowledge, Power and International Policy Coordination*), pp. 187–224.

Haas, Peter M. (1992) 'Introduction: Epistemic Communities and International Policy Coordination', *International Organization*, vol. 46 (Winter 1992 special issue on *Knowledge, Power and International Policy Coordination*), pp. 1–36.

Herring, Richard J. and Robert E. Litan (1995) *Financial Regulation in the Global Economy*. (Integrating National Economies series.) Washington, DC: Brookings, 1995.

Holtham, Gerald (1989) 'German Macroeconomic Policy and the 1978 Bonn Economic Summit', in

Richard N. Cooper et al., *Can Nations Agree? Issues in International Economic Cooperation*, Washington, D.C.: The Brookings Institution, 1989.

Horne, Jocelyn and Paul R. Masson (1988) 'Scope and Limits of International Economic Cooperation and Policy Coordination', *International Monetary Fund Staff Papers*, 35 (June 1988), pp. 259–96.

Horsefield, J. Keith, Margaret G. de Vries and others (1969) *The International Monetary Fund, 1945–1965*, Washington, DC: International Monetary Fund, 1969. Three volumes: I, Chronicle; II: Analysis; III: Documents.

Ikenberry, G. John (1993) 'Salvaging the G-7'. *Foreign Affairs*, 72 (Spring 1993), 132–39.

International Monetary Fund (1999) *International Standards and Fund Surveillance – Progress and Issues*. Prepared by IMF Staff. Washington, DC: International Monetary Fund, August 16, 1999.

International Monetary Fund (1999) *Report of the Managing Director on Progress in Strengthening the Architecture of the International Monetary System*. Washington, DC: International Monetary Fund, April 1999.

International Monetary Fund (1999) *Report of the Managing Director to the Interim Committee on Progress in Strengthening the Architecture of the International Financial System*. Washington, DC: International Monetary Fund, September 24, 1999.

International Monetary Fund (2000). *Report of the Acting Managing Director to the International Monetary and Financial Committee on Progress in Reforming the IMF and Strengthening the Architecture of the International Financial System*. Washington, DC: International Monetary Fund, April 12, 2000.

Kenen, Peter B. (1992) *EMU After Maastricht*. Washington, DC: Group of Thirty, 1992.

Kenen, Peter B. (1995) *Economic and Monetary Union in Europe, Moving Beyond Maastricht*. Cambridge: Cambridge University Press, 1995.

Kenen, Peter B., ed. (1996) 'Making EMU Happen, Problems and Proposals: A Symposium', *Princeton Essays in International Finance*, No. 199. Princeton, NJ: International Finance Section, Princeton University, August 1996.

Lane, Philip and Gian Maria Milesi-Ferretti (1999) 'The External Wealth of Nations: Measures of Foreign Assets and Liabilities for Industrial and Developing Countries'. *CEPS Discussion Paper Series*, No. 2231, International Macroeconomics. London: Centre for Economic Policy Research, September 1999.

Lane, Timothy, Atish R. Ghosh, Javier Hamann, Steven Phillips, Marianne Schulze-Ghattas and Tsidi Tsikata (1999) *IMF-Supported Programs in Indonesia, Korea and Thailand: A Preliminary Assessment*. IMF Occasional Paper No. 178. Washington, DC: International Monetary Fund, 1999.

Masson, Paul R. (1996) 'Fiscal Dimensions of EMU', *Economic Journal*, Vol. 106, No. 437 (July 1996), pp. 996–1004.

Masson, Paul R., Thomas H. Krueger and Bart G. Turtelboom, eds. (1997) *EMU and the International Monetary System*. Washington, DC: International Monetary Fund, 1997.

Møller, J. Ørstrøm (1995) *The Future European Model: Economic Internationalization and Cultural Decentralization*. Westport, Conn.: Praeger, 1995.

Newhouse, John (1997) *Europe Adrift*. New York: Pantheon Books for the Council on Foreign Relations, 1997.

Obstfeld, Maurice (1998) 'EMU: Ready or Not?' *Princeton Essays in International Finance* No. 209. Princeton, NJ: International Finance Section, Princeton University, July 1998.

Polak, Jacques J. 1981. 'Coordination of National Economic Policies'. *Occasional Paper, Group of Thirty*, No. 7 (New York: Group of Thirty, 1981).

Polak, Jacques J. 1991. 'International Policy Coordination and the Functioning of the International Monetary System', in H.J. Blommestein, ed., *The Reality of International Economic Policy Coordination*, Amsterdam: North Holland, 1991.

Putnam, Robert D. and C. Randall Henning (1989) 'The Bonn Summit of 1978: A Case Study in

Coordination', in Richard N. Cooper et al., *Can Nations Agree? Issues in International Economic Cooperation*, Washington, D.C.: The Brookings Institution, 1989, pp. 12–140.

Putnam, Robert D. and Nicholas Bayne (1987) *Hanging Together: Cooperation and Conflict in the Seven-Power Summits*. Revised edition (first edition 1984). Cambridge, MA: Harvard University Press, 1987.

Radelet, Steven and Jeffrey D. Sachs (1998) 'The East Asian Financial Crisis: Diagnosis, Remedies, Prospects'. *Brookings Papers on Economic Activity*, 1998:1, 1–90.

Sbragia, Alberta M., ed. (1992) *Euro-Politics: Institutions and Policymaking in the 'New' European Community*, Washington, DC: Brookings Institution, 1992.

Sebenius, James K. (1992) 'Challenging Conventional Explanations of International Cooperation: Negotiation Analysis and the Case of Epistemic Communities', *International Organization*, vol. 46 (Winter 1992), pp. 323–66.

Solomon, Robert. (1982) *The International Monetary System, 1945–1981*, New York: Harper & Row, 1982. (Updated and expanded edition of *The International Monetary System 1945–76*, published in 1977.)

Solomon, Robert (1991) 'Background Paper' in *Partners in Prosperity: The Report of the Twentieth Century Fund Task Force on the International Coordination of National Economic Policies*, New York, N.Y., Priority Press Publications, 1991.

Solomon, Robert (1994) *The Transformation of the World Economy, 1980–93*. London: Macmillan, 1994.

Sykes, Alan O. (1995) *Product Standards for Internationally Integrated Goods Markets*. (Integrating National Economies series.) Washington, DC: Brookings Institution, 1995.

Ungerer, Horst (1997) *A Concise History of European Monetary Integration – From EPU to EMU*. Westport, CT: Quorum Books, Greenwood Publishing Group, 1997.

Wallace, William (1994) *Regional Integration: The West European Experience*. (Integrating National Economies series.) Washington, DC: Brookings Institution, 1994.

Williamson, John, ed. (1994) *Estimating Equilibrium Exchange Rates*. Washington, DC: Institute for International Economics, 1994.

Williamson, John (1977) *The Failure of World Monetary Reform, 1971–74*, New York: New York University Press, 1977.

Working Group on Exchange Market Intervention (1983) *Report of the Working Group on Exchange Market Intervention*. Phillippe Jurgensen, Chairman. Commissioned at Versailles Economic Summit in June 1982. Released by, among others, U.S. Department of the Treasury, March 1983.

2. International Monetary Policy Coordination*

TORSTEN PERSSON[†] and GUIDO TABELLINI[‡]
[†] *IIES, Stockholm University; CEPR; NBERR*
[‡] *IGIER, Bocconi University; CEPR; Ces-Ifo*

In a world of free trade and capital mobility, monetary policy is strongly interdependent across countries via international spillover effects on inflation and employment. These interdependencies create strategic interactions in policymaking. This chapter introduces some of the main ideas from the large literature on international monetary policy coordination which deals precisely with the strategic aspects of policymaking. This literature is extensively surveyed also in Canzoneri and Henderson (1991), Currie and Levine (1993), Ghosh and Masson (1994) and Persson and Tabellini (1995).

The international policy spillovers discussed in this chapter and in much of the literature operate through the exchange rate. A devaluation shifts demand away from foreign goods, towards domestically produced goods. This increases employment and inflation at home, but has opposite effects abroad. With no coordination, these spillover effects are not internalized. Thus, both countries may have an incentive to engage in so called "competitive devaluations" to boost domestic employment, and their policy response to supply shock is also distorted. In the chapter we discuss how these incentive problems interact with lack of domestic credibility, and how to design monetary institutions accordingly.

Section 1 presents a simple static model. It is a two-country version of a popular closed economy model discussed at length in our book, Persson and Tabellini (2000). This open economy version borrows from Persson and Tabellini (1995) and (1996). The model focuses on international spillovers via the real exchange rate and is consistent with the reduced form of the more extensive models in Rogoff (1985), or Canzoneri and Henderson (1988, 1991), among others. Each country has a prospective credibility problem in monetary policy. But it also has a latent incentive to engage in competitive devaluations, which implies a conflict over the real exchange rate. Section 2 shows that the equilibrium of this model suffers from two sets of distortions, in the absence of mechanisms for inducing international coordination and enhancing credibility. On the one hand, lack of domestic credibility implies that inflation is too high and too variable. On top of that, there is also a stabilization bias showing up as suboptimal fluctuations in real macroeconomic variables; this second distortion is due to the failure of individual central banks to internalize international spillovers. In this section, we also reproduce a result demonstrated by Rogoff (1985), namely that monetary policy coordination may be counterproductive

*This is a slightly edited version of chapter 18 in our book, *Political Economics: Explaining Economic Policy*, MIT Press, 2000. We are grateful to MIT Press for granting us permission to reproduce it here.

A. H. Hallett et al. (eds), Challenges for Economic Policy Coordination with European Monetary Union, 27–43.

if governments lack credibility. The argument appeals to the same kind of second-best reasoning discussed in the literature on credibility – cf. for instance Persson and Tabellini (2000), Chapter 12: coordination removes the second distortion, but aggravates the domestic credibility problem. In Section 3, we ask how to sustain desirable policies. Here, we highlight the role of institutions in supporting desirable policies. We show that a pair of optimally chosen inflation targets removes the policy distortions. But we also discuss alternative institutions that may go some way towards implementing desirable policy outcomes. The discussion puts in perspective some historical experiments with multilateral regimes for pegging the exchange rate, such as the Bretton-Woods agreement or the EMS.

I. A stylized model

There are two countries, each specializing in the production of a single good. Monetary policy can stabilize the economy in the short run, but is subject to a credibility problem. Furthermore, policy has spillover effects abroad, and each country has an incentive to engage in competitive devaluations.

All variables are defined as rates of change. The change in the log of the real exchange rate, z, is defined as:

$$z = s + p^* - p, \tag{1.1}$$

where s denotes the rate of nominal depreciation of domestic currency. We let letters without an asterisk denote variables in the "home country" and variables with an asterisk denote variables in the "foreign country". Thus, p and p^* denote producer price inflation rates in the two countries. We start by describing the home country. CPI-inflation π is given by

$$\pi = p + \alpha z, \tag{1.2}$$

where α is the share of foreign goods in the home country's consumption basket. Producer price inflation, in turn, satisfies

$$p = m + v, \tag{1.3}$$

where m is the rate of money growth, and v is a demand, or velocity, shock.

Employment x is determined by an expectations-augmented Phillips-curve:

$$x = \theta + (p - p^e) - \varepsilon, \tag{1.4}$$

where θ is the (stochastic) natural rate of employment, ε is a supply shock and p^e is the rationally expected value of p. The natural rate θ is observed by wage setters when wages are set (p^e are formed), whereas the supply shock ε is not. As we shall see below, in this setting the central bank enjoys an information advantage over wage setters with regard to the shock ε, and thus it can stabilize output fluctuations in the face of such shocks.

Relative prices of the two goods, z, depend on the relative supply of outside goods, $(x - x^*)$, in relation to its relative demand. We assume that relative demand is an increasing function of z. The equilibrium real exchange rate satisfies:

$$z = \delta(x - x^*) + \phi, \tag{1.5}$$

where $\delta > 0$ is the inverse (relative) demand elasticity of outside goods. A lower supply of home goods (lower x) thus creates relative excess demand for home goods and depreciates the real exchange rate (reduces z). We interpret ϕ as a "speculative shock" to the nominal exchange rate. By (1.1) and (1.5), the nominal exchange rate satisfies:

$$s = \delta[x - x^*] + p - p^* + \phi.$$

The shock ϕ captures all forces moving the nominal exchange rate, other than the current output and price fundamentals. In particular, ϕ may reflect expectations of future inflation and devaluations, fear of government defaults, financial crises, or other future events that may induce current capital outflows or inflows. It would thus make sense to relate the shock ϕ to variables determining the systematic incentives to inflate and engage in competitive devaluations. Such variables would be future values of the natural rate θ and of other parameters in the loss function (see below). These links could be made precise in a less stylized, multi-period, model. We assume that the structural shocks v, v^*, ε, ε^* and ϕ are independently distributed with an expected value of zero.

The policy instrument m is chosen by the home country's central bank. Policy preferences are given by the loss function

$$L = \frac{1}{2}[\pi^2 + \lambda x^2 + \mu(z - \chi)^2], \tag{1.6}$$

where λ and μ are positive weights. We thus implicitly assume that the inflation and employment targets are both zero. Assuming $\mathsf{E}(\theta) < 0$ creates a systematic "inflation bias", as in the standard literature on policy credibility – cf. Persson and Tabellini (2000), Chapter 15. We assume that fluctuations in z are costly in their own right, even aside from their possible effects on inflation and employment. This may capture distributional effects, relocation costs or financial repercussions of unexpected changes in international relative prices, that do not show up in macroeconomic performance but nevertheless affect national welfare. The policy target χ for the real exchange rate is assumed to be observable to wage setters but may be subject to shocks. Assuming $\mathsf{E}(\chi) > 0$ is a simple, albeit *ad hoc*, way of introducing a systematic incentive to engage in competitive devaluations. Informally, we can interpret shocks to χ as capturing variations in the clout of the export industry, lobbying for higher profitability through a weaker exchange rate.[1]

The foreign country is modeled in exactly the same way, with the exception of z entering with an opposite sign. We assume that the parameters, α, λ, and μ, and the shock θ to the natural rate are identical across countries (that is, we assume $\theta = \theta^*$ throughout).[2] But we allow for cross-country differences in the real exchange rate targets ($\chi \neq \chi^*$) in the variances of all shocks ($\sigma_\varepsilon^2 \neq \sigma_{\varepsilon^*}^2$, say) and for arbitrary covariance across pairs of structural shocks ($\sigma_{\varepsilon\varepsilon^*} \gtrless 0$, say).

Events in the model unfold as follows: (i) Observable shocks collected in the vector $\vartheta = (\theta, \chi, \chi^*)$ are revealed, (ii) private expectations (p^e, p^{*e}) are formed, (iii) structural shocks collected in the vector $\omega = (\varepsilon, \varepsilon^*, v, v^*, \phi)$ are revealed, (iv) policies (m, m^*) are simultaneously set, (v) macroeconomic outcomes are realized.

II. Incentives

In this section, we show how decentralized policymaking may give rise to different policy distortions. To establish a normative benchmark for the analysis, we first study the hypothetical situation when the two central banks can commit to cooperation ex ante.

COMMITMENT AND COOPERATION

Suppose that before stage (i) in the model; the two central banks can commit themselves to optimal state-contingent policy rules for m and m^*, minimizing their joint losses, subject to the constraint that private expectations are formed rationally, given available information. Concretely, we thus seek the state-contingent monetary policy rules $(\Psi(\vartheta, \omega)), \Psi^*(\vartheta, \omega))$ minimizing $\mathsf{E}(L + L^*)$, subject to $p^e = \mathsf{E}(p \mid \vartheta)$ and $p^{*e} = \mathsf{E}(p^* \mid \vartheta)$. ($\mathsf{E}(u)$ denotes the unconditional expectation of u, whereas $\mathsf{E}(u \mid \vartheta)$ denotes the conditional expectation of u, given the realization of ϑ). The first-order condition for the optimal choice of $\Psi(\vartheta, \omega)$ in an arbitrary state can be expressed as:[3]

$$\pi(\vartheta, \omega) + \lambda(x(\vartheta, \omega) - \theta) + 2\mu\delta z(\vartheta, \omega) + \alpha\delta(\pi(\vartheta, \omega) - \pi^*(\vartheta, \omega)) = 0. \tag{2.1}$$

The optimal policy rule thus trades off stabilization of domestic inflation around its target (the first term) and prices and employment around the natural rate (the second term). But it also takes into account the effect of policy on domestic and foreign losses of induced changes in z, both directly (the third term) and indirectly through CPI-inflation (the fourth term). Given the corresponding set of first-order conditions for $m^*(\vartheta, \omega)$ and the model structure, we can solve for the optimal policy rule in terms of underlying shocks. Straightforward, but tedious, algebra gives

$$m = \Psi(\vartheta, \omega) = \psi_\varepsilon \varepsilon - v + \psi_{\varepsilon\varepsilon^*}(\varepsilon - \varepsilon^*) - \psi_\phi \phi, \tag{2.2}$$

where the ψ's are complicated expressions in the model's parameters. The central bank thus stabilizes the price and output effects of domestic supply shocks somewhat (one can show that $0 < \psi_\varepsilon < 1$) and domestic demand shocks completely. But it also adopts a more restrictive monetary policy so as to stabilize asymmetric and negative foreign supply shocks, $\varepsilon - \varepsilon^* < 0$. Similarly, it meets speculative shocks against its own currency, $\phi > 0$ by a more contractionary policy, so as to partially offset the real depreciation (one can also show that $\psi_\phi > 0$).

Notice an important aspect of the solution: none of the observable shocks in ϑ enters the optimal policy rule. The reason should be familiar from the literature on rational expectations and monetary policy – cf. for instance Fischer (1977), Walsh (1998). As these variables are observable, any systematic policy response to these variables would be anticipated by wage setters. Furthermore, the real variables in the model are neutral to expected policy. A central bank which indeed has the ability to make a binding commitment to a policy rule is therefore best off by ignoring these shocks, thus keeping expected and actual inflation anchored at zero.

DISCRETION AND NON-COOPERATION

Suppose now, more realistically, that ex ante commitments are infeasible. Furthermore, each central bank chooses its policy ex post at stage (iv) of the model, in a non-cooperative fashion. The home country's central bank thus minimizes L with respect to $m(\vartheta, \omega)$, taking foreign policy $m^*(\vartheta, \omega)$, as well as private expectations $\mathsf{E}(p \mid \vartheta)$ and $\mathsf{E}(p^* \mid \vartheta)$, as given. The first-order condition for $m(\tau, \omega)$ can be written as

$$\pi(\vartheta, \omega) + \lambda(x(\vartheta, \omega) - \theta) + 2\mu\delta z(\vartheta, \omega) + \alpha\delta(\pi(\vartheta, \omega) - \pi^*(\vartheta, \omega))$$
$$= -\lambda\theta + \mu\delta\chi + \mu\delta z(\vartheta, \omega) - \alpha\delta\pi^*(\vartheta, \omega). \tag{2.3}$$

The condition has been written such that its left-hand side coincides with the expression in (2.1). Thus, the right-hand side of (2.3) captures the forces that induce a deviation from the benchmark optimum. One of these, captured by the first term on the right hand side of (2.3), is familiar. The "credibility" (ex post optimality) constraint makes the outside central bank ignore the effect of its policy on private expectations formation: the ex post incentive to stimulate growth gives a permanent inflation bias – recall that $\mathsf{E}(\theta) < 0$. The "individual rationality" constraint, associated with non-cooperative policymaking also makes the outside central bank ignore the spillover effects on the monetary union. The second term on the right hand side, $\mu\delta\chi$, captures this effect and gives rise to a permanent competitive depreciation bias – recall $\mathsf{E}(\chi) > 0$. Since the incentives to expand employment and depreciate the real exchange rate are correctly anticipated by the private sector, the equilibrium rate of expected inflation is higher without any effect on real variables.

To see this result more clearly, consider the following special case. All structural shocks appearing in $\boldsymbol{\omega}$ are zero, and the real exchange rate targets coincide in the two countries: $\chi = \chi^* > 0$. In this symmetric situation, it is easy to see that – whatever the policy regime – both countries will pursue the same policies, $m(\vartheta, \mathbf{0}) = m^*(\vartheta, \mathbf{0})$, and have the same realized inflation, $\pi(\vartheta, \mathbf{0}) = \pi^*(\vartheta, \mathbf{0})$. Absent unobservable shocks, policies are perfectly anticipated. Thus, inflationary expectations are correct, and by (1.4) employment in each country is at the natural rate $x(\vartheta, \mathbf{0}) = x^*(\vartheta, \mathbf{0}) = \theta$. By (1.5), it follows that the real exchange rate is constant, $z(\vartheta, \mathbf{0}) = 0$. Given these results, it follows immediately from (2.3) that inflation under commitment and cooperation would be zero:

$$\pi^{C,C}(\vartheta, \mathbf{0}) = 0.$$

In the regime of discretion and non-cooperation, (2.3) instead implies:

$$\pi^{D,N}(\vartheta, \mathbf{0}) = \frac{1}{1 + \alpha\delta}(-\lambda\theta + \mu\delta\chi). \tag{2.4}$$

Inflation in the discretionary non-cooperative regime is thus too high and too variable compared to the benchmark optimum. The inflation bias is more pronounced, the larger is the gap between the employment target (of zero) and the natural rate, and the larger is χ governing the incentive for a competitive devaluation. Notice, though, that inflation is lower the higher is α, the share of foreign goods in the consumption basket. The reason is that an expansionary policy depreciates the exchange rate which adds to the marginal cost of inflation. Thus, more open economies have a smaller incentive to inflate. This prediction was used by Romer (1993) in his well known empirical study of the determinants of inflation. He found the prediction to hold. In his broad cross-section of countries, larger openness, in the sense of this model, was indeed significantly associated with lower inflation. The result did not hold for the subsample composed of the richest countries, though. The aforementioned, and more comprehensive, study by Campillo and Miron (1997) subsequently confirmed these results.

The two remaining terms on the right-hand side of (2.3) capture a distorted stabilization of shocks, implying too much volatility, not only in inflation but also in employment and real exchange rates. This stabilization bias arises because central bankers do not internalize the international spillover effects of their policies. How this modifies policymaking depends on the shocks. To clarify the nature of the policy distortion relative to the benchmark, we consider another special case that has received considerable attention in the literature on international policy coordination. This special case assumes that all observable shocks in ϑ are zero, implying that no inflation bias is present. Furthermore, the only structural shocks are symmetric supply shocks $\varepsilon = \varepsilon^*$. Again, in both policy regimes, symmetry implies equal policies, $m(\mathbf{0}, \varepsilon) = m^*(\mathbf{0}, \varepsilon)$, equal employment in the two countries, and an unchanged exchange rate, $z(\mathbf{0}, \varepsilon)$. It follows that producer-price inflation and CPI-inflation coincide: $\pi(\mathbf{0}, \varepsilon) = p(\mathbf{0}, \varepsilon) = \pi^*(\mathbf{0}, \varepsilon) = p^*(\mathbf{0}, \varepsilon)$. Finally, the absence of an inflation bias means that expected inflation is zero. It follows from the Phillips curve (1.4) that $x(\mathbf{0}, \varepsilon) = x^*(\mathbf{0}, \varepsilon) = \pi(\mathbf{0}, \varepsilon) - \varepsilon$. With these preliminaries in hand, (2.4) allows us to solve for the inflation rate in the benchmark optimum:

$$\pi^{C,C}(\mathbf{0}, \varepsilon) = \frac{\lambda}{1 + \lambda}\,\varepsilon.$$

This is exactly the same result as in the closed economy literature on credibility. Suppose we have a negative supply shock, $\varepsilon = \varepsilon^* > 0$. The optimal policy rule trades off the domestic employment benefits of expansionary policy against the domestic inflationary cost, at a rate depending on the relative weight of these objectives in the loss function. Under discretion and non-cooperation, (2.3) implies instead

$$\pi^{D,N}(\mathbf{0}, \varepsilon) = \frac{\lambda}{1 + \lambda + \alpha\delta}\,\varepsilon.$$

Evidently, the equilibrium policy is not expansionary enough. The central bank recognizes that expansionary policy has additional inflationary costs at home, as it depreciates the exchange rate. But it does not consider the fact that depreciation induces deflation abroad and thus worsens the tradeoff faced by the foreign central bank. Each central bank thus attempts to export some of the necessary adjustments abroad. Thus, it does not sufficiently stabilize employment. As the other central bank has similar incentives, however, the effect on the exchange rate is nullified in equilibrium. The end result is thus that policy is *too contractionary* in both countries. This kind of argument was a common explanation in the monetary policy coordination literature of the early 1980s as to why non-coordinated policy responses in the major countries may have worsened the recession that followed upon the first two oil shocks.

DISCRETION AND COOPERATION

Suppose now that policymakers cannot make ex ante commitments to a policy rule. Nevertheless, they can find a way of enforcing a cooperative policy agreement at the ex post policymaking stage, i.e. at stage (iv) of the model. It is not immediately clear why the latter is possible while the former is not, as there are also incentives to deviate from the cooperative agreement. Let us postpone that discussion to the next section, though.

Formally, the two policymakers set their policy instruments so as to maximize the sum of their loss functions, taking expected inflation $\mathsf{E}(p|\boldsymbol{\vartheta})$ and $\mathsf{E}(p^*|\boldsymbol{\vartheta})$ as given. The condition for optimal home money growth $m(\boldsymbol{\vartheta}, \boldsymbol{\omega})$ in this regime of discretion and cooperation is:

$$\pi(\boldsymbol{\vartheta}, \boldsymbol{\omega}) + \lambda(x(\boldsymbol{\vartheta}, \boldsymbol{\omega}) - \theta) + 2\mu\delta z(\boldsymbol{\vartheta}, \boldsymbol{\omega}) + \alpha\delta(\pi(\boldsymbol{\vartheta}, \boldsymbol{\omega}) - \pi^*(\boldsymbol{\vartheta}, \boldsymbol{\omega}))$$
$$= -\lambda\theta + \mu\delta(\chi - \chi^*). \tag{2.5}$$

It is obvious that the policy coincides with the benchmark optimum, when the inflation-bias problem is absent. That is, when $\theta = \theta^*$ and $\chi = \chi^*$ then (2.5) and (2.1) coincide.

The ability to coordinate policy internationally is thus advantageous when the only problem of policymaking is connected with stabilizing structural shocks. The advantages of cooperation are not general, however. To demonstrate this, let us return to the case with symmetric observable shocks and zero structural shocks. Exploiting the symmetry of the solution, namely $x = \theta$, $z = 0$, $\pi = \pi^*$, we can use (2.5) to write equilibrium inflation as:

$$\pi^{D,C}(\boldsymbol{\vartheta}, \mathbf{0}) = -\lambda\theta + \mu\delta(\chi - \chi^*). \tag{2.6}$$

Comparing (2.6) and (2.4), we see that $\pi^{D,C}(\boldsymbol{\vartheta}, \mathbf{0})$ could be higher or lower than $\pi^{D,N}(\boldsymbol{\vartheta}, \mathbf{0})$: under discretion and with no $\boldsymbol{\omega}$ shocks, inflation could be higher and more volatile with cooperation than without it. As real output is exactly the same (since we assumed $\boldsymbol{\omega} = \mathbf{0}$), the outcome under cooperation could be worse for both countries.

What is the reason for this result? It is quite simple. We have seen that *not-cooperating* central banks perceive an additional marginal effect of expanding m. For a given foreign monetary policy, an expansion generates a real depreciation. This can be either good or bad: on the one hand, higher prices of imported goods add to CPI-inflation; hence, depreciation is costly. On the other hand, a depreciation could take the real exchange rate closer to the target χ, and this would be a benefit. But when policymakers cooperate, they ignore this effect – or more correctly, they recognize and internalize the cost of the corresponding deflation and appreciation abroad. The perceived cost of expansionary policies could thus be lower, in which case equilibrium inflation is higher with cooperation.

In other words, if $\pi^{D,N}(\boldsymbol{\vartheta}, \mathbf{0}) < \pi^{D,C}(\boldsymbol{\vartheta}, \mathbf{0})$, it means that perceived exchange rate effects provide a disincentive to inflate: monetary policy without cooperation has a contractionary bias. This contractionary bias is a vice when coupled with international conflict over how much to stabilize structural shocks. But it becomes a virtue when coupled with domestic incentive problems, tied to the temptation of using monetary expansion to boost employment and real exchange rates. This insight is originally due to Rogoff (1985b), and it was further elaborated upon by Kehoe (1989) with regard to capital taxation.

Naturally, also allowing for the unobservable (structural) shocks, $\boldsymbol{\omega}$, adds to the benefits of cooperation. Cooperation is now also helpful in promoting more efficient stabilization, though it could still aggravate the domestic credibility (or political) problems. Whether the benefits outweigh the cost depends on whether the coordination problem is more serious than the credibility problem. An *ex ante* assessment of which regime would be preferable would have to rely on comparing the expected value of the loss under specific assumptions about the distributions for ϑ and ω. Rogoff took this ambiguity to imply that gains from cooperation can be ensured only under appropriate institutions. This point brings us right into the topic of the next section.

III. Institutions

Much of the early literature on international policy coordination stopped at the point of making the case for a coordinated policy. It is not enough to demonstrate that the policy outcome under cooperative policymaking is superior, though, as individual countries generally have incentives to deviate from the cooperative policy. The argument is therefore incomplete unless coupled with an argument for how the suggested solution might be enforced. In his discussion of the main obstacles to successful international policy coordination, Frankel (1988) emphasized precisely the difficulty of enforcing cooperation. The literature has shown that reputational incentives may relax the short-run incentives to deviate when policymakers repeatedly interact over time. The general argument is well-known and is discussed for instance in Persson and Tabellini (2000). Its specific application to monetary policy coordination is well summarized in Canzoneri and Henderson (1991, Chs. 4–5), and in Ghosh and Masson (1994, Ch. 8). Hence, we do not deal with it here. Instead, we discuss what institutions might enforce desirable policy outcomes. We start in the abstract, by showing how a pair of optimal inflation contracts are capable of implementing the optimal policy rule under cooperation and commitment. Next, we discuss variations on this argument, attempting to link the theory to real-world international monetary arrangements.

OPTIMAL LINEAR INFLATION CONTRACTS

Assume that two central banks set policies independently under discretion at stage (iv) in the model of this chapter. But before stage (i) an "international principal" has the ability to design institutions, thereby trying to implement a beneficial policy. We model institutions as "performance contracts", that is as arrangements or contracts that punish or reward the central bank depending on its performance, however defined. At a constitutional stage (o), the international principal formulates a publicly observable complete contract for each central bank which assigns state-contingent transfers (rewards if positive, punishments if negative), conditional on realized inflation. The question is what constitutes an optimal contract from the point of view of the benevolent international principal who cares about both countries from an ex-ante perspective, and what kind of behavior it induces on the agent.

Specifically, assume that each central bank is faced with a linear, but state-contingent, performance contract in realized inflation. First, consider the national central bank. It thus obtains a transfer given by:

$$T(\pi(\vartheta, \omega); \vartheta, \omega) = t_0(\vartheta, \omega) - t_1(\vartheta, \omega)\pi(\vartheta, \omega). \tag{3.1}$$

Our goal is to optimally set the terms t_i, $i = 0, 1$, that define the contract. The central bank minimizes the difference between its loss function in (1.6) and the transfer in (3.1). This formulation implies risk neutrality by the central bank with regard to the transfers.

It is easily verified that this modifies the first-order condition under discretion and non-cooperation (2.3) at one point only: an extra term appears on the right-hand side, namely: $(1 + \alpha\delta)t_1(\vartheta, \omega)$. It then follows directly from (2.3) and (2.1) that the central bank indeed has the appropriate incentives to implement the ex ante cooperative policy, if the marginal reward for low inflation is set at:

$$t_1(\vartheta, \omega) = \frac{1}{1 + \alpha\delta}[-\lambda\theta + \mu\delta\chi + \mu\delta z(\vartheta, \omega) - \alpha\delta\pi^*(\vartheta, \omega)], \tag{3.2}$$

where z and π^* are understood to be evaluated at the ex ante optimum. Solving for z and π^* in the ex-ante optimum, the marginal reward can be rewritten in terms of the structural shocks:

$$t_1(\vartheta, \omega) = \frac{1}{1 + \alpha\delta}[-\lambda\theta + \mu\delta\chi - t^{\varepsilon^*}\varepsilon^* - t^{\varepsilon\varepsilon^*}(\varepsilon - \varepsilon^*) + t^{\phi}\phi]. \tag{3.3}$$

The coefficients t^{ε^*}, $t^{\varepsilon\varepsilon^*}$, and t^{ϕ}, like the ψ-coefficients in (2.2), are complicated expressions (with a likely positive sign) in the structural parameters.

The marginal reward in these expressions has an intuitive interpretation. The first two terms balance the central bank's systematic incentives to expand employment and depreciate the real exchange rate; the stronger these incentives, the stiffer the optimal penalty. This is similar to the result in the closed economy literature that the reward scheme should be tailored to state-dependent incentives to inflate – cf. Persson and Tabellini, Chapter 17. The additional terms correct the stabilization bias deriving from the failure of the home country's central bank to internalize the foreign spillover effects of its policy. In particular, the reward should be weaker if the *foreign* country suffers a negative supply shock (ε^* positive), a less severe asymmetric supply shock ($(\varepsilon - \varepsilon^*)$ positive), or a speculation against its currency (ϕ negative). In these three cases, the impact of the shock is to generate foreign inflation $\pi^* > 0$ and foreign depreciation (home appreciation) of the real exchange rate $z < 0$. The home country's uncorrected non-cooperative policy is too contractionary, which calls for a weaker marginal reward for low inflation.

The incentive scheme for the foreign central bank should be structured in a similar way – the marginal reward $-t_1^*$ should satisfy

$$t_1^*(\vartheta, \omega) = \frac{1}{1 + \alpha\delta}[-\lambda\theta + \mu\delta\chi^* - t^{\varepsilon}\varepsilon + t^{\varepsilon\varepsilon^*}(\varepsilon - \varepsilon^*) - t^{\phi}\phi], \tag{3.4}$$

where $t^{\varepsilon} = t^{\varepsilon^*}$ and, $t^{\varepsilon\varepsilon^*}$, t^{ϕ} are identical to the coefficients appearing in (3.3). As this expression reveals, the correction of the stabilization bias is symmetric across the two central banks. When it comes to the inflation bias, the country with a worse credibility problem or a stronger incentive to engage in competitive devaluations, should face stronger average rewards for approaching its zero inflation target. In general, the marginal rewards implementing the desired policy thus depend on the sign and size of the shocks.

OPTIMAL TARGETING

Our linear model implies that state-contingent contracts over *any* pairs of nominal variables can implement the ex ante optimum policies.[4] As argued in Persson and Tabellini (1993, 1995), however, complete state-contingent contracting is unlikely to be feasible. Simplicity and verifiability problems may require the penalties and rewards in any central bank incentive scheme to be state-independent. One may therefore conjecture that the design of international monetary institutions must necessarily tackle a second-best problem, along the lines of the simple contracting solutions discussed in the closed economy literature – see Persson and Tabellini (2000), Chapter 17. A moment's reflection, however, suggests that this conjecture is not necessarily correct. A recent paper by Jensen (1999) explains why, in a model similar to the one in this chapter, except that central banks do not value exchange rate stability as such and do not have the incentives for competitive devaluations.

We can grasp the idea by inspecting the first-order conditions for the ex ante optimal cooperative policy (2.1) and the ex post optimal non-cooperative policy (2.3). The stabilization bias, associated with the last two terms on the right-hand side of (2.3), appears because the home central bank sets policy ignoring its effects on the foreign central bank's loss function via spillover effects on the real exchange rate and foreign inflation. As these terms are linear, an appropriately structured reward, which is *quadratic* in these variables, could thus provide the right marginal incentives. Specifically, suppose that the transfer to the home central bank is given by:

$$T(\pi, \pi^*, z) = t_0 - [t_\pi(\pi - \pi^B)^2 + t_{\pi^*}(\pi - \pi^*)^2 + t_z z^2]/2. \tag{3.5}$$

Thus, the central bank obtains an additional rewards or penalties for stabilizing inflation around an absolute level, π^B, for stabilizing the difference between home and foreign inflation, and for stabilizing the real exchange rate.

Suppose, as before, that when faced with this scheme, the central bank minimizes the difference $L - T(\cdot)$ at stage (iv) of the model. The optimal policy is then given by a condition identical to (2.3), except that the following expression also appears on the left-hand side:

$$\begin{aligned} t_\pi \frac{\mathrm{d}\pi}{\mathrm{d}m}(\pi - \pi^B) + t_{\pi^*}\left(\frac{\mathrm{d}\pi}{\mathrm{d}m} - \frac{\mathrm{d}\pi^*}{\mathrm{d}m}\right)(\pi - \pi^*) + t_z \frac{\mathrm{d}z}{\mathrm{d}m} \\ = -t_\pi(1 + \alpha\delta)\pi^B + (t_\pi(1 + \alpha\delta) + t_{\pi^*}(1 + 2\alpha\delta))\pi \\ - t_{\pi^*}(1 + 2\alpha\delta)\pi^* + t_z\delta z. \end{aligned}$$

Suppose further that the domestic incentive problems are state independent and known at the institution design stage, in the sense that $\theta < 0$ and $\chi > 0$ are known constants. Then, we can find an incentive scheme implementing the ex ante cooperative policy, by equating the above expression, term by term, with the expression on the right-hand side of (2.3). Straightforward algebra gives the following solution.

$$t_z = \mu > 0, \qquad t_{\pi^*} = \frac{\alpha\delta}{(1+2\alpha\delta)} > 0,$$
$$t_\pi = -\frac{\alpha\delta}{(1+\alpha\delta)} < 0, \quad \pi^B = \frac{-\lambda\theta + \mu\delta\chi}{\alpha\delta} > 0. \tag{3.6}$$

The coefficients on relative inflation and the real exchange rate are thus positive, while the coefficient on $(\pi - \pi^B)^2$ is negative. That is, this scheme in (3.5) rewards the central bank for targeting foreign inflation, π^*, and for achieving stability of the real exchange rate. As $t_\pi < 0 < \pi^B$, the central bank is also rewarded for *deviating* from π^B, that is for keeping inflation below the threshold π^B. The combined effect of t_π and t_{π^*} makes the net marginal rewards independent of the level of π; control of the credibility problem instead relies on the inflation target π^B. The latter implies a constant marginal cost of inflation, mimicking the incentives in the optimal linear inflation contract in the same way as in Svensson (1997a). Here however, unlike in Svensson (1997a), π^B can be interpreted as an upper threshold, not as a target: the closer we get to π^B, the more the central bank is punished (as $\pi^B > 0$ while society's favored inflation rate is zero by assumption).

By the linearity of the model, other targeting schemes could also implement the optimum, but are perhaps less intuitive, as they are not related to the underlying policy distortions in the same direct way. If the domestic incentive problem associated with the observable shocks θ and χ is state dependent (in the sense that θ and χ are also random variables), then the state independent targeting approach discussed here can handle the average distortion associated with $\mathsf{E}(\theta) < 0$ and $\mathsf{E}(\chi) > 0$, although the inflation rate would still be too variable.

INTERNATIONAL MONETARY ARRANGEMENTS

The discussion above is quite abstract in assuming an institution design stage, where an "international principal" sets up some mechanism to induce desirable behavior by the central banks of individual countries. Can we think of plausible real-world counterparts to these theoretical constructions? Both the Bretton-Woods system and the EMS did indeed grow out of an initial and lengthy period of multilateral negotiations – like the institution design stage of the model above. Both arrangements also had a codified set of prospective rewards and sanctions tied to the behavior of central banks – like the contractual transfers in the model.[5] Finally, both arrangements amounted to an explicit or implicit policy assignment among the member countries. The US Fed and the German Bundesbank would direct their policies towards a domestic target, providing a nominal anchor to the system. The other central banks would instead have an adjustable exchange rate target vis-a-vis the central currency, whereby they would capture some credibility from the anchor country.

Why would these real-world international monetary arrangements involve the exchange rate as a key intermediate target, rather than a more symmetric arrangement? One possible answer is that the exchange rate is used as a target because it is so easily monitored. However, exchange rate stability would only work well as a coordination mechanism if the two countries were subject to symmetric shocks. A classical paper by Canzoneri and Gray (1985) shows that under such circumstances, no international enforcement is needed to reach the cooperative optimum. In the model of this chapter, suppose that the supply shocks are symmetric $\varepsilon = \varepsilon^*$ and that speculative shocks are absent, $\phi = 0$. Suppose, further, that the foreign country's central bank faces a strong enough penalty that it always chooses a policy keeping the nominal exchange rate constant, $s = 0$. Suppose finally, that the home country has appropriate monetary institutions to take care of any domestic credibility problem. If the home country pursues an optimal non-cooperative policy, taking the pegging of the foreign country into account, this is enough to implement the ex ante cooperative optimum (see Persson and Tabellini (1995) for a formal derivation of this result).

When these conditions are not satisfied, however, international enforcement of exchange rate stability is necessary. In the previous section, we have also seen that asymmetric shocks or speculative shocks call for exchange rate changes, both in the cooperative and the non-cooperative solutions. How can these changes take place without disrupting cooperation too much? Perhaps by combining rules and discretion in a simple way. Bretton Woods system and the EMS can be described as mechanisms for implementing a simple rule with an escape clause. In normal circumstances, the central-currency country would pursue a restrictive monetary policy and the exchange rate against the central currency would remain pegged. But temporary slippage of the monetary anchor and realignments would be allowed under exceptional circumstances.[6]

In the model above, an international principal could implement such an escape-clause equilibrium by replacing the contracts in (3.6) and (3.4) with a pair of non-linear, state-independent, contracts. Deviations from a fixed exchange rate $s = 0$ and a specific home money growth rate m would be punished by a pair of non-contingent negative lump-sum transfers (c^s, c^m). How often the escape clause would be triggered would depend on (c^s, c^m). The lower their value, the more realizations of ϑ and ω would induce the central banks at stage (iv) to break the contract and pursue a decentralized, discretionary policy associated with an exchange rate realignment.

Such a multilateral peg system would be suboptimal, relative to the hypothetical benchmark of the *ex ante* cooperative optimum; just how suboptimal depends on the properties of the shocks. Frequent realizations of high values of θ, χ and χ^*, low or negative correlation between ε and ε^*, or a high variance of the speculative shock ϕ, would imply a frequent breach of the simple rule. But with limited credibility problems of monetary policy, a central country with a great deal of credibility, relatively parallel macroeconomic development in the participating countries, and low capital mobility, the incentives to deviate from the simple rule would be small. Describing the fifties and (most of) the sixties under the Bretton Woods system, as well as the eighties under the EMS, in just those terms might not be too far-fetched.

But asymmetric or speculative shocks might make a monetary arrangement that creates strong incentives for convergent monetary policies worse than no arrangement at all. Such shocks are therefore especially likely to put a strain on the simple rule and, potentially, on the whole mechanism. It is interesting to note that the eventual breakdown of both the Bretton Woods system and the EMS was indeed preceded by asymmetric shocks to the central currency country: the US fiscal shock in connection with the Vietnam war and Johnson's great society program, and German unification, respectively. The breakdown was also preceded by increasing capital mobility among the relevant countries: the expansion of the euromarkets in the late 1960s and the abolishment of capital controls inside the European Community in the late 1980s.

IV. Discussion

The complete form of monetary policy cooperation would be full monetary union, with a single money managed by a *single* central bank. The previous discussion suggests that full monetary union would be a suboptimal arrangement with large asymmetric shocks. But if the cooperative optimum under commitment is infeasible, we face a second-best institution design problem, namely a choice between different suboptimal alternatives. In the last decade we have witnessed the 1992–1994 turmoil in European markets, followed by the effective breakup of the EMS and the subsequent creation of the EMU, as well as the Asian and Latin-American crises in the late nineties. We have also seen a very recent trend towards inflation targeting cum floating exchange rates in developing countries. These events suggest that the only relevant choice may be between floating rates (and appropriate domestic institutions) under high capital mobility and full monetary union. Moreover, we have confined our analysis to stabilization policies. Savings on transactions costs (Casella (1992)) or microeconomic benefits in other areas of integration (Basevi, Delbono, and De Nicolò (1992)), may be additional gains from a full monetary union.

Whatever its motivation, a monetary union raises several interesting questions. First, under which circumstances should a single country join a monetary union? To the list starting with Mundell's (1961) high labor mobility, and including the predominant type of macroeconomic shocks, the recent literature on "optimum currency areas" has added large domestic incentive problems in monetary policy. But there is also an interesting systemic question: how does the design of the common central bank resolve conflicting interests of member countries and shape the union's monetary policy? In keeping with our approach in this chapter, these positive and normative questions could be productively analyzed, by drawing on principal-agent theory and contract theory. A common central bank is an instance of common agency: this common agent serves multiple principals (the member countries) with partly common, partly conflicting, interests. The analysis would have the following ingredients: participation constraints must be respected, particularly with asymmetric countries, and the specific collective decision-making mechanism shapes the policy outcome, as well as the distribution of costs and benefits. Dixit (1998) and (1999) takes precisely this approach to discuss policymaking by the European Central Bank. These papers, and others mentioned below, suggest that the question of how to design a common central bank cannot be analyzed without paying close attention to the broader political and institutional framework in which the member countries interact.

V. Notes on the Literature

The model in this chapter has been adapted from Persson and Tabellini (1995) and (1996) who, in turn, essentially formulated a reduced form of the static models in Canzoneri and Henderson (1988, 1991). It also encompasses the models in other well-known papers of the traditional policy coordination literature, as Canzoneri and Gray (1985) and Rogoff (1985).

Several of the papers in Bryant et al. (1988) discuss the empirical importance of international policy spillovers. Home and Masson (1988) and Fischer (1988) survey a number of studies attempting to empirically measure the gains from coordination. Most studies seem to find relatively modest gains from coordination, a fact that Canzoneri and Henderson (1991) attribute to the nature of the exercise: the studies allow for gains from joint stabilization, but not from eliminating permanent conflicts. One might speculate that allowing for domestic incentive problems in empirical studies may give rise to larger prospective gains from coordination, but only to the extent that coordination serves to eliminate first-order losses, due to these domestic incentive problems.

Miller and Salmon (1985) derived the Rogoff (1985) result on the ambiguity of gains from cooperation in a dynamic policy game, based on a two-country version of the sticky-price Dornbusch overshooting model. van der Ploeg (1988) demonstrated the same result in a model where the private sector in each country is modeled as a forward-looking and intertemporally maximizing representative agent. A related paradox can be found in Frankel and Rockett (1988), who demonstrate that the coordination of monetary policies may lead to worse outcomes, if policy-maker's disagree on how the world economy works. Oudiz and Sachs (1985) found that when policymakers do not cooperate, having access to commitment may not improve the outcome in a model with a truly forward-looking private sector; it is exposed in a two-period model by Canzoneri and Henderson (1991, Ch. 5). Similar results can also be found in Levine and Currie (1987) and in Currie, Levine, and Vidalis (1987). International policy cooperation can be counterproductive in the presence of other incentive problems, not just when there is lack of credibility. Tabellini (1990) considers a model of fiscal policy where there would be benefits from coordination because of terms of trade effects. But if a domestic political distortion leads to excessive fiscal deficits, then international cooperation exacerbates the effects of this distortion and may be counter-productive. Vaubel (1985) makes a similar point in a more general – though less formal – setting.

The book by Obstfeld and Rogoff (1996) summarizes the new microfounded approach to open economy macroeconomics. This approach can be used to discuss proper welfare issues in policy coordination, as suggested by Corsetti and Pesenti (1998) and Ghironi (1998).

The volume edited by Bordo and Eichengreen (1993) contains many useful studies of the Bretton Woods system, analytical as well as descriptive. Useful collections of articles on the EMS and on monetary union in Europe can be found in de Cecco and Giovannini (1989) and Canzoneri, Grilli and Masson (1992). Martin (1992) compares optimal monetary policy delegation in a monetary union and under flexible exchange rates. Giavazzi and Pagano (1988) discuss the EMS and the incentives created by the practice of not allowing full compensation for inflation differentials at EMS realignments. Cohen and Wyplosz (1989) specifically emphasize the role of the EMS as a coordination device.

A large recent literature has studied positive models of monetary policy within the institutional framework of the European Central Bank (ECB). See in particular L. Svensson (1999) and the literature quoted therein. Besides the papers by Dixit (1998) and (1999b) quoted above, other earlier papers by Casella and Feinstein (1989), Alesina and Grilli (1992) and von Hagen and Süppel (1994) have studied collective decision making inside a common central who sets policy for several countries. More recent contributions on the incentive or collective choice problems faced by the ECB include Bottazzi and Manasse (1998), Gruner (1999), Lippi (1999), Muscatelli (1998), Sibert (1998) and Terlizzese (1999).

Notes

1. An alternative (but perhaps equally ad-hoc) way of modeling the incentive to engage in competitive devaluations would be to let z enter the right-hand side of the supply function, (??), with a positive sign: a real depreciation would then lead to higher output growth (see Canzoneri and Gray (1985) and Martin (1995)). Most of the results would apply to this different specification. Note also that a political interpretation of χ (a result of lobbying by special interests rather than true social welfare) would not change our normative conclusions. The reason is that the equilibrium real exchange rate on average is always zero, under all institutional arrangments – this follows from the assumed neutrality of expected policy over real variables.
2. This assumption simplifies the algebra but entails no loss of generality as far as the main results are concerned.
3. To derive (2.1) we have exploited the fact that, in equilibrium and given our assumption that $\theta = \theta^*$, we have:

$$\frac{\partial \mathrm{E}(L + L^* \mid \vartheta)}{\partial p^e} = -\lambda\theta - \mu\delta(\chi^* - \chi).$$

The first term on the right hand side is the marginal cost of a reduction of output below the natural reate, the second term captures the marginal welfare costs of a real depreciation (as p^e rises, z falls).

4. As discussed in Persson and Tabellini (1993), (2000), this equivalence also remains in more general settings; however, performance contracts written over variables other than π are more informationally demanding, if there are non-linearities in the constraints describing the economy.
5. Examples were the obligation to inform and consult the IMF or other countries before exchange rate changes, the conditional rights to draw on SDR's to finance balance of payments deficits and the possibility of IMF conditionality in the case of the Bretton-Woods system, the short-run credit facilities, the ties to other EG institutions like the CAP, and the practice not to allow full restoration to parity of overvalued currencies at realignments, in the case of the EMS.
6. The classic formulation in Article IV of the Bretton Woods agreement about allowing devaluations in situations of "fundamental disequilibrium" only, reminds us precisely about the notion of a rule with an escape clause.

References

Alesina A. and Grilli, V. (1992) 'The European central bank: Reshaping monetary politics in Europe'. In M. Canzoneri, V. Grilli and P. Masson, eds., *Establishing a Central Bank. Issues in Europe and Lessons from US*. Cambridge: Cambridge University Press.

Basevi, G., Delbono, F. and Denicolo, V. (1992) 'International monetary cooperation under tariff threat'. *Journal of International Economics* 28:1–23.

Bordo, M. and Eichengreen, B. (1993) *A Retrospective on the Bretton Woods System.* Chicago: Chicago University Press.

Bottazzi, L. and Manasse, P. (1998) 'Bankers' vs workers' Europe: Asymmetric information in EMU:' IGIER Working Paper No. 127.

Bryant, R., Henderson, D., Holtham, G., Hooper, P. and Symansky, S. (1988) *Empirical Macroeconomics for Interdependent Economies.* Washington DC: Brookings Institutions.

Campillo, M. and Miron, J. (1997) 'Why does inflation differ across countries?' In C. Romer and D. Romer, eds. *Reducing Inflation: Motivation and Strategy.* Chicago: Chicago University Press.

Canzoneri, M. and Gray, J. (1985) 'Monetary policy games and the consequences of noncooperative behavior'. *International Economic Review* 26: 547– 5647

Canzoneni, M., Grilli, V. and Masson, P., eds., 1992. *Establishing a Central Bank: Issues in Europe and Lessons from the U.S.* Cambridge: Cambridge University Press.

Canzoneri, M. and Henderson, D. (1988) 'Is sovereign policy making bad?' *Carnegie Rochester Conference Series* 28:93–140.

Canzoneri, M. and Henderson, D. (1991) *Monetary policy in interdependent economies: A game-theoretic approach.* Cambridge: MIT Press.

Casella, A. (1992) 'On markets and clubs: economic and political integration of regions with unequal productivity'. *American Economic Review Papers and Proceedings* 87: 115–121.

Casella, A. and Feinstein, J. (1989) 'Management of a common currency'. In M. de Cecco and A. Giovannini, eds., *A European Central Bank?* Cambridge: Cambridge University Press.

Cohen, D. and Wyplosz, C. (1989) 'European monetary union: An agnostic evaluation'. In R. Bryant et al., eds., *Macroeconomic Policies in an Interdependent World.* Washington D.C.: Brookings Institution.

Corsetti, G. and Pesenti, P. (1998) 'Welfare and macroeconomic interdependence'. Mimeo.

Currie, D. and Levine, P. (1993) *Rules, Reputation and Macroeconomic Contracts.* Cambridge UK: Cambridge University Press.

Currie, D., Levine, P. and Vidalis, N. (1987) 'International cooperation and reputation in an empirical two-bloc model'. In R. Bryant and R. Portes, eds., *Global Macroeconomics: Policy Conflict and Cooperation.* London: Macmillan Press.

de Cecco, M. and Giovannini, A., eds. (1989) *A European Central Bank?* Cambridge: Cambridge University Press.

Dixit, A. (1998) 'Equilibrium contracts for the European central bankers'. Mimeo. Princeton University.

Dixit, A. (1999) 'A repeated game model of monetary union'. Mimeo. Princeton University.

Fischer, S. (1988) 'International macroeconomic policy coordination'. In M. Feldstein, ed., *International Economic Cooperation.* Chicago: Chicago University Press.

Frankel, J. (1988) 'Obstacles to international macroeconomic policy coordination'. International Finance Section Paper. Princeton University.

Frankel, J. and Rockett, K. (1988) 'International macroeconomic policy coordination when policymakers disagree on the model'. *American Economic Review* 78: 318–340.

Ghironi, P. (1998) 'U.S-Europe economic interdependence (I): Positive analysis'. Mimeo. University of California, Berkeley.

Giavazzi, F. and Pagano, M. (1988) 'The advantage of tying one's hands: EMS discipline and central bank credibility'. *European Economic Review* 32: 1055–75.

Ghosh, A. and Masson, P. (1994) *Economic Cooperation in an Uncertain World.* Oxford: Blackwells.

Gruner, H. (1999) 'On the role of conflicting national interests in the ECB council'. CEPR Discussion Paper No. 2192.

Horne, J. and Masson, P. (1988) 'Scope and limits of international economic cooperation and policy coordination'. *International Monetary Fund Staff Papers* 35: 259–296.

Jensen., H. (1999) 'Optimal monetary policy cooperation through state-independent contracts with targets'. Forthcoming in *European Economic Review*.

Levine, P. and Currie, D. (1987) 'Does international macroeconomic policy coordination pay and is it sustainable? A two country analysis'. *Oxford Economic Papers* 39: 38–74.

Lippi, F. (1999) 'Median voter preferences, central bank independence and conservatism'. Discussion Paper. Banco d'Italia.

Martin, P. (1992) 'Choosing central bankers in Europe'. Mimeo. Graduate Institute of International Studies.

Martin, P. (1995) 'Free riding, convergence and two speed monetary unification in Europe'. *European Economic Review* 39: 1345–1364.

Miller, M. and Salmon, M. (1985) 'Policy coordination and dynamic games'. In W. Buiter and R. Marston, eds., *International Economic Policy Coordination*. Cambridge: Cambridge University Press.

Mundell, R. (1961) 'A theory of optimum currency areas'. *American Economic Review* 51: 657–665.

Muscatelli, A. (1998) 'Optimal inflation contracts and inflation targets with uncertain central bank preferences: Accountability through independence?' *Economic Journal* 108: 529–542.

Obstfeld, M. and Rogoff, K. (1996) *Foundations of International Macroeconomics*. Cambridge: MIT Press.

Oudiz, G. and Sachs, J. (1985) 'International policy coordination in dynamic macroeconomic models'. In W. Buiter and R. Marston, eds., *International Economic Policy Coordination*. Cambridge: Cambridge University Press.

Persson, T. and Tabellini, G. (1993) 'Designing institutions for monetary stability'. *Carnegie-Rochester Conference Series on Public Policy* 39: 53–89.

Persson, T. and Tabellini, G. (1995) 'Double-edged incentives: Institutions and policy coordination'. In G. Grossman and K. Rogoff, eds., *Handbook of International Economics*, Vol. III. Amsterdam: North-Holland.

Persson, T. and Tabellini, G. (1996) 'Monetary cohabitation in Europe'. *American Economic Review Papers and Proceedings* 86: 111–116.

Persson, T. and Tabellini, G. (2000) *'Political Economics – Explaining Economic Policy'*, Cambridge: MIT Press. Forthcoming.

Rogoff, K. (1985) 'Can international monetary policy coordination be counterproductive?' *Journal of International Economics* 18: 199–217.

Romer, D. (1993) 'Openess and inflation: Theory and evidence'. *Quarterly Journal of Economics* 107: 869–903.

Sibert, A. (1998) 'The reputation of the European central bank'. Paper presented at the workshop 'The Euro and its Effects on the Spanish Economy', Donostia-San Sebastian, 26–27 November, 1998.

Svensson, L. (1999) 'Monetary policy issues for the eurosystem'. CEPR Discussion Paper No. 2197.d

Tabellini, G. (1990) 'Domestic politics and the international coordination of fiscal policies'. *Journal of International Economics* 28: 245–265.

Terlizzese, D. (1999) 'A note on lexicographic ordering and monetary policy'. Mimeo. Bank of Italy.

van der Ploeg, F. (1988) 'International policy coordination in interdependent monetary economies'. *Journal of International Economics* 23: 1–23.

Vaubel, R. (1985) 'International collusion or competition for macroeconomic policy coordination'. *Recherches Economiques de Louvain* 51: 223–240.

von Hagen, J. and Suppel, R.1994. 'Central bank constitutions for federal monetary unions'. *European Economic Review* 38: 774–782.

3. Policy Making in an Integrated World: From Surveillance to ... ?[1]

BARRY EICHENGREEN*
University of California, Berkeley

The adequacy of multilateral surveillance and of the institutions charged with carrying it out has been cast into doubt by the series of escalating crises that has punctuated the 1990s. No one questions that domestic policies have important cross-border repercussions in a world of interdependent economies. No one questions the *prima facie* case for surveillance to foster a consensus on the nature of those repercussions, to encourage countries to adjust their policies to better take cross-border spillovers into account, and to monitor governments' compliance with the terms of their agreements. But the adequacy of existing mechanisms for discharging these functions has come under a cloud following the European currency crisis of 1992–3, the Tequila crisis of 1994–5, the Asian crisis of 1997 and the global emerging-markets crisis of 1998 and as a result of the inability of the official community to do much about either the causes or consequences of financial crises.

These recognitions are evident in the drumbeat of criticism directed at the IMF and in calls to convene a new Bretton Woods Conference. But these same statements are revealing of the absence of agreement of how to strengthen surveillance and, in particular, to better avert and manage crises. Respectable voices call for expanding the IMF, shrinking the IMF, merging it with the World Bank and the BIS, spinning off its surveillance and lending functions to regional monetary funds, and even abolishing the institution. The vague and peculiar nature of the term "international financial architecture" that is used to denote the entity that is the object of all this reformist effort is further revealing of the lack of definition that characterizes the debate.

This paper marshals some suggestions of where to go from here. Section 1 focuses on surveillance *qua* surveillance. I first consider the need for a major push in the area international standards as the centerpiece for multilateral surveillance in the 21st century, highlighting what I see as the shortcomings of official initiatives in this area. I describe an idea for reforming the IMF to make it a more effective vessel for the surveillance function. Section 2 turns from crisis prevention to crisis management, considering how to make the Fund a more effective crisis manager and the prospects for expanding private-sector burden sharing when a crisis strikes.

Section 3 discusses the role of policies toward the capital account and the exchange

*I am grateful to the Federal Reserve Bank of Boston for granting me permission to reprint this article here.

A. H. Hallett et al. (eds), Challenges for Economic Policy Coordination with European Monetary Union, 45–63.

rate. Section 4 is a skeptical aside on the economics and politics of regional funds. Section 5, in concluding, sketches the policy agenda going forward.

I. Surveillance

The IMF has been criticized for expanding its surveillance and conditionality from the monetary, fiscal and exchange rate policies that are its traditional bread and butter to prudential supervision, auditing and accounting, bankruptcy procedures, corporate governance and competition policy, among other issues. Its intrusion into everything from the Suharto family's clove monopoly to Indonesia's national car program is attacked as invasive, unnecessary and counterproductive (Feldstein 1998, Rodrik 1999). It is invasive because it interferes with the traditional prerogatives of sovereign states. It is unnecessary, in the view of the critics, because microeconomic and structural conditions are inappropriate for dealing with currency and financial crises that are essentially macroeconomic in nature. And it is counterproductive because different institutional arrangements are appropriate for different economic, legal and cultural settings and because ignoring this, and trampling on national prerogatives, runs the risk of provoking a populist backlash.

THE CASE FOR STANDARDS[2]

The counter-argument is that high capital mobility makes it impossible to fix the international financial system without first fixing the domestic financial systems of countries active on international markets. International financial stability requires domestic financial stability, given the scope for financial problems to spill across borders. And domestic financial stability can only be attained through institutional reform. This is why Feldstein's conclusion, that the IMF should stick to giving advice on monetary and fiscal policies and avoid meddling in the other internal arrangements of countries, will not do. Stabilizing a country's financial system requires institutional reforms extending well beyond policies toward external trade and payments. Few would question that creating a stable financial environment presupposes disclosure requirements for banks and corporations to make available the information required for market discipline to work, and prudential supervision to compensate for theshortcomings of banks' and firms' own risk-management practices.[3] In a world of information asymmetries and highly-leveraged institutions, in which financial crises can spread contagiously, the international community has a common interest in seeing that all countries active on international markets adopt minimally-acceptable domestic arrangements in these areas. Some will argue that this is as far as the IMF and the international community should go in intruding into countries' internal affairs. I find it impossible to resist the conclusion that they must go further – that the need for domestic institutional reforms with implications for the stability of international financial markets extends beyond this point. It extends to the use of internationally-recognized auditing and accounting practices, in whose absence lenders will be unable to accurately assess the financial condition of the banks and corporations to which they lend. It extends to effective creditor rights, in whose absence claimants will be unable to monitor and control the economic and financial decisions of managers. It extends to investor-protection laws to prevent insider trading, market cornering and related practices, in whose absence securities markets will not develop. It extends to fair and expeditious corporate bankruptcy procedures, without which debt problems can cascade from borrower to borrower. Countries can satisfy these desiderata in different ways, but in a world of capital market integration there is no avoiding the need to satisfy them.

The fear, however, is that international pressure for reform will force all emerging markets to don what Thomas Friedman (1999) refers to as the "golden straitjacket", denying them the opportunity to design regulatory institutions sensitive to their distinctive economic, cultural and legal traditions. This is where standards come in. International standards, which define criteria that must be met by all countries but permit them to satisfy them in different ways, offer a way of reconciling the common imperatives created participation on international markets with the existence of diverse domestic economic systems and traditions.[4] The complaint that the IMF's structural interventions are arbitrary and capricious at least partly explains the backlash they have provoked; with the promulgation of international standards there will exist an objective set of criteria to which the Fund can refer when it demands structural changes.

Realism requires acknowledging that neither the IMF nor the G-7's newly-created Financial Stability Forum possesses the competence and resources required to design detailed international standards in all the relevant areas. This is where my recommendations depart from those of the official community. I favor relying as heavily as possible on the private sector: on the International Accounting Standards Committee, the International Federation of Accountants, the International Organization of Supreme Audit Institutions, Committee J of the International Bar Association, and the International Corporate Governance Network, among others. Most of these self-organizing bodies include a full complement of emerging-market members; some also have subcommittees concerned with issues particularly relevant to emerging markets. The multilaterals should of course participate in the deliberations of these bodies as a way of taking "ownership" of the standards they set. But the private sector must take the lead.

Promulgating standards is one thing, enforcing them another. Effective market discipline will require someone to issue blunt assessments of national practice. Each self-organizing should be encouraged to rate countries' compliance with their standards and to establish an electronic bulletin board where such information can be centralized. Hyperlinks should be provided to the Fund's own electronic bulletin board (as they already are, to a limited degree, for macroeconomic and financial data). Where the self-organizing committee is comprised of national regulators, the rating function could still be privatized; it could be spun off to commercial concerns like Fitch-IBCA. If the assessments made by these private-sector bodies are subject to the kind of criticism presently levied at credit-rating agencies – namely, that changes in their evaluations lag changes in market conditions – then the Fund will have to take on the compliance-evaluation function itself. The best way for it to do so would be by publishing an annual report in which it rated each of its member's compliance in each of the relevant sub-areas (perhaps in conjunction with its annual or biannual Article IV consultations, and with help from the World Bank and the BIS).[5] But lenders having a limited attention span, the IMF will have to reinforce market discipline by offering the carrot of concessionary interest rates on its loans to countries that comply and by conditioning its programs on steps to bring national practice into conformance.[6]

AN INDEPENDENT AND ACCOUNTABLE IMF

Unfortunately one worries that the IMF, for the same reasons that it has been reluctant to criticize its members' exchange-rate and macroeconomic policies, will hesitate to criticize them for failing to meet these newly-promulgated international financial standards. The Fund, as a political animal, finds it hard to call its members to task. National governments, which are its shareholders and ultimately call the shots, find it hard to criticize other national governments. They are reluctant to point out shortcomings in national policies for fear of embarrassing foreign heads of state.

This is a specific instance of a more general problem – that IMF decision-making is excessively politicized. To put the point another way, excessive weight tends to be attached to national interests, interfering with the IMF's ability to pursue its broader social mandate. It has been argued, for example, that several of the Fund's recent programs, like those for Mexico, serve the interests of creditor countries by providing financial assistance that allowed foreign portfolio investors to be repaid at the expense of the taxpayers of the crisis country. Here the implication is that IMF policies were used to advance creditor interests, at the expense of future moral hazard and considerable cost to the Mexican taxpayer. It is similarly argued that the U.S. Government arm-twisted the Fund into agreeing to continued disbursements for Russia in 1997– 8, despite evidence that economic and financial reform there off track, in an effort to prop up what it perceived as a reform-minded government and out of concern that failure would bring to power extremists who could not be trusted with the country's nuclear capability. Again, the implication is that IMF policies were used to further U.S. security objectives rather than in the pursuit of financial stability, aggravating moral hazard rather than furthering reform. It is argued that the conditionality the Fund attached to its Asian programs, requiring the crisis countries to open their financial markets and distribution systems to foreign competition, served the interests of advanced-industrial countries seeking market access more than the crisis countries themselves.

If the problem is that the Fund's decisions are distorted by the parochial concerns of national governments, then greater independence from those governments is the logical solution. The obvious way of achieving this is by amending the Articles of Agreement to enhance the independence of the Executive Board, as argued in De Gregorio et al. (1999). Executive Directors could still be appointed by national governments or groups of governments, just as central bank governors in some federal systems are appointed by state or regional governments.

But if Directors are too inclined to take advice from those governments, then the Articles should be amended to discourage them from doing so. If the Statute of the European System of Central Banks prohibits members of the ECB Board from taking advice from their governments, in other words, why shouldn't the IMF's Articles of the Agreement impose the same prohibition on Executive Directors?[7]

Many readers will object that doing so would vest too much power in an all-powerful board of monetary technocrats. This worry could be addressed by amending the Articles to give Directors an explicit mandate – for example to maintain economic and financial conditions and facilitate the pursuit of economic and financial policies that maximize stability, prosperity and growth – and by insisting on greater transparency, notably by requiring more decisions to be taken on the basis of up-or-down votes and releasing the results. In addition, Directors should be required to explain their decisions, and the substance of Board discussions should be made public. If Directors have idiosyncratic objectives, greater transparency of decision making will reveal their hidden agendas, which will in turn strengthen their incentives to pursue the Fund's mandate. Directors' ultimate constituencies will then be able to judge whether their representatives supported or resisted a particular Fund policy, and Directors, rather than going along to get along, will have an incentive to register their dissents.

Ultimately, a specific body must have the power to hold the Executive Board accountable for fulfilling its mandate. The obvious candidate is the Interim Committee. Individual Directors or even the entire Board could be dismissed by a supermajority vote of the Interim Committee.[8] The French Government among others has suggested vesting additional power with the Interim Committee as a way of reinvigorating the Fund. Making provision for the Interim Committee to hold Directors accountable is a way of achieving this end without politicizing the activities of the Fund.[9]

Is this proposal realistic? More than a few readers will be inclined to dismiss it out of hand. But who could have imagined a few years ago how many countries would have moved to establish independent central banks? In an age when some observers call for abolishing the IMF and other recommend creating a "true international lender of last resort", enhancing the independence of its Board is a limited reform. For those who recognize that financial markets are imperfect and acknowledge that those imperfections create the need for an institution to backstop the markets, but who at the same time worry that national agendas too often distort IMF decision making, this is a logical way to proceed.

II. Crisis Response

Amending the Articles of Agreement to enhance the independence of the Board also speaks to the concern that the IMF is too inclined to provide support for unsustainable currency pegs and to let private investors off the hook. If the temptation is always to provide one more bailout now and worry about the consequent moral hazard later, then the solution – by analogy with Rogoff's (1985) argument for delegating monetary policy to conservative central bankers to offset the inflationary bias imparted by the time inconsistency of optimal policy – is to delegate decision-making to independent Executive Directors temperamentally disinclined to bail.

RULES AND MECHANISMS FOR IMF LENDING

Thoughtful Executive Directors, whether independent or not, need guidelines for how and when to intervene. I believe that there are two circumstances justifying IMF intervention, which in turn call for the creation of two different IMF facilities.

Moral hazard may always be with us, but the concern attached to it by observers of IMF policy waxes and wanes. Concern seems to have peaked following the Mexican and Asian crises, when the IMF relaxed its rules governing the size of rescue packages, disbursements reached unprecedented levels, as international investors (in what they referred to as the "moral hazard play") poured money into Russia in the expectation that, if debt-servicing difficulties developed, the Fund would respond with additional finance.[10] When Russia unexpectedly defaulted and investors took losses, this assurance was shattered. Commentators began to question whether the decisions of international investors were really so strongly distorted by the readiness of the IMF to backstop the market.[11] Moreover, the severity of the credit crunch that developed in the autumn of 1998 and the perceived threat to the stability of global financial markets made even the U.S. Congress, previously reluctant to agree to an increase in IMF quotas, recognize that moral hazard was not the sole consideration. Rather, sensible policy requires balancing moral hazard risk against meltdown risk.

Doing so means proceeding as follows. First, moral hazard must be limited by putting the genie of ever-bigger bailouts back in the bottle. There will continue to be occasions when the IMF should assist a country experiencing a sudden reversal in capital flows. That assistance may be justified to support demand and production and minimize the severity of the recession while resources are shifted from the nontraded- to the traded-goods sector. It may be justified to give the government the resources needed to recapitalize an insolvent banking system. It may even be justified to permit the government to repay selected foreign creditors whose goodwill is viewed as essential for the maintenance of credit market access. But the Fund cannot countenance ever bigger bailouts to pay off ever more numerous foreign creditors, or it will create a truly unsupportable moral hazard problem.

The solution is for the Fund to resume its earlier policy of loaning a country no more than 100 per cent of quota in a year and 300 per cent over three years.[12] In addition to addressing moral hazard, this would deal with the fact that the Fund's resources are chronically inadequate to underwrite its activities.[13] While multilateral assistance would still be there to help a government carry out its core functions, it would not always suffice to pay off all existing creditors, preventing the moral hazard problem from getting out of hand. Again, the Articles of Agreement could be amended to eliminate the facilities and provisions that allow exceptions to this rule. If the feeling of shareholders is that the growth of capital markets requires growth in IMF packages, then they should address this directly by using existing mechanisms to agree to a quota increase. In this connection, it would be important to change the way quotas are allocated, placing a higher weight on international capital transactions and a lower weight on current transactions.[14] But the bottom line is that loans for addressing *country* problems should be limited.

Systemic problems which pose a threat to the stability of global financial markets are another matter. Exceptional finance may be required for truly exceptional circumstances. To address these circumstances, the Fund needs a "contagion window" to provide short-term emergency loans to countries with fundamentally strong policies at risk of being destabilized by adverse financial developments abroad.[15] It now possesses something along these lines in the form of its awkwardly named "contingent finance facility" (established by the Executive Board at the end of April). To access this facility, countries have to demonstrate that their policies are fundamentally sound, that they are suffering from events affecting international capital markets originating in other parts of the world, and that the problem is temporary. They will be allowed to access this facility more quickly than other IMF loans, and disbursements will be large and front loaded. Repayment maturities will be short. Interest rates will be high to discourage excessive recourse to the facility.

It is too early to tell whether the Contingent Credit Facility will be good, bad or irrelevant. If the conditions for access are very tightly enforced, the CCF may never be activated, in which case it will prove irrelevant. If, on the other hand, those conditions are loosely enforced, it may turn out to be a serious engine for moral hazard. Thus, we need Goldilocks policy, neither too hot nor too cold. To continue with the metaphor, the proof of the pudding will be in the eating.

ORDERLY WORKOUTS

A credible commitment by the IMF not to automatically run to the rescue of a country that would otherwise find it impossible to keep current on its obligations presupposes the existence of a tolerable alternative mechanism for dealing with outstanding debts. It is easy to *say* that the Fund should no longer bail out governments and their creditors, but it is hard not to *do* so as long as there do not exist other way of reasonably addressing financial problems when they arise. The shortcoming of existing arrangements is that they make workouts excessively difficult. Since many international bonds include provisions requiring the unanimous consent of bondholders to the terms of a restructuring agreement, there is an incentive for "vultures" to buy up the outstanding debt and hold the process hostage by threatening legal action. Unlike syndicated bank loans, most such bonds lack sharing clauses requiring individual creditors to share with other bondholders any amounts recovered from the borrower and thereby discouraging recourse to lawsuits.

Those who believe that countries may have to take occasional recourse to suspensions and subsequent restructurings argue that these provisions in bond covenants should be modified. Majority voting and sharing clauses would discourage maverick investors from resorting to lawsuits and other ways of obstructing settlements beneficial to the debtor and the majority of creditors alike. Collective-representation clauses, which specify who represents the bondholders and make provision for a bondholders committee or meeting, would allow orderly decisions to be reached. This was suggested in 1996 by the G-10 in its post-Mexico report and echoed in a series of recent G-22 and G-7 reports and declarations.[16] In February of this year the G-7 placed the issue on its work program for reforming the international financial system with the goal of reaching a consensus by the Cologne Summit in June.

If this is a good idea, why then have the markets not done it already? One answer is moral hazard. Neither debtors nor creditors may wish to weaken the bonding role of debt by altering loan agreements in ways that might tempt borrowers to walk away from their obligations. Making it easier for debtors to restructure might cause investors to fear that the debtor was prepared to do so at the first sign of trouble and prompt them to liquidate their holdings of his securities, precipitating precisely the kind of bond-market crisis that the international policy community is concerned to avoid.

But if the bonding role of debt was the be-all and end-all, we would also abolish domestic bankruptcy procedures and re-institute debtor's prison to prevent domestic borrowers from ever defaulting on their obligations. In fact, in the domestic context we balance the temptation for debtors to walk away from their obligations against the efficiency advantages, for debtors and creditors alike, of clearing away unviable debt overhangs and restoring the financial health of fundamentally viable enterprises. The argument for collective action clauses in bond covenants is an argument for establishing a similar balance in the international bond market. Majority-voting, sharing, and non-acceleration may make it easier to renegotiate defaulted debts, but if this permits a long deadlock to be avoided, there will be no reason for investors to shun bonds with these features.[17]

A better explanation for why the market has not solved the problem is adverse selection. It is an intrinsic feature of the capital market that lenders know less than borrowers about the latter's willingness and ability to pay. Hence, for the same reason that only patients who anticipate succumbing to a fatal disease will buy expensive life insurance, only countries that anticipate with high probability having to restructure their debts may wish to issue securities with these provisions. Left to its own devices, neither market may function. The danger is that adverse selection would render the market in these modified bonds illiquid and thereby impair the ability of emerging economies to borrow.

The G-10's 1996 report, where the idea of collective action clauses was first mooted, said little about this dilemma. While acknowledging the first-mover problem and suggesting that official support for contractual innovation should be provided "as appropriate", it failed to specify concrete steps to be taken by the authorities. The G-22 subsequently recommended that unnamed governments, presumably those of the United States and United Kingdom, should "examine" the use of such clauses in their own sovereign bond issues. The G-7 recommended that its members should "consider" them. Treasury Secretary Rubin, in a speech designed to set the tone for the Interim Committee's April 1999 meeting, reiterated that the international community should "encourage" their broader use.[18] But the official community needs to do more than examine, consider and encourage. Given the adverse selection problem, progress is unlikely without the introduction of legislation and regulations in the creditor countries. And without progress on this front, the international community will lack credibility when it insists that it will not automatically run to the rescue of crisis-stricken countries.

The way forward would be for the IMF to urge its members to make the inclusion of majority-representation, sharing, non-acceleration, minimum-legal-action threshold, and collective-representation clauses to international bonds a condition for admission to domestic markets. It should provide an incentive for countries to do so by indicating that it is prepared to lend a more attractive interest rates to countries that issue debt securities featuring these provisions.[19] U.S. and UK regulators, for their part, could make the admission of international bonds to their markets a function of whether those bonds contain the relevant sharing, majority voting, minimum legal threshold, and collective representation provisions. They could include these same provisions in their own debt instruments.

Short-term bank credits are a thornier issue. They tend not to be governed by contracts, making it harder to deal with them by specifying contractual provisions.

Litan et al. (1998) have suggested somehow requiring countries to pass legislation that would provide for an automatic reduction of the principal of all foreign currency loans extended to banks in their countries that are not rolled over in the event of a crisis. Foreign creditors could get still out, but only at a loss. The prospect of that loss would strengthen their incentive to stay in, to address their collective action problem, and to restructure the debt.

The danger with this approach is that it could precipitate the very crises that the authorities are concerned to avoid. Banks anticipating that they might wish to get out in the near future but that they could do so only at a loss would scramble out today. A government decree that all foreign bank credits had to be forceably rolled over or written down would be much more disruptive to the markets than collective action clauses in individual bond contracts, which would come into play at the discretion of the individual borrower(s) and lender(s).

The problem remains of what to do about short-term bank-to-bank credits, whose flightiness can threaten the stability of the domestic banking system. Gaining voluntary agreement of the banks to roll over their credits, as in Korea at the end of 1997, is desirable when possible, but possible it will not always be.[20] The best solution, I will argue, is to avoid excessive dependence on short-term foreign credits in the first place. I now develop this point.

III. Policies Toward the Exchange Rate and the Capital Account

The single most robust leading indicator of crisis risk in emerging markets is short-term external debt, the short-term external debt of the banking system in particular.[21] Short-term debt is liquid, and if investors choose to liquidate it, serious financial problems can arise. When the debt in question is debt of the banking system, whose assets are relatively illiquid (by definition, since banks are in the business of providing intermediation services to information-impacted segments of the economy), the result can be bank runs and banking crises. The consequences are especially disruptive in developing countries, where the informational prerequisites for securitized markets are lacking and banks dominate the market in intermediation services.

POLICIES TOWARD THE CAPITAL ACCOUNT

Central banks and governments address this problem by providing deposit insurance and lender-of-last-resort services. But the central bank cannot print the foreign exchange needed to pay off foreign depositors. This is where IMF loans come in, of course, but it is also where they create moral hazard. The dilemma is stark: the expectation of large IMF support packages will encourage an excessive dependence on short-term foreign funding, but the absence of large IMF support packages will leave the lender of last resort powerless in the face of flight by foreign-currency depositors.

In the best of all worlds, banks would internalize these risks, hedging their exposures and avoiding excessive dependence on risky short-term foreign funding. In a second-best world, domestic regulators would require them to limit their exposures, close their positions, and manage their risks. But in the real world, where too few banks can adequately manage risk and too few regulators have the capacity to correct these deficiencies, it may be necessary to intervene directly with policies designed to prevent excessive reliance on short-term foreign funding.

Capital requirements can be used on both the borrowing and lending sides to apply appropriate incentives, although there are reasons to worry about their effectiveness in politicized environments where capital is all too rarely written down. Holding-period taxes a la Chile can be used to lengthen the maturity structure of the debt, but to work they must be universal in coverage.[22] The lesson of Thailand is that simply requiring the banks to close their positions may only encourage them to shift the foreign-currency exposure to corporates, who are no better able to handle it. The bottom line is that short-term foreign-currency-denominated debt is a time bomb waiting to explode, and that holding-period taxes on all capital inflows are the appropriate way of defusing it.

More generally, this perspective suggests that caution should be the watchword when opening the capital account, at the short end in particular. The worst of all possible policies were those followed by Thailand and South Korea before the crisis, which encouraged bank borrowing abroad at the expense of other foreign borrowing and short-term foreign funding over inward foreign direct investment and corporate bond flotations. The now standard lesson the Asian crisis – that exposing badly-regulated banks to an open capital account is akin to offering a recovering alcoholic a drink – implies the need to upgrade bank regulation but also to go slow in opening the capital account.

POLICIES TOWARD THE EXCHANGE RATE

The other way to discourage banks and corporates from developing an excessive dependence on short-term, unhedged foreign debt is by pursuing policies of greater exchange rate flexibility. Allowing the exchange rate to fluctuate is the only credible way of encouraging agents to hedge their exposures. A pegged rate provides an irresistible incentive for the private sector to accumulate unhedged foreign debts. To defend the peg, the government is inevitably forced to insist that there is absolutely no prospect that it will change. How many CFO's will then be rewarded for purchasing costly exchange-rate insurance before the fact? If the currency is allowed to fluctuate on a day-to-day basis, banks and firms will learn the importance of using forward and futures markets to purchase insurance against currency swings.[23] Then, when the exchange rate does move by an unexpectedly large amount, they will not be thrust into bankruptcy by the increase in the cost of servicing short-term foreign debts. A currency crash will not automatically mean a financial crash, as it did for example in Indonesia in 1998, and the greater stability of the domestic financial system will turn stabilize the exchange rate.

All of this assumes the existence of an active interbank market in currency forwards and an exchange-based market in futures. Greater exchange rate flexibility itself provides an incentive for the development of these markets, although prudent governments will use their regulatory powers to provide further encouragement. This is one illustration of how the adoption of a more flexible exchange rate should encourage the development of a more resilient, crisis-resistant financial system.

The other side of this coin is more limited access to foreign capital. A fluctuating currency makes it less attractive for foreign investors to lend, especially in the currency of the borrowing country. Capital flows, especially short-term portfolio capital flows, are less.[24] This effect is apparent in the strikingly low correlation of savings and investment in particular regions of larger countries, in contrast to the much higher correlations for countries as a whole.[25] Another way to put the point is that a fluctuating (or potentially fluctuating) currency which discourages foreign investors from lending in the currency of the borrowing country also limits the ability of banks and firms to hedge their foreign-currency exposures in the aggregate. They can reshuffle those exposures so as to avoid dangerous concentrations, but the overall level of foreign-currency exposure is a given. Greater exchange rate flexibility which creates an incentive to hedge these risks shows up in a lower overall level of foreign borrowing.

Some countries may therefore want to go all the way in the other direction, to dollarization, to obtain freer access to capital flows. Making dollarization work means installing a host of supportive domestic policies. The banking system must be internationalized to compensate for the absence of a lender of last resort. The labor market must be "flexiblized" to compensate for the absence of the exchange rate as an instrument of adjustment. Countries that adopt these policies will enjoy freer access to foreign lending as a result. But the number that are able and willing to go "whole hog" is likely to remain few.

The story would be different were it possible for Mexico or Argentina to obtain a seat on the Federal Reserve Board and exert at least some influence over the stance of their monetary policy. Knowing that they retained at least some say over their monetary destinies, Mexicans and Argentines would be more inclined to embrace dollarization. But the day when the United States is prepared to grant Mexico or Argentina a seat on the Open Market Committee, or even extend U.S. bank regulation and limited lender-of-last-resort services to the country, is still very far away.

If the United States is not prepared to enter a monetary union with Argentina, then the latter may instead wish to contemplate one with Brazil, Uruguay and Paraguay. Importing Brazilian monetary policy is no bargain, but a common monetary policy for Mercosur, like a common monetary policy for Europe, has the potential to create a more stable monetary zone by virtue of the custom union's sheer size and economic diversity.[26] Through one avenue or another, some countries will eventually resolve their dilemma through monetary unification.

But if there is one lesson from Argentina's recent attempt to encourage the U.S. to contemplate this option, it is that the day when the political and economic prerequisites exist for more European-style monetary unions remains very far away. Monetary unification may be the vision of the future, but more flexible exchange rates are the reality for today.

IV. Regional Monetary Funds

The idea of an Asia Fund to supplement the IMF was advanced by the Japanese Government following the outbreak of the Asian crisis; it has been developed further by a number of academics and officials.[27] At least four rationales for the approach can be distinguished. While I analyze them in the Asian context, the conclusions are more general.

First, peer pressure may work better at the regional level. Europe, where mutual surveillance has a long history and a procedure by that name has been enshrined in the Maastricht Treaty, is frequently cited a case in point. But in contrast with Europe, Asia (and other regions) lack institutions with track records comparable to those of the EU's Monetary Committee and Ecofin Council. Nor do Asian countries appear ready to negotiate an international treaty which makes provision for serious sanctions and fines like those of the Maastricht Treaty for countries that fail to adjust their domestic policies. More fundamentally, Asia lacks the tradition of integrationist thought and the web of interlocking agreements that works to encourage monetary and financial cooperation in Europe. There is no counterpart to the social and political "pillars" of the Maastricht Treaty to support the application of peer pressure. There is no wider web of political and diplomatic agreements to be placed at risk by a failure to cooperate on monetary and financial matters.

A second argument is that, because economic structures and conditions vary by region, neighboring countries have a comparative advantage in diagnosing their distinctive economic problems and crafting appropriate solutions. All Asian economies have bank-based financial systems and highly-geared corporate sectors, which the IMF overlooked, the argument goes, when prescribing interest-rate hikes to deal with the crisis; an Asian Monetary Fund would not have committed such an egregious error. This seems to me to greatly exaggerate both structural similarities within the region and the ability of policy makers to gain insight into conditions in neighboring countries from local experience. It is hard to think of three more structurally different economies than Japan, Indonesia, and China, for example.

Third, and related to the preceding, it is argued that the creation of regional monetary funds will intensify competition in the market for ideas. If countries in crisis could appeal to both the IMF and a regional monetary fund, whose assistance was conditioned on different policy actions, then a genuine market in ideas would develop, and only institutions giving sound advice would be able to retain a customer base. If it has a poorer understanding of the roots of the Asian crisis and what measures should be taken to address it than experts employed by the Asia Fund, the IMF will lose business to its regional competitor. Unfortunately, the analogy with market competition is questionable. In a competitive economy, the firm with the best ideas produces the best product, makes the most profits, and ends up dominating its market. It is not clear that the same is true of the market in policy advice and official financial assistance. Intergovernmental organizations do not behave like profit-maximizing firms. A multilateral that offers inferior advice does not necessarily end up losing market share and "filing for bankruptcy". The IMF is paid before other creditors whether its advice is good or bad. It does not follow that a regional fund which lent to governments at unrealistically low interest rates would be driven out of business, since it would more likely than not have its coffers replenished by the high-income countries that were its principal shareholders.

Fourth and finally, the fact that the cross-border repercussions of policies are disproportionately regional is seen as justifying a regional response.[28] Because Asian countries are so heavily export oriented and sell into the same markets, they may need additional intergovernmental credit lines to deal with shared trade-related risks.

Because their bank-based financial systems send few price signals (compared to securitized markets), they may be disproportionately vulnerable to contagious bank runs and currency crises, justifying the creation of a regional monetary fund. In the same way that a community targeted by burglars may wish to create a neighborhood watch to supplement the municipal police force, countries in a region exposed to common risks may wish to create a fund empowered to provide additional financial assistance to one another.

While analytically sound, this argument is likely to be of limited practical relevance. The problem pointed up by the Asian crisis is not that multilateral financial assistance is too little; to the contrary, the IMF's packages were of unprecedented size. To be sure, authors like Radelet and Sachs (1998) have criticized IMF assistance as tardy and tranched. (The Fund doled out its assistance a drop at a time, as the stricken government showed signs of complying with its conditions.) But it is unrealistic to assert that a regional fund would behave differently.

Governments are not willing to extend unlimited support to their foreign counterparts, even when they are the governments of neighboring countries, without evidence that the latter is prepared to undertake the adjustment measures needed to pay the money back. Even in Europe, where the EMS Articles of Agreement technically committed strong-currency countries to provide unlimited support to their weak-currency counterparts, the former have in practice refused to freely underwrite the financial needs of the latter. In any case, ever bigger bailouts, whether supplied by the IMF or a regional monetary fund, are not a sustainable way of coping with financial crises. For those who take the moral hazard problem seriously, the task at hand is rather to provide an alternative approach to crisis management and resolution.

Thus, while the idea of regional funds to supplement the crisis-prevention and crisis-management functions of the IMF has intuitive appeal, closer scrutiny reveals serious problems with the approach.

V. Where We Stand

In my 1999 book, I argued that the new international financial architecture should be organized around four pillars: international standards for financial arrangements and practices, Chilean-style taxes on short-term foreign borrowing as a form of prudential regulation, greater exchange rate flexibility for the majority of emerging-market economies, and collective-action clauses in loan contracts to create an alternative to ever-bigger IMF bailouts. All four elements have to be adopted simultaneously, I argued, to make the world a safer financial place. The good news is that all four elements are on the policy agenda (see Table 1). Each of them has been embraced by either Europe or the United States. The bad news is that not all four elements have been embraced by *both* Europe and the United States.

International standards are one element on which everyone agrees, although there is not yet the necessary commitment to working with the private sector on their promulgation or agreement on steps to encourage compliance. The United States has endorsed greater exchange rate flexibility for emerging markets and expressed sympathy for the use of Chilean-style capital-inflow taxes.[29] But it is still reluctant

Table 1. G7 Timetable for Reform of the International Financial System

- G7 compliance with IMF good practice code on fiscal transparency
- G7 report on strengthening national financial regulation, particularly of highly leveraged institutions
- IMF to complete manual for implementing fiscal transparency good practice code and to start monitoring code's implementation
- IMF (supported by BIS and others) to complete code of best practice for monetary and financial transparency
- IMF to strengthen data dissemination standards
- Early findings of BIS committees on disclosure standards for private sector financial institutions and international capital flows
- World Bank/IMF interim report on establishing insolvency and debtor-creditor regimes
- IMF to report on progress of its policy to lend to countries in arrears to their other creditors
- World Bank interim report on development of principles of best practice in social policy
- IMF to report on proposals for it and other international financial institutions to publish more information
- IMF to report on progress towards formal evaluation mechanism for assessing its own effectiveness

At G7 Spring meeting: discuss progress on:

- Proposals to strengthen World Bank and IMF's Interim and Development Committees
- Examining scope for stronger prudential regulation in industrialized countries and emerging markets
- Considering necessary elements for maintaining sustainable emerging market exchange rate regimes
- Developing new crisis response, including new forms of official finance and ways to include private sector
- Strengthening IMF's crisis prevention and response procedure
- Policies to protect the most vulnerable in society

By OECD Ministerial meeting in May:

- OECD to complete code of principles for sound corporate governance

By G7 Cologne summit in June:

- G7 to convene first meeting of Financial Stability Forum
- G7 consensus on how to proceed on strengthening national financial regulation, particularly of highly leveraged institutions
- G7 consensus on how to promote more collective action clauses in bond issues

By end June 1999:

- G7 to disseminate information on government and central bank foreign exchange liquidity position

By IMF/World Bank Annual Meeting in October:

- IMF and standard-setting bodies to prepare strategy for implementing accounting, corporate33 governance, data and monetary and fiscal policy transparency standards. Joint paper on this by IMF and World Bank
- IMF to finalise structure for transparency reports

By end 1999:

- G7 report on private sector compliance with corporate governance and accounting transparency standards

By January 2000:

- G7 to comply with strengthened IMF data dissemination standard **Others:**
- G7 compliance with best practice code on monetary and financial policy transparency, once code is agreed
- IMF to continue policies of trade liberalization, eliminating soft loans by states to favored industries and non-discriminatory insolvency regimes

Source: *Financial Times* (22 February 1999), p.5.

to do more than utter some encouraging words to bring about the introduction of collective action clauses into loan agreements. Without the addition of renegotiation-friendly provisions to loan contracts, the IMF cannot credibly promise to stand aside when a country is pushed to the brink. And if the IMF cannot credibly refuse to organize a financial rescue, then the incentives for emerging markets to adopt greater exchange rate flexibility and short-term inflow taxes will remain weak.

European policy makers, for their part, are even more concerned about private sector burden sharing. They are less reluctant to legislate and regulate the introduction of new provisions in loan contracts (Jones 1999). But given their own experience, they are less understanding of the need for exchange rate flexibility. Without greater exchange-rate flexibility, the temptation to engage in excessive short-term foreign borrowing will remain, and the adverse financial consequences of large exchange-rate changes, when they come, will be all the more devastating. Again, asserting that the IMF could simply stand aside and let events play themselves out is not credible.

Thus, the task for the short term is to reconcile these differences within the G-7 and to bring the emerging markets into the architecture dialogue. Looking further into the future, it is possible to envisage more radical reform at both the national and international levels. Some countries may want to contemplate dollarization, so long as they are truly prepared to put in place the entire constellation of economic and financial policies needed for it to work. They may want to contemplate the formation of monetary unions, so that those who wish to eliminate the problem of exchange-rate risk are not reduced to the status of passengers who are permitted to ride in the car but never to drive. They may want to amend the Articles of Agreement of the IMF to create a Fund capable of making credible commitments and of carrying out its mandate without succumbing to political pressures. But these are reforms for the future, to be undertaken after completing the tasks at hand.

Notes

1. Prepared for the Federal Reserve Bank of Boston's Conference on Policy Making in an Interdependent World, Cape Cod, 7–9 June 1999. This paper relies even more heavily than usual on the insights of my collaborators in various joint projects related to this topic: to the other authors of the Geneva Report on the World Economy (*An Independent and Accountable IMF)*: Jose de Gregorio, Takatoshi Ito and Charles Wyplosz; to Morris Goldstein, David Lipton and other members of the Council on Foreign Relations Task Force on Strengthening the International Financial System; and to Fred Bergsten and others at the Institute for International Economics, which published my book, *Toward a New International Financial Architecture: A Practical Post-Asia Agenda*. Obviously, the opinions expressed here are not always theirs; for reasons of temperament and space, I may have put some of our conclusions in blunter and less nuanced ways than they would prefer.
2. The arguments of this subsection are from Eichengreen (1999), where they are elaborated in much more detail.
3. And to take systemic risk into account.
4. None of this is to deny that compromise will be required. Indeed, not just emerging markets but the United States itself will be forced to compromise for significant progress to be achieved. Thus, U.S. reservations about the adequacy of international accounting standards, whether parochial or even well justified, hardly encourages other countries to sign on to an agreement that it itself resists.

5. This would appear to be the British Government's preferred approach to this aspect of the international financial architecture. The Fund has begun to explore the feasibility of this task by carrying out a series of pilot reports ("experimental studies in transparency").
6. There remains the question of whether these incentives will be enough. Only a fraction of IMF member countries is subject to a program at any point in time, and there are good reasons to question whether market discipline will be prompt and systematic in its application. This creates an argument for reinforcing these other incentives to comply by having national regulators key capital requirements for foreign lending to whether the IMF rates the borrowing country as in compliance with the relevant international financial standards.
7. Statutory independence may not be enough; effective independence may require an amendment to the Articles specifying that Directors will be appointed to multi-year terms of office and creating high hurdles to their dismissal. Their independence will be strengthened if they receive adequate compensation. (History suggests that this should not be a problem.) It may be desirable to include a provision barring them from moving laterally into government or finance for a specified period following their term on the Board (although enforcement of such a provision would not be straightforward). True independence may in addition require budgetary independence. All large international rescue packages in the 1990s have been cobbled together out of contributions from the IMF, other multilaterals, and national governments. Given the rapid expansion of international liquidity, IMF resources alone have not been enough. The Fund's dependence on financial supplementation from national governments would be another check on the institution's independent Directors. It may be desirable therefore to amend the Articles of Agreement to give the Fund the option of borrowing on the market, subject to the concurrence of a supermajority of the Board.
8. Requiring a supermajority (members of the Interim Committee holding 80 per cent of quotas and votes in the Fund, for example) would protect Directors against arbitrary dismissal and buttress their political independence but at the same time hold them accountable to their mandate and apply sanctions in the event of dereliction of duty.
9. Other reforms of the Interim Committee may also be desirable. In fact, there are a variety of sensible proposals on the table (courtesy of the British and Italian governments, among others). In particular, strengthening the legitimacy of the Interim Committee and the Fund more generally may require updating quota and constituency system to take into account ongoing changes in the world economy, from rapid economic growth in Asia (which should increase the representation of that region) to monetary unification in Europe (which, by eliminating balance-of-payments problems among its members, should reduce its representation). The IMF's review of quotas, now underway, provides an opportunity to take a first step in this direction.
10. A compendium of warnings to this effect is McQuillan and Montgomery (1999).
11. See for example Institute of International Finance (1999).
12. Except under exceptional circumstances, as detailed below.
13. This follows in part from the fact that only a fraction of the currencies in which countries subscribe are usable in the Fund's international operations. Presumably this problem will moderate as more countries graduate to the club of middle- and high-income members with stable finances and convertible currencies.
14. The IMF has recent commissioned a study of how the allocation of quotas should be changed to better reflect changes in the world economy. Updating that formula would strengthen the legitimacy of returning to a quota-based policy of regular access.
15. Note that this differs from existing GAB/NAB arrangements, which govern IMF resources rather than IMF disbursements and may be activated to deal with the problems of a country that is the source of the threat to the international system rather than the victim.
16. See Group of Ten (1996), Group of Twenty Two (1998) and Group of Seven (1998), respectively.
17. To be sure, this is no panacea. Private placements would not be affected. New provisions could

be added to existing loans only through a voluntary exchange of existing bonds for new ones. Not only might some bondholders resist, but any one country that attempted to first to carry out the exchange might be seen as signaling that it was contemplating imminent default and precipitate a crisis. The average term to maturity of international bonds may be on the order of five years, but some have as long as 20 years to run. All this means the incorporation of sharing, majority-voting, non-acceleration, and minimum-legal-threshold provisions into bond covenants will be slow. But slow progress is better than no progress.

18. See Rubin (1999).
19. The Fund has recently signaled its willingness to do so by mentioning the adoption of collective action clauses as one of the criteria that it will consider when determining whether or not countries qualify for its Contingent Credit Facility.
20. The special circumstances that made this possible in Korea are unlikely to be replicated. Korea had the advantage of a newly-elected democratic government committed to pushing through economic reforms. Where the government has less credibility and concerted lending is seen as relieving the pressure for economic adjustment and reform, foreign creditors may not be so inclined to stay in. In addition, the sovereign guarantee extended first to Korean banks and then to the bonds into which the bank credits were converted was viable only by virtue of the sovereign's relatively light debt load, an advantage that not all governments will enjoy.
21. For evidence, see Frankel and Rose (1996) and Rodrik and Velasco (1999). Note that these authors define crises in entirely different ways but reach very similar conclusions.
22. The Chilean authorities discovered, inter alia, that limits on bank borrowing abroad simply encouraged the mining companies to borrow for the banks and on-lend the proceeds. There is an enormous debate over the effectiveness of these taxes. Some critics complain that evasion remains a problem. Others observe the lack of evidence that Chile's taxes limited the overall level of foreign borrowing. The second objection can be dismissed on the grounds that the goal was never to limit the overall level of foreign borrowing but to alter its average maturity, and on the maturity front the evidence is compelling (see Hernandez and Schmidt-Hebbel (1999) for the definitive analysis). As for the first objection, it is important to recall that such a measure, to effectively lengthen the maturity structure of the debt, need not be evasion free. The last word on this subject should go to Chile's finance minister, who has asked (I paraphrase), "If these capital-import taxes are so easily evaded, then why do we have so many non-interest-bearing foreign deposits at the central bank?"
23. Montiel (1999) cites Colombia and Chile in the early 1990s as examples of cases where greater exchange rate flexibility worked to discourage short-term unhedged foreign borrowing. To be clear, the argument is not that central banks and governments should follow policies of benign neglect toward the exchange rate. Freely floating rates are unattractive to most emerging markets, since their economies are small, their financial markets are shallow, and their exports are disproportionately concentrated in a few commodities. Governments may still want to intervene to damp currency fluctuations. My argument is that they will have to learn to intervene less and that countries with open capital markets will have avoid orienting monetary policy around an explicit exchange rate target, which ends up creating one-way bets for currency speculators. I return to the currency-board exception below.
24. For evidence, see again the case studies discussed by Montiel (1999) and the econometrics of Bachetta and van Wincoop (1998).
25. Bayoumi and Rose (1993) provide evidence of this for the regions of the UK, while Bayoumi (1997) does the same for the regions of Canada.
26. In other words, a larger, more economically diversified monetary zone would be less vulnerable to the world-price shocks that have traditionally destabilized Latin American economies heavily dependent on a few primary-commodity exports.
27. See Ito, Ogawa and Sasaki (1999).
28. The evidence and its implications are pursued in Rose (1998).

29. The U.S. position was previewed by Secretary Rubin in his April 21st speech, in which he attempted to signal a new toughness on the need for greater exchange rate flexibility (the headline in the next day's *Financial Times* was "US Urges End to IMF Funds to Back Pegged Currencies"), and a new sympathy for the use of capital-import taxes ("Mr. Rubin also went further than previously in accepting that a Chilean-style tax on short-term capital inflows could be appropriate", the *Financial Times* correspondent wrote).

References

Bachetta, Philippe and Eric van Wincoop (1998) 'Does Exchange Rate Stability Increase Trade and Capital Flows?' NBER Working Paper no. 6704 (August).

Bayoumi, Tamim (1997), *Financial Integration and Economic Activity*, Manchester: Manchester University Press.

Bayoumi, Tamim and Andrew Rose (1993) 'Domestic Saving and Intra-National Capital Flows', *European Economic Review* 37, pp.1197–1202.

De Gregorio, Jose, Barry Eichengreen, Takatoshi Ito and Charles Wyplosz (1999), *An Independent and Accountable IMF*, Geneva Report on the World Economy 1, London: CEPR (forthcoming).

Eichengreen, Barry (1999), *Toward a New International Financial Architecture: A Practical Post-Asia Agenda*, Washington, D.C.: Institute for International Economics.

Feldstein, Martin (1998) 'Refocusing the IMF', *Foreign Affairs* 77, pp.20–33.

Frankel, Jeffrey and Andrew Rose (1996) 'Currency Crashes in Emerging Markets: An Empirical Investigation', *Journal of International Economics* 41, pp.351–366.

Friedman, Thomas (1999), *The Lexus and the Olive Tree*, New York, Farrar, Straus, Giroux.

Goldstein, Morris et al. (1999), *Report of the Task Force on International Financial Architecture*, New York: Council on Foreign Relations.

Group of Seven (1998), *Declaration of G-7 Finance Miniters and Central Bank Governors*, http://www.imf.org/external/np/g7/103098dc.htm.

Group of Ten (1996), *Resolving Sovereign Liquidity Crises*, Washington, D.C.: Group of Ten.

Group of Twenty Two (1998), *Report of the Working Group on International Financial Crises*, Washington, D.C.: Group of Twenty Two.

Hernandez, Leonardo and Klaus Schmidt-Hebel (1999) 'Capital Controls in Chile: Effective? Efficient? Endurable?' unpublished manuscript, Central Bank of Chile.

Institute of International Finance (1999), *Report of the Working Group on Financial Crises in Emerging Markets*, Washington, D.C.: Institute of International Economics (January).

Ito, Takatoshi, Eiji Ogawa and Yuri Nagataki Sasaki (1999) 'Establishment of the East Asian31 Fund', Chapter 3 of Institute for International Monetary Affairs (ed.), *Stabilization of Currency and Financial Systems in East Asia and International Financial Coordination*, Tokyo: Institute for International Monetary Affairs.

Jones, Tim (1999) 'Italian Plan to be Discussed At Dresden', *European Voice* (15 April).

Litan, Robert, et. al (1998) 'Statement of the Shadow Financial Regulatory Committee on International Monetary Fund Assistance and International Crises', Statement No. 145, Shadow Financial Regulatory Committee.

Montiel, Peter J. (1999) 'Policy Responses to Volatile Capital Flows', unpublished manuscript, Williams College.

McQuillan, Lawrrence J. and Peter C. Montgomery (1999), *Tbe International Monetary Fund: Financial Medic to the World?* Stanford, CA: Hoover Institution Press.

Radelet, Steven and Jeffrey Sachs (1998) 'The East Asian Financial Crisis: Diagnosis, Remedies, Prospects', *Brookings Papers on Economic Activity* 1, pp.1–74.

Rodrik, Dani (1999) 'Governing the Global Economy: Does One Architectural Style Fit All?' unpublished manuscript, Harvard University.

Rodrik, Dani and Andres Velasco (1999) 'Short-Term Capital Flows', unpublished manuscript, Harvard University and New York University (April).

Rogoff, Kenneth (1985) 'The Optimal Degree of Commitment to an Intermediate Monetary Target', *Quarterly Journal of Economics* 100, pp.1169–1189.

Rose, Andrew (1998) 'Limiting Currency Crises and Contagion: Is There a Case for An Asian Monetary Fund?' unpublished manuscript, University of California, Berkeley.

Rubin, Robert (1999) 'Remarks on Reform of the International Financial Architecture to the School of Advanced International Studies', *Treasury News* (21 April), RR-3093.32

4. International Macroeconomic Policy Coordination: Any Lessons for EMU? A Selective Survey of the Literature

PETER MOOSLECHNER and MARTIN SCHUERZ
Oesterreichische Nationalbank, Economic Analysis and Research, P.O. Box 61, A-1011 Vienna, Austria

I. Introduction

International economic policy coordination is not merely an economic issue, it is and has also to be treated as a political topic. Consequently, this article aims to provide a selective survey not only of relevant economic literature, but also of political economy literature on international macroeconomic coordination.[1] Particular emphasis will be placed on surveying the literature both on an analytical level, with a focus on divergent methodologies, and on a level of substance, where the coordination topic's key questions are touched upon.[2]

In the section on methodologies three analytical approaches for dealing with economic policy coordination are distinguished: (i) policy optimization analysis, (ii) regime analysis and (iii) international relations approaches. These three analytical perspectives do not necessarily exclude each other but, rather, overlap and demonstrate a difference in the scope of analytical interest. While some empirical approaches cannot be easily subsumed under this typology or simply do not fit this scheme, this differentiation, nevertheless, proves to be helpful to understand analytical differences between the approaches.[3]

In the section on the substance of the coordination literature the coordination literature will be surveyed along the lines of their particular relevance for understanding the policy process and its conflicts. The treatment of the coordination literature will also be related to a number of relevant coordination questions emerging within the context of European Monetary Union.

The survey is organized as follows. After a short introduction Section II starts by reviewing the variety of definitions of coordination. Subsequently Section III considers the rationale for coordination on the one hand or non-coordination on the other. Section IV deals with coordination from the perspective of three different analytical approaches, whereas the likely empirical gains of coordination are evaluated in Section V. The following two sections in particular discuss the role of shocks and other difficulties encountered in coordination, as for example uncertainty. Finally some analytical questions relevant for the topic of coordination in EMU are outlined. An extensive bibliography is attached.

A. H. Hallett et al. (eds), Challenges for Economic Policy Coordination with European Monetary Union, 65–90.

II. Definition of Economic Policy Coordination

Unfortunately the term coordination has been used in a confusing variety of ways.

Wallich (1984, p. 85) provides the classical definition of coordination as "*a significant modification of national policies in recognition of international economic interdependence*". This definition is quoted extensively in the economic literature. However, it does not distinguish independent policy-making that considers international factors from internationally negotiated adjustments to national policies. It rather assumes that policymakers will first formalize policies without recognizing actions by others and then modify these policies.

The definition of coordination by Webb (1995, p. 11), – "*negotiated mutual adjustment that causes states to pursue different policies than they would have chosen had policy-making been unilateral*", which resembles Keohane's definition of cooperation in "*After hegemony*" (1984, pp. 51–52) and also the understanding of Kenen (1990, p. 66) that "*Coordination is the most rigorous form of economic cooperation, because it involves mutually agreed modifications in the participants national policies. In the macroeconomic domain, it involves an exchange of explicit, operational commitments about the conduct of monetary and fiscal policies*", is for analytical purposes therefore preferable. Coordination in a strong sense will involve jointly designed mutual adjustments of national policies – about the time paths of policy instruments and not merely aspirations about the time paths for ultimate-target variables.

Less ambitious forms of interaction are often called economic cooperation. Rather confusing is that in game theory, however, "*cooperation*" involves the existence of a binding agreement (that has to be enforced by an outside authority).[4]

Following Currie, Holtham and Hughes Hallett (1989, p. 24) we may distinguish different levels of cooperation. The spectrum of policy cooperation might comprise:

1. In the simplest case, cooperation might consist only of the exchange of information. Policymakers may exchange information about policy targets and priorities, but they will take their decisions in an autonomous way.
2. Coordination in the form of crisis management will have ad hoc character and will be limited to reactions on episodes of particular difficulties.
3. Policymakers may agree on targets such as the exchange rate or intermediate monetary targeting. A variable might be used as a kind of surrogate for coordination.
4. Partial coordination would involve agreeing on policy assignments.
5. In the form of full coordination, policymakers aim at a bargain across all targets and policy instruments.

III. The Rationale for Coordination and for Non-coordination

"*Coordination of macroeconomic policies is certainly not easy; maybe it is impossible. But in its absence, I suspect nationalistic solutions will be sought – trade barriers, capital controls and dual exchange-rate systems. Wars among nations with these weapons are likely to be mutually destructive. Eventually, they, too, would evoke agitations for international coordination.*" James Tobin (1987, p. 68).

There is broad concurrence in the economic literature on the rationale for coordination. Almost every economic textbook explains that international macroeconomic coordination in an interdependent world economy[5] is desirable when externalities and public goods are important (e.g., Buiter and Marston, 1985). The presence of international linkages implies that policy actions in one country will have spill-over effects into other countries. Spill-over effects may arise from changes in fiscal or monetary policy, taxation, trade or industrial policy.

From a policy perspective the concern is that non-coordination might lead to sub-optimal results. For example a tightening of monetary policy to fight inflation in one country might lead to an appreciation of the currency and to inflationary pressures in other countries whose currencies depreciate. When all countries tighten monetary policy under worldwide inflationary pressures, the result may be an overtightening of monetary policy worldwide (see Oudiz and Sachs, 1984; Miller and Salmon, 1985). A mismatch between fiscal and monetary policy will be characterized by high fiscal deficits and a tight monetary policy. This combination would result in a tendency toward appreciation in the exchange rate and an unbalanced policy mix. The other negative alternative would be an easening of monetary policy combined with loose budgetary policies. The policy mix would be growth supportive in the short run but damaging in the long run.

Some economists have argued that international economic policy coordination will have undesirable effects. Vaubel (1983) concluded that policy coordination is harmful because it reduces competition among governments. Coordination could raise the cost of policy errors if the wrong approach is followed collectively. And Fischer (1988, p. 12) underlined: "*It would in general be far better if the major industrial countries concentrated on the pursuit of sound domestic economic policies and reserved the pursuit of international cooperation for those subjects like international trade and national security in which cooperation is truly essential.*"

Their main argument is that coordination might deflect the attention of national governments from domestic policy issues – which should have a higher priority. However, it is hard to see the exclusiveness of alternatives, i.e., either the pursuit of sound domestic economic policies or the search for coordinated solutions.

Another argument by Rogoff (1985) against coordination has been considered extensively in the literature. Rogoff constructed a two-country model based on a complete rational-expectations framework that includes a role for interest rates. Explicit coordination might be counterproductive if a subgroup of players cooperate in the absence of relevant third parties (in Rogoff's theoretical model it is the private sector which is excluded).[6] The theoretical consideration of the Rogoff paper of likely negative effects of coordination has not been supported by empirical studies (see Section V). Carraro and Giavazzi (1991) provide a counterexample in which with three players – government, firms and trade unions – cooperation is welfare enhancing. They rightly point out that a comparison of the outcome of a game in which central banks cooperate and wage setters expect them to cooperate with a game in which monetary authorities do not cooperate and are not expected to cooperate is misleading, as the case where central banks cooperate is not an equilibrium of the sequential game.

The academic economic literature on international policy coordination started already with the work of Meade (1951) stressing the importance of the problem of policy conflicts. In the studies of Cooper (1968) strategic monetary interdependence was analyzed under a fixed exchange rate system. Cooper argued that a lack of economic policy coordination becomes costly because increasingly interdependent economies complicate the achievement of national policy goals.

International coordination of macroeconomic policies attracted much attention in the academic literature in the 1970s after the regime shift from a system of fixed exchange rates to a system of flexible exchange rates. The techniques of game theory have provided useful tools for analyzing the strategic aspects of policy conflicts and coordination. Much of the analysis took place within a regime of fixed exchange rates.[7] Starting with the contributions of Hamada (1974, 1976, 1979) rigorous game-theoretical techniques have been applied to questions of policy coordination. Hamada's studies were limited to simple symmetrical two-country models without dynamics – interdependence was analyzed in terms of a single-shot game – and implicitly assumed backward-looking expectations of the private sector. In a static game non-coordinated economic policy is typically inefficient because of a prisoner's dilemma in policy choices.

The results of coordination analysis change by moving from a static to a dynamic analysis. In the case of repeated games the variety of outcomes will increase. If strategic interactions are repeated then analysis has to focus on the path and not on the single move. Important are models with structural time dependence where the welfare loss in any period depends on actions in the past as well as present actions.

The question of time consistency of policies gained importance in the 1980s.[8] The interest in such studies was linked to a general revival of political interest in policy coordination. From 1985 onwards the focus of policy interest was mainly on monetary policy and foreign exchange interventions. Research on international economic coordination since then has been mainly developed along two lines, firstly, by analyzing in simplified models the theoretical aspects of strategic behavior and, secondly, by exploring in empirical structural models the interaction of economies.

The focus is on expectational interactions among national policymakers and between governments and the private sector. Special emphasis is given to time consistency and the possibility that policymakers may renege on implicit agreements with the private sector. Information or signals get a crucial role in dynamic games (see Currie and Levine, 1985). Conditional for these models is a high degree of information; the correct model is assumed to be known to all actors participating in the strategic game, and there is the assumption of perfect knowledge about the type of economic disturbances.[9] Dynamic games come up with two kinds of solutions: an open-loop solution and a closed-loop solution. The former considers cases where policymakers set the complete time path of strategies as a function of time. In dynamic games with closed-loop solutions the strategy of the policymaker does depend on time and on state variables.

IV. Diverging Analytical Perspectives on Policy Coordination

There are a number of differences in the analytical perspective between policy optimization and regime analysis and, consequently, rather diverging policy conclusion will result. Both approaches tend from a policy perspective to be rather normative, as they concentrate on likely advantages of coordination achieved either by international optimization or by agreed rules of the game. International relation approaches remain in comparison more descriptive ("*story-telling*") and are more concerned with the political process itself that leads to a coordinated outcome, focusing on power, norms and institutional issues. None of the three approaches consistently has a leading position in explaining coordination but each of them catches important elements of political economy.

POLICY-OPTIMIZATION ANALYSIS

The economic literature on macroeconomic policy cooperation is dominated by policy-optimization analysis. Policy optimization concentrates on explicit coordination. What is the economic outcome when policymakers set economic policy in a coordinated way?

The notion of policy interdependence has been operationalized in the framework of a policy-optimizing approach. In such an analysis the agents are national governments, which have well-defined, exogenously given preferences (loss functions). The interactions among national economies (the way in which policies and shocks originating in one country affect other countries) and the alternative strategies available to national governments are exogenous to the analysis. The decisions of national governments are treated as cooperative or non-cooperative games.[10] Each national government is a unitary decision-making agent who acts in a strategic way according to its interests which are biased towards domestic welfare.

In a non-cooperative game structure, policymakers try to maximize their own country's welfare, taking the policies of other national governments as given. Unilateral national behavior is often modeled as Nash or Stackelberg non-cooperative behavior.[11] A *Nash equilibrium* is deemed to be the optimal non-cooperative decision, it is the result of a strategic game in which each party maximizes its objectives by taking the action of the other party or parties as given. In a Nash equilibrium all parties are on their reaction curve and are acting in a credible way.

Stackelberg behavior results when one nation takes a leadership position vis-à-vis others. Such a leader-follower solution to two-country models provides a kind of halfway point between the Nash and cooperative equilibria. This behavior will be contrasted with cooperative approaches and the incentives to deviate from cooperative outcomes are studied. In a cooperative game structure the national governments will jointly maximize a weighted average of their individual welfare (a joint welfare function).[12] Cooperative games will generate Pareto-optimal outcomes.

The policy-optimizing approaches rest on rational choice assumptions and on the hypothesis of an unitary-actor.[13] One of the problems of economic arguments relating to the international macroeconomic coordination is the assumption that policy-making is a technical exercise in welfare maximization. According to this approach nations have well-defined loss functions and act to optimize their decisions accordingly. This suggestion is far from convincing. Macroeconomic policy-making might rather be understood as government actions to achieve a variety of conflicting aims. Many of these goals might have more to do with domestic policy than with policy optimization.

Apparently, the typical assumption of policy optimization that each government can be treated analytically as a unitary actor does not represent the political and institutional facts of life. A multiplicity of domestic players with different interests should make analysis a lot more difficult. In reality it will be difficult to define a uniform national interest. There will rather be conflicting interests between influential groups such as producers and consumers, trade unions and employers organisations or exporters and importers. And in any case, coordination does not necessarily reflect national interests. It rather reflects each government's perception of its own interest, which may differ from what independent experts define as national interests.

REGIME ANALYSIS

Regime analysis studies policy coordination from a different standpoint, namely assuming that policy coordination is needed in order to produce certain public goods, such as stability. However, the contrast between policy optimization and regime analysis is not a sharp one. If policy optimization concentrates on explicit coordination then regime analysis might be said to concentrate on international economic coordination through presumptive rules. It should be noted that we do not understand the term regime as a substitute for the hegemon's role but rather as an alternative to explicit coordination.[14]

The general mode of cooperation in a regime is mutual recognition by participants of the rules, which are at least to some degree subject to multilateral surveillance. Rules are expected to have a number of advantages: It is often argued that policymakers prefer to follow well-designed rules that are easily monitored and that will be appreciated by the public. The expected advantages of reputation and credibility might be viewed by policymakers as favorable even if policy rules will exert discipline on the policy-making process. In addition rules are expected to protect the small players against the large ones.

The questions posed by regime analysis are: What kind of rules of the game help to achieve the most efficient economic outcome? In practice policymakers (and the literature) have focused almost exclusively on the exchange rate.[15]

The performance of alternative international regimes which are confronted with various shocks in relation to a certain goal is evaluated by structural multi-country models.[16]

Policy coordination in practice may be directed mainly to regime preservation and not to policy optimization. Exchange rate cooperation in the 1980s would in this terminology be called regime preservation, and we will argue that coordination under EMU would also fall in this category.

There is the famous Williamson-Miller (1987) extended target zone approach proposing that fiscal policy should be used to aim at internal nominal demand growth, while monetary policy focuses at the external balance by holding exchange rates within wide bands around an *equilibrium exchange rate level*. Currie and Wren-Lewis (1989a, 1989b, 1990) found that the extended target scheme could have improved the economic performance over the period 1975–1986.[17]

Taylor (1989) examined a number of monetary rules under different exchange rate regimes.[18] In the comparison of a fixed exchange rate system with a flexible exchange rate system in which monetary policies has different aims – such as stabilizing the price level or nominal income or both price and output with different elasticities – the conclusion of the study is that a *mixed price-real output rule* is likely to have better stabilization properties in the case of exogenous shocks to the economy than a *pure rule based on either prices or nominal GNP*.

In conflict with these results is the outcome of a study by Hughes Hallett, Holtham and Hutson (1989), which, based on the MCM model of the Federal Reserve Board, analyzed the advantages of a combination of exchange rate targeting and pursuing at the same time independent policies. Their conclusion is that there are prospects for improving policy coordination by exchange-rate management.

Levine et al. (1989) concludes by using a reduced two-bloc version of the OECD Interlink model that policy coordination can be effective when the rules are kept simple and that there is scope to use simple rules as a surrogate for stronger versions of coordination. In the study of Bryant at al. (1993) it was tried to rank regimes according to their performance.[19] One of the robust generalizations emerging was the relatively poor performance of exchange rate targeting relative to the other international regimes studied.[20] In general the performance of simple policy rules depended on the nature of shocks facing the economies.

To a certain degree regimes work as a kind of substitute for coordination. In the gold standard system the adjustment mechanism – the famous price specie flow variant – worked in an automatic way.[21] The rules of the game – an asymmetric fixed exchange rate system – were explicitly defined. Policymakers of non-reserve currency countries had to intervene in order to keep exchange rates fixed, while the policymaker of the reserve country could follow an independent monetary policy. The rules of the game were therefore clear and the interplay of policies was determined by these rules of the game.

INTERNATIONAL RELATIONS APPROACHES

The term international relations approaches is rather broad as it comprises realist, neorealist and liberal institutionalist approaches in international relation theory.[22] International relations approaches have tended to focus on the systemic level of analysis, on the sources of and constraints on cooperative behavior among states as a function of the international system. Much of this literature has also used game theory and interpreted the prisoners' dilemma as the key element of international politics. Reference to the social context will be of help for an adequate understanding of the process of economic policy coordination.[23]

In political economy literature the issue of power is underlined for strategic problems (Webb 1995, chapter 2) and leadership becomes a key element for successful coordination. Power – following the definition by Krasner (1983, p. 342) "*the ability to determine who plays the game, or to define the rules, or to change the values within the payoff matrix*" – shapes the distribution of burden of adjustment to international macroeconomic imbalances, and international bargaining power is crucial for understanding why policy coordination has happened and why not, and also for the question why the burden of adjustment is distributed as it is among countries.

Webb argued (1995, p. 46ff) that "*the record of international macroeconomic coordination ... suggests that the key issue in international negotiations has been determining how burdens of adjustment ... will be distributed among countries, not overcoming obstacles to cooperation posed by the fear of cheating in an anarchic world*". In the case of the Bonn summit 1978 the outcome helped influential groups in each country to achieve domestic aims.

Krasner (1991) pointed out that in the case of pure coordination games, distributional conflicts over Pareto-optimal outcomes are likely to be resolved through the exercise of power. International bargaining power is considered to be of greater importance for governments than concerns about maximizing welfare (which motivates the discussions of international policy coordination in the framework of policy-optimizing approaches as we have seen in chapter 2.1).[24] However, political scientists themselves often follow rather abstract approaches such as improving the states' international power position. And very similar to the policy optimization approach in realism, states are treated as unitary and rational actors engaged in the pursuit of national self interest.

As there is not one theory of cooperation in international relations literature we have to concentrate on the hypotheses with which the divergent approaches came up: Hegemony is often understood as the key for understanding the extent of policy coordination. The leadership of a hegemon may facilitate a desirable outcome (see Kindleberger, 1973; Gilpin, 1975; and Keohane, 1984).[25] If stability can be understood as a public good, all countries benefit from it irrespective of whether they contribute to its production or not.[26]

Two propositions have to hold simultaneously: First, the presence of a dominant actor should lead to the provision of greater stability in the international environment, and second this greater stability has to benefit all states in the system. In the *benevolent strand of hegemony theory* literature (Snidal, 1985) the hegemon is willing to pay an undue part of the short-run costs of the public good either because he expects to gain in the long run and/or because he expects gains in other fields (Kindelberger, 1986, p. 8).[27] The *coercive strand of hegemony theory* describes the idea how a hegemon might use its power to create an international economic system. Rather than providing the public good unilaterally by adjusting its policy, the hegemon could offer rewards and threat with punishment to persuade other countries to adjust their policies.

Realism takes a rather pessimistic view of state behavior. The realist assumption is that states are egoistic and that policymakers will act rational on the basis of what they perceive as their self interest. The realist approach has important limitations for a general understanding of the sources of defection from cooperation. The overemphasis on the state has explanatory disadvantages. Keohane urges to reformulate realism "*because it fails to take into account that states' conceptions of their interests, and of how their objectives should be pursued, depend not merely on national interests, and the distribution of world power, but on the quantity, quality, and distribution of information*" (Keohane, 1984, p. 245).

In concentrating on the state as an actor, the ways in which other actors might use institutions is neglected and the way in which the state interest is changed by actions of institutions is not considered. State interest can be shaped by epistemic communities or by institutional structures: *Institutionalism* refers to the regimes set up by hegemons. The regimes consist of principles, norms and rules and decision-making procedures on which the expectations of actors converge. The importance of institutions – a set of practices and expectations – is underlined because they help policymakers to pursue their own interest through cooperation. Regimes might reduce uncertainty and make cooperation easier as they provide transparency and information to relieve likely fears that arise in a multipolar world (e.g., the fear that countries will act unilaterally). Regimes create the expectation that all participating parties will interact indefinitely and that a defection of one party will be punished by another party's non-cooperation in the future. Regime members calculate reputational gains from coordination. This would imply that regimes shape preferences of the members and encourage cooperation (Moravcsik, 1993).

An *epistemic community* might be viewed as a prerequisite for cooperation. It means "*a professional group that believes in the same cause-and-effect relationships, truth tests to accept them and shares common values; its members share a common understanding of a problem and its solution*" (Haas, 1992, p. 55). When uncertainty is high, decision-makers might be more willing to permit scientific elites access to the policy process with the chance that their views get institutionalized in the policy process, and might change national preferences. It remains an open issue why and when an epistemic community will have an impact on the domestic policy system.

One strand of the literature focuses on the issue whether the source of state preferences is *international* or *domestic*. The use of game theory with its assumption of unitary and rational actors has influenced the decision in literature to neglect domestic politics. Unlike the state-centric theories, a two-level approach considers domestic conflicts as inevitable. Policymakers will have to reconcile domestic and international imperatives (Putnam, 1988). In "*two level game theory*"[28] policymakers act at two levels – a domestic one and an international one. Milner (1992) suggested that domestic political situations often leave states unable to implement internationally cooperative policies. The key obstacles to strengthening policy coordination were interpreted to be domestic, not international (Webb, 1995). Monetary and especially fiscal policies were traditionally considered as policies designed to internal goals.[29]

A further hypothesis is that "*the prospects for cooperation diminish as the number of players increases*" (Oye, 1986, p. 18). This view is shared in economic literature by Taylor (1987), who believes that difficulties of monitoring compliance tend to increase with the number of participants, but has been challenged by others. The point that a large number of states creates collective action problems, because the probability of defection will increase and the feasibility to sanction the defector will be reduced, has explanatory weaknesses. A large number of players provides more opportunities for exchanges and side payments (Grieco, 1988).

The international relations literature on coordination remains to a large part game-theoretic. It has been guided by a systemic focus and by observations of problems that compel coordination among governments. Even if the simplifying assumption of policy-optimizing approaches were left and analysis was located in the social context that is almost excluded in economic analysis, the international relations approaches have a number of drawbacks. Their hypothetical character makes them vulnerable to empirical counter-examples. As strategic processes are often described in a metaphorical way the concepts lack explanatory power. It is remarkable that to a large extent international relation literature neglects domestic politics. Similar to economic literature on coordination, international relations approaches rely heavily on unexamined assumptions about the determination of the payoff structures of states, the likely strategies to alter systemic conditions and the capacity of states to ratify and implement cooperative arrangments.[30]

V. Gains from Economic Policy Coordination?

In empirical studies (Oudiz and Sachs, 1984; McKibbin and Sachs, 1989; Taylor, 1985) the results of a welfare function, where each country maximizes its welfare (weights are assigned to various economic objectives in each country), are compared with the values when countries maximize a joint welfare function. The difference between the two calculations is taken as a measure of the gains to coordination.

In their pioneering study, Oudiz and Sachs (1984) investigated the quantitative gains to international policy coordination by treating policy formulation as a static game.[31] They estimated that the gains from cooperation among the G3 countries in the mid-1970s would be about 0.5% of GDP to each country compared with the best Cournot-Nash non-cooperative outcome. In a more general analysis Hughes Hallett (1986) estimated the gains to be between 0.5% and 1.5% of GNP for USA, EEC and Japan.

Gains of this size are not much bigger than the forecast standard of errors of the target variables. But the question whether the gains from coordination are sizable is in fact not well defined. The standards of comparison for this judgement are unclear and the results are sensitive to the choice of weights. It is impossible to distinguish welfare improvement resulting from economic policy coordination from improvement attributable to less ambitious forms of cooperation (e.g., consultation). The counterfactual outcome – optimization by policymakers in the Nash noncooperative equilibrium – is not necessarily convincing. A comparison between optimal coordinated policies and optimal non-coordinated policies is not realistic as it should be more relevant to compare sub-optimal coordinated policies with sub-optimal non-coordinated policies.

In addition, measurement of gains can be sensitive to the range of policies considered. The magnitude of gains might increase if not only macro- and microeconomic factors but also non-economic issues are considered. A wide domain of policies considered will change the results on coordination gains.

Small demonstration models (Currie and Levine, 1985; Miller and Salmon, 1985; Oudiz and Sachs, 1985; Levine and Currie, 1987) where each economy is represented by a few simplified equations suggested that the gains from coordination are likely to be small but significant. However, the equations restrict the framework to a world of two identically symmetric economies with either no dynamics or steady state dynamics. The policy responses are known with certainty and there are no information innovations. The results are similar in simple but estimated models of Carlozzi and Taylor (1985), Sachs and McKibbin (1985) and Taylor (1985).[32]

A great advance in the 1980s has been the increasing flow of empirically based results that would make the theoretical research more relevant for policy makers. There are a huge number of studies based on large-scale empirical multi-country models (see e.g., Canzoneri and Minford, 1988; Currie, Levine and Vidalis, 1987; Currie and Wren Lewis, 1990; Frankel, 1990b; Frenkel, Goldstein and Masson, 1989; Hughes Hallett, Holtham and Hutson, 1989; McKibbin and Sachs, 1989, 1991; and Taylor, 1985, 1989).

Studies agree on the conclusion that the gains from coordination are not evenly distributed. Oudiz and Sachs 1984 came up with the result that gains are distributed approximately 2:1 in favor of Germany relative to the USA in two different models. Hughes Hallett (1986) found, by using a range of bargaining models, gains to be distributed 2:1 in favour of the EEC relative to the USA. This result is somewhat sensitive to alternative types of exogenous shocks (Hughes Hallett, 1987). Cooperation in the form of an agreement on the exchange rate path might lead to an asymmetrical distribution of gains among the G-5 countries (Hughes-Hallett, 1989).

Policy optimization and international relation approaches converge in stressing the argument that significant gains may result merely from information exchange between policymakers and from strategic rather than myopic actions (Keohane, 1984; Bryant, 1987; Currie, Holtham and Hughes-Hallett, 1989). Canzoneri and Edison (1989) concentrate on the selection of a "*good*" non-cooperative solution from a set of Nash equilibria. The differences in Nash solutions may result from information sharing and surveillance, the choice of policy instruments and the adoption of reputational strategies. They conclude that coordination in terms of information and surveillance is far more important than coordination of instruments. Even limited cooperation such as information exchanges should bring gains in terms of more efficient noncooperative policies – outcomes reached without proper coordination. Information exchanges about the initial conditions of economies and about expected shocks may help to reduce uncertainty, they "*appear to be a key part of the co-ordination process, irrespective of the model or the time period*" (Currie and Levine, 1991, p. 402). Also the institutionalist literature underlines the importance of mere consultations and information exchange (see Keohane, 1984). Information exchange and regular consultations about policy intention will yield benefits in any case but will be of particular help when serious crises emerge.

A number of factors caution against drawing policy conclusions from the studies on gains of coordination. Firm evidence on the signs and sizes of the spillover effects among countries is not available. The results may be sensitive to specific features of the chosen model.

A number of gains of policy coordination – to be expected because of issue-linkages and package deals in other policy areas – will not be caught by the policy-optimizing approaches because of its narrow focus.

VI. The Specific Role of Shocks in Policy Coordination

The role of shocks has drawn attention in a number of studies. Canzoneri and Minford (1988), Curie et al. (1987) found relatively small gains in the absence of major shocks, based on calculations from versions of the Liverpool and OECD models for the USA and the EEC or OECD respectively. The mix of shocks (the size and nature of exogenous shocks) can affect the gains form coordination. Persistent shocks and the existence of "*reputation*" increase the importance of coordination (Curie et al., 1987).

McKibbin and Sachs (1991) have shown that the benefits from monetary policy coordination are quite limited, because of the importance of supply-side spillover effects arising from fiscal policy. If policy is more constrained, then the benefits from coordination will fall.

Currie et al. (1987) found in a dynamic analysis – a reduced version of the OECD model – the gains of coordination to be small in the face of temporary disturbances. But benefits will increase as the persistence of the disturbance rises and the existence of "reputation" increase the importance of coordination. However, it is not clear why a non-coordinated outcome should not also be affected by exogenous shocks.

Canzoneri and Henderson (1991) make a difference between symmetric and asymmetric shocks. They showed that the Cournot-Nash equilibrium is overcontractionary for symmetric shocks. In the case of asymmetric shocks it can be overcontractionary for one country and overexpansionary for the other country. Fratianni and von Hagen (1992) conclude that the desirability of the European Monetary System (EMS) critically depended on the relative size of asymmetric and symmetric shocks and on the correlation pattern between them.

A further contribution by Canzoneri and Henderson (1991) was the development of an analytical framework in which policymakers are confronted with periodic supply shocks. When monetary authorities in the case of a negative supply shock are only concerned with the inflationary impact and not with the consequence for the foreign country – a real depreciation of its currency – then the worldwide monetary expansion would turn out to be too low.

VII. Difficulties for Macroeconomic Policy Coordination

In the case of models which assume perfect knowledge about the type of economic disturbances and of the policymakers' reaction function, the analysis had to concentrate on the problem of inefficient equilibria. However, the results from studies assuming perfect foresight by policymakers may be biased against finding large gains of coordination.

UNSUSTAINABILITY

A point made by several authors is, that coordination without reputation might be counterproductive (see Miller and Salmon (1985); for a standard illustrative model incorporating the key international spillover effects see Levine and Currie (1987) and Currie, Levine and Vidalis (1987); and for a static model Canzoneri and Henderson (1988), Currie and Levine (1991)).[33] Without government reputation vis-a-vis the private sector cooperation between policymakers may not pay, and when it does the benefits would be minimal.[34]

A coordination solution will be unsustainable when policymakers do not stick to their commitment and cheat by deviating in their future policies from the agreed policy stance. Analytically this issue is treated by considering forms of reneging.

With the passage of time a country or more countries might come to a point where there is an incentive to renege on the cooperative outcome. Such cooperative agreement will lack credibility, and rational policymakers will not enter into such an agreement. The *folk theorem of repeated games* stresses the point that even if players have an incentive to renege (to deviate from the coordinated outcome) they will not do so because they fear to lose payoffs when other players can punish them in the subsequent periods.

The traditional method to restore sustainability is to devise an incentive mechanism through sanctions against reneging. If there are supranational institutions which can legally enforce the coordinated solution then policy will be credible. The institution will prevent that policymakers renege on each other or on the private sector. This implies a "*loss of sovereignty*" as Canzoneri and Henderson (1988) contrast it with a sovereign policy-making process whereby countries co-ordinate on an agreed outcome and employ trigger mechanism to enforce that outcome.

As Cooper already pointed out in 1985, the term "*time inconsistency*" may be inappropriate for reference to the policy process as it refers only to a particular analytical framework for choosing optimal policy over a finite period of time. Cooper concluded that the problem of forward-looking expectations has been exaggerated within that framework. What in his view is more important is a lack of trust. But as there is no empirical evidence on this issue a definitive judgement results difficult.

Following Kenen (1990) and Bryant (1995) the issue of reneging and cheating (Hughes Hallett, 1986b) stressed in literature has to be considered as exaggerated by looking to historical experiences. What seems to be far more important is the question of uncertainty.

UNCERTAINTY

"*... uncertainties about the effects of one country's policies on the economies of other countries make it impossible to be confident that coordinated policy shifts would actually be beneficial*" Feldstein (1988).

The literature on coordination, which in the 1970s mainly focused on the choice of policies and policy bargains, moved on to analyze also the implications of the choice of models and model bargains. Model uncertainty – which means the technical reference to uncertainty about the *true* model – was explicitly introduced in the theoretical analysis by Ghosh and Masson (1987, 1991, 1994), Masson (1992), Frankel (1988, 1990) Frankel and Rockett (1988).

Frankel and Rockett (1988) were pessimistic about the gains from coordination under conditions of uncertainty. They provided a static framework for evaluating a specific type of policy uncertainty – namely uncertainty about the true model of the economy. Their analysis is based on ten large multi-country models (USA and Europe), with the assumptions that each country uses its own model to measure the gains of a coordination solution and that governments do not exchange information but that they agree to coordinate when their own calculation of welfare effects shows that it will be beneficial for them. In other words: each government believes in its own model and knows the other models. They showed that misperceptions about economic behaviour can lead to-welfare worsening policy bargains.

Some caution about these results seems to be necessary as the assumption that policymakers do not consider the possibility that the models used by their counterparties might be correct is not convincing. The results – that the gains to one country that unilaterally discovered the correct model and adjusted its policies accordingly are much greater than the potential gains from coordination – are of little help for policymakers as we may doubt that they will ever find the *true* model.[35]

In addition, a number of studies have reversed these results. The presence of model uncertainty may provide an additional incentive to coordinate policies, provided that policymakers recognize that they cannot know the true model. In particular Ghosh and Masson (1991) showed that, by allowing for the possibility of learning that the model used by others may be correct, coordination dominates uncoordinated regimes.[36] Under the assumption of Bayesian learning the ex post gains from coordination turn out to be positive in their simulation exercises.

In the case of uncertainty not only the interaction among policymakers is of relevance but also epistemic communities, i.e., "*networks of professionals with recognized expertise and competence in a particular domain and an authoritative claim to policy-relevant knowledge* ..." (Haas 1992, p. 3), might get an important role as a source of information that will contribute to overcome uncertainty about policy coordination.[37] In economic literature the term used is not epistemic communities, but consensus on ideas is also underlined (Frankel, 1988; Cooper et al., 1989; Eichengreen, 1997).

Coordination literature has concentrated on game-theoretic dilemmas of collective actions and on uncertainty. In reality there are multiple obstacles to successful coordination, such as differences in policy objectives between policymakers, the lack of a coherent common understanding how macroeconomy works and how it should work, heterogenous national institutions, and contingent political and social factors. If there are differences in fundamental matters such as the role of the state or in the degree of necessary liberalization then coordination will result extremely difficult. In reality coordination will be complicated by political, bureaucratic and legal constraints on jurisdictional divisions within governments. Looking back in monetary history we may conclude that coordination has been successful in cases where it was systematically institutionalized and where the political consensus was broad.

VIII. Future Policy-Oriented Research Areas: Coordination within EMU?

Without doubt, the formation of a Monetary Union in Europa has raised a large number of new and important questions concerning policy coordination and, in fact, led to new and increasing interest in the topic. A large number of future policy-oriented research areas in this field can be identified which deserve our interest.[38]

First of all, the EMU regime might be interpreted as a surrogate for far-reaching forms of policy coordination. More ambitious forms of coordination aiming at explicit coordination so as to optimize the policy mix in EMU are confronted in any case with coordination constraints imposed by the EMU regime, such as the independence provision of the ESCB and the supreme monetary policy goal of maintaining price stability.

The central argument is that the EMU game is mainly about regime preserving, i.e., about preserving monetary dominance. For example, the tight fiscal rules of the Stability and Growth Pact should increase further the credibility of the single monetary policy and should ensure compliance with the independence requirement of the ESCB.

The basic characteristic of playing according to the rules of the EMU game is that policies have to be compatible with the operation of the regime. If policies become incompatible the rules of the game will point to the need for adjustment.

International cooperation understood as a two-level process (Bryant, 1995)[39] means that in exceptional periods negotiations take place at the top level (e.g., Treaty on the European Union, Stability and Growth Pact). The ongoing policy decisions at the lower level will then be influenced by the rules of the game agreed at the higher level. Now that the EMU regime – a kind of monetary dominance regime – has actually been put in place the participants have moved on to the subgame of how to play in EMU.

Three areas of particular interest can be selected on which policy oriented research in the field of coordination in EMU might focus. All approaches will have to assign importance to all kinds of uncertainty.

Exceptional crises/shocks (asymmetric or symmetric):The *rules of the EMU game* – as perhaps the rules of all games we can think about – can never cover all contingencies. A threat that therefore has to be considered in any regime – but in EMU in particular because of its multi-level structure – is that under a given set of rules defects might emerge which cannot be resolved through calls for discipline by the leader. Historical experience has taught that international regimes are threatened by crises (in EMU, e.g., the risk of a pan-European crisis) and that the issue of coordination might be reformulated as a question for the adequate form of crisis management.

Social context of EMU: Rule-based regimes cannot by themselves create credibility.

They "*depend for their effectiveness on adherence to the spirit as well as to the letter of the agreed rules*" (Cooper, 1985, p. 1229) and as Frankel (1990, p. 110) pointed out "*if a cooperative regime is to be successful, it must be built on an accumulation of trust*". Trust may be particular fragile in EMU, which is after all no political Union and not founded in a world of surrendered sovereignty, rather the contrary.

In this respect the importance of scientific research on the question of social context was underlined in the literature survey. The advantages of a rules-based regime can be realized if it is not only strongly backed by macroeconomic and structural policies but also by the political will. This means on the one hand that the rules of the EMU game will have to be based on a consensus relating to the economic policy paradigm among policymakers, epistemic communities, institutions and the monetary authority. Paradigms have changed – e.g., with the demise of the Keynesian consensus in the 1970s and early 1980s, and might change again. But on the other hand, the political will itself has to be based on a social consensus. A lack of credibility, which signifies in a broad sense political sustainability, might emerge if the policy mix of the EMU regime turns out unfavorable.

Further political science research is needed on the question whether a technical institution such as the ECB might get into trouble by playing a strategic role in the European policy process. Viewed from a normative democratic-oriented approach, a monetary dominance regime lacks legitimacy. As the principal cannot transfer its legitimacy to the agent, the legitimacy of the latter depends on the outcome and remains fragile.

As an issue such as democratic accountability in EMU cannot not be limited to the question of transparency it will not be sufficient for the ESCB to be, first, transparent about its policy intentions in monetary policy, second, to demonstrate technical competence in monetary policy and, third, to leave no doubt about monetary leadership in the regime.

Preferences in society about the interplay of monetary policy with other policies, the solution of trade-offs between policy objectives and the institutional possibilities in the case of crises may diverge. This fact is bound to complicate, in every scenario, the coordination process. A strategy of clear division of responsibilities among monetary and fiscal authorities seems to be more feasible in a national context where technical solutions aiming at efficiency are based on a consensus. It is an open issue whether a game of monetary leadership is socially sustainable in the long run.

Structure of incentives/strategic interactions: An analysis of the EMU regime has to take account of a changed incentive structure of players in EMU. The monetary authorities are involved in a game with private-sector wage- and price setters and fiscal authorities. For the outcome of this game, it will be decisive whether the design of the EMU regime is robust vis-à-vis non-coordination, this means if policymakers and social partners undertake exactly those policies that are required to sustain the regime. Even from the point of efficiency, a threat strategy of the Eurosystem – to announce countervailing action in the case of loose fiscal policy or excessive wage policies – might be dangerous as it concentrates on misbehavior and does not extend adequately on the policy reaction in the case of sound macroeconomic behavior.

The independent ECB might opt on the basis of its strategic leadership role for a less or more cooperative policy equilibrium. In any case it will be decisive whether EU governments and social partners are willing to take the role of Stackelberg followers of the Eurosystem that has the possibility of disciplining other policy areas in order to achieve the aims of the Maastricht Treaty. To establish credibility of its price stability target by neglecting the costs for the policy mix will be sub-optimal.

As a rule-based regime can by no means be a substitute for far-reaching co-ordination it is preferable to regard the three analytical approaches presented in the survey as rather complementary. The key weakness of the EMU regime is that it was never conceptually coherent but marks rather a further step in an open integration process of the EU, which has to be kept in mind in each policy-oriented analysis of coordination in EMU.

IX. Concluding Remarks

The theoretical case for international coordination was well established, and presumed settled, in the 1970s. In the mid-1980s, the focus of research shifted to intertemporal aspects of economic interdependence. In the early 1990s, the subject no longer generated as much interest among economists as it might have deserved from an economic policy perspective. With EMU, the topic of coordination has once again found its way onto the political and scientific agenda.

The standard approach followed in coordination literature is policy optimization. The contribution of this strand of literature is rather methodological and the models it employs point to a number of possible explanations and patterns of interaction.

As the assessment of potential gains is at best tentative, assessment results do not allow for straightforward policy conclusions. The strength of policy optimization literature on coordination lies in its axiomatic structure, which permits analytical rigor and specificity. However, this explanatory vigor can also be seen as the source of the policy optimization approach's main weaknesses.

Economists' and political scientists' studies on coordination will not be suited to serve as blueprints of policy coordination for policymakers to follow at summit meetings. As a matter of fact, the practical information value to be gained from theoretical analysis and empirical models can only be described as limited. However, the research helps to clarify policymakers' incentive structures in the face of different kinds of policy conflicts. Coordination literature, overall, provides useful analytical insights in the structure of coordination. And an improved analytical understanding of macroeconomic interaction is a prerequisite for more successful efforts at policy coordination.

Even if the key question, how much relevance the abundant literature on co-ordination may hold for the "real world", could not be answered definitely, at least the survey may be seen as an attempt to *deconstructing the rhetoric of coordination.*

Notes

1. See further literature surveys on coordination in chronological order by Cooper (1985), Artis and Ostry (1986), Kenen (1987), Currie and Levine (1991), Bryant (1995a) and Hamada and Kawai (1997).
2. For a review of historical perspectives on international economic policy coordination see Putnam and Bayne (1987), Dobson (1991), the appendix in Ghosh and Masson (1994) and Eichengreen (1985).
3. Bryant (1995a) suggests a similar categorization in his literature survey on coordination.
4. In this survey the term coordination will be used despite its strict meaning in a rather vague and broad sense as it has been used in the literature rather arbitrarily.
5. Macroeconomic interdependence will not only increase the number of disturbances but will also alter the magnitude of disturbances.
6. Other welfare-decreasing outcomes of cooperative solutions are considered by Miller and Salmon (1985), who focus on time-consistent solutions in a two-country model with forward-looking expectations, Levine and Currie (1987), for an empirical two-bloc model where the gains from cooperation without reputation can be negative, and for issues of fiscal coordination Kehohe (1987, 1989).
7. In a symmetric fixed exchange rate system each country has to share the adjustment burden of international reserves in a symmetric way with the aim to keep exchange rates fixed.
8. See many of the papers in Buiter and Marston (eds.) 1985 which provide thorough analyses of problems emerging in dynamic games, Bryant and Portes (eds.) 1987, Currie and Levine 1993.
9. The importance of the time-consistency problem might have been exaggerated in theory. We follow the conclusion of Kenen (1987, p. 34) that "*policy changes do not necessarily call into question a government's credibility or damage its reputation, except in the theorist world, where everyone knows enough to identify each new disturbance immediately and thus to decide whether the government is exploiting a time inconsistency in its current policy plan or revising that plan appropriately to deal with a new disturbance.*"
10. A game consists of a set of players, a set of strategies and a payoff function for each player.
11. For a reference to this analytical perspective see e.g., Canzoneri and Henderson (1991).
12. Usually an arithmetic or geometric average of the welfare functions of the national states.
13. Putnam and Henning (1989, p. 106): "*The right question is not whether the unitary-actor assumption is unrealistic, but whether it is misleading. Unfortunately we believe that it is the latter.*"
14. There is an ambiguous use of the term regime in coordination literature: Hamada and Kawai (1997) use the term regime choice approach, Kenen (1990) distinguishes regime choice from

regime preserving; Bryant (1995b) labels the term regime environment. In any case the economic terminology has the disadvantage that the term regime is used in the international relation literature quite differently and in rather broad terms, comprising principles, norms and rules and decision-making procedures on which the expectations of actors converge. Currie, Holtham and Hughes Hallett (1989) distinguish between relative and absolute coordination.

15. For a proposal for presumptive rules see Williamson and Miller (1987) and Frankel (1990b).
16. A well studied example of a regime is the Bretton Woods System where countries aimed to maintain fixed exchange rates and domestic policies were constrained by the balance of payment and their reserve positions, or the EMS where policy cooperation to a large extent became endogenous.
17. It was not tested how robust the scheme would be under alternative models (e.g., models involving forward looking expectations). For targeting regimes being an impefect substitute for full coordination as a general proposition see Hughes Hallett (1994).
18. Assumptions of the models are sticky nominal wages and potential output and fiscal policy are exogenous.
19. Bryant et al (1993) includes analyses with simplified theoretical models, deterministic simulations and stochastic simulations.
20. As Bryant (1995) mentioned the project focused only on simple rules for domestic monetary policies and not on the combined functioning of monetary policy and fiscal policy operating regime (Bryant 1995, p. 417).
21. Eichengreen (1985, p. 171) quotes "*a story which illustrates central bankers' attitudes toward policy coordination and consultation. It seems to have been the tradition at the Netherlands Bank for the President and the Directors to personally count the bank notes withdrawn from circulation at a meeting held directly after lunch. One day in 1912 or 1913 two Directors of the Reichsbank paid a visit to Amsterdam, and the President of the Bank had the novel idea of taking them to lunch. The conversation was 'highly interesting', and the President arrived at the bank note meeting fifteen minutes late with what he thought was an adequate excuse. The oldest of the Directors was unappeased and commented, 'Your work is here, not in coffeehouses'.*"
22. For a realist analysis see Gilpin (1975), Krasner (1976). For a critique and a liberal institutionalist approach see Kindleberger (1986), Keohane (1984), Grieco (1988).
23. "*the main comparative advantage of political science has been not so much theoretical formalization as sensitivity to institutions and contexts – in short story-telling*" (Putnam and Henning, 1989, p. 13).
24. However also in economic literature the importance of the issue of *dominant* players is recognized (see Hamada and Kawai, 1997).
25. Kindleberger (1981) argued that American hegemony worked as a substitute for coordination. For Kindleberger a hegemon must be lender of last resort and play the role of providing countercyclical financing, discounting in times of crises and ensure an open market.
26. We understand stability as an outcome that is likely to maintain itself over time; it can be measured in terms of the persistence of the rules and procedures that characterize a particular international regime. Webb rightly concludes that analysts may be mistaking stability for policy coordination.
27. Keohane (1984) maintained that hegemony uniquely facilitates cooperation and that cooperation was therefore most extensive when the USA was at the peak of power in the 1950s and 1960s. Eichengreen (1989) offered two examples of hegemons: the UK in the classical gold standard and the USA in the Bretton Woods System. He concluded that a system predicated on the existence of a hegemon may be dynamically unstable.
28. However, the term "*theory*" is misleading as it is rather a metaphor. Its power to describe reality has to be demonstrated empirically case by case. In the case of the Bonn summit 1978 the provocative conclusion of Putnam and Henning (1989) is that the agreement was possible only because each of the major governments was internally divided.

29. For a chronological analysis of negotiated mutual adjustment of monetary and fiscal policies since the late 1970s see Webb (1995, chapter 5).
30. For an evaluation of strengths and weaknesses of international theories of cooperation see Milner (1992).
31. Oudiz and Sachs uses policy multipliers from a number of large-scale models of the world economy.
32. Currie and Levine (1985), Miller and Salmon (1985), Oudiz and Sachs (1985) and Taylor (1985) extended the static game approach and considered identically symmetric economies and dynamic decisions; Canzoneri and Gray (1985) explored on static decisions and allowed asymmetric spillovers.
33. Kehohe (1991) showed in the context of capital taxation how a lack of credibility can make policy coordination counterproductive.
34. Non-reputational policies might be considered as non-cooperation between the public and the private sector.
35. Bryant (1988) criticized in his comment the analysis of Frankel and Rockett (1988) as "*too much of a mechanical bean counting exercise. It classifies outcomes as welfare increasing or reducing merely by looking at the signs of the effects; it gives very small gains or losses the same weight as large gains and losses*".
36. Ghosh and Masson (1987) chose a single two region macro-econometric model and introduced parameter uncertainty at the structural level of the model. Ghosh and Masson (1991) adopted a general, two-country Mundell-Fleming model with sticky prices and rational exchange rate expectations. Estimations were done on the basis of the IMF's MULTIMOD model.
37. For example, Central bankers that formed part of the Delors committee at the end of the 1980s can be considered as an epistemic community.
38. Many of the ideas and suggestions raised in this section are based on the intensive debate of the subject at the OeNB Workshop, where a preliminary version of the paper was presented.
39. This two-level game characteristics are quite similar to the two-level metaphor (domestic and international) from Putnam and Henning (1989).

References

Allsopp, C. and Vines, D. (1998) 'The Assessment: Macroeconomic Policy After EMU', *Oxford Review of Economic Policy* **14**(3), 1–24.

Artis, M. and Ostry, S. (1986) *International Economic Policy Coordination*, Chatham House Papers 30. The Royal Institute of International Affairs, London.

Artis, M. and Winkler, B. (1997) 'The Stability Pact: Safeguarding the Credibility of the European Central Bank', *National Institute Economic Review*.

Axelrod, R. (1984) *The Evolution of Cooperation*, New York: Basic Books.

Barrell, R. and Whitley, J. (eds.) (1992) Macroeconomic Policy Coordination in Europe. The ERM and Monetary Union. SAGE Publications. National Institute of Economic and Social Research.

Barro, R.J and Gordon, D. (1983) 'Rules, Discretion and Reputation in a Model of Monetary Policy', *Journal of Monetary Policy* **12**, 10–121.

Blackburn, K. (1993) 'Monetary Policy and Reputation', in Fratinanni, M. and Salvatore, D. (eds.) (1993) *Monetary Policy in Developed Economies. Studies in Comparative Economic Policies Volume 3*, North-Holland, Amsterdam, pp. 125–164.

Blackburn, K. and Overgaard Ravn, M. (1995) 'Growth, Human Capital Spillovers and International Policy Coordination', *Scandinavian Journal of Economics* **95** (4), 495–515.

Blommestein, H.J. (ed.) (1991) *The Reality of International Economic Policy Coordination. Contributions to Economic Analysis*, Amsterdam: North-Holland.

Branson, W.H., Frenkel, J.A. and Goldstein, M. (eds.) (1990) International Policy Coordination and

Exchange Rate Fluctuations. A National Bureau of Economic Research Conference Report. The University of Chicago Press.

Buiter, W.H. and Marston, R.C. (eds.) (1985) *International Economic Policy Coordination*, Cambridge University Press.

Bryant, R.C. (1987) Intergovernmental Coordination of Economic Policies: An Interim Stocktaking in International Monetary Cooperation: Essays in Honor of Henry C. Wallich, *Essays in International Finance No. 169*. Princeton University Press.

Bryant, R.C. and Portes, R. (eds.) (1987) *Global Macroeconomics. Policy Conflict and Cooperation*, CEPR, Macmillan Press.

Bryant, R.C., Currie, D.A., Frenkel, J.A., Masson, P.R., Portes, R. (eds.) (1989) *Macroeconomic Policies in an Interdependent World*, The Brookings Institution/CEPR/IMF.

Bryant, R.C. and Hodgkinson, E. (1989) 'Problems of International Cooperation', in Cooper, R.N. et al. (eds.), *Can Nations Agree? Issues in International Economic Cooperation*, The Brookings Institution Washington D.C., pp. 1–12.

Bryant, R.C. et al. (1993) *Evaluating Policy Regimes: New Research in Empirical Macroeconomics*, Brookings Institution Washington D.C.

Bryant, R.C. (1995a) *International Coordination of National Stabilization Policies*, The Brookings Institution. Washington D.C.

Bryant, R.C. (1995b) 'International Cooperation in the Making of National Macroeconomic Policies: Where Do We Stand?' in Kenen, P.B. (ed.), *Understanding Interdependence. The Macroeconomics of the Open Economy*, New Jersey: Princeton University Press, Princeton.

Canzoneri, M.B. and Gray, J. (1985) 'Monetary Policy Games and the Consequences of Non-cooperative Behavior', *International Economic Review* **26**(3), 547–564).

Canzoneri, M.B. and Minford, P. (1988) 'When International Policy Coordination Matters: An Empirical Analysis', *Applied Economics*, **20**, 1137–1154.

Canzoneri, M.B. and Henderson, D.W. (1988) 'Is Sovereign Policy Making Bad', in Carnegie-Rochester Conference Series on Public Policy 28 (spring), pp. 93–140.

Canzoneri, M.B. and Edison, H.J. (1989) A New Interpretation of the Coordination Problem and its Empirical Significance. International Finance Discussion Paper No. 340. Board of Governors of the Federal Reserve System. Washington D.C.

Canzoneri, M.B. and Henderson, D.W. (1991) Monetary Policy in Interdependent Economies: A Game-theoretic Approach. Cambridge/London: The MIT Press.

Canzoneri, M.B. and Diba, B. (1996) Fiscal Constraints on Central Bank Independence and Price Stability in: CEPR Discussion Paper 1463.

Caporale, G.M. (1996) International Economic Policy Coordination: A Brief Survey of the Literature. Discussion Paper No. 22–96 Center for Economic Forecasting/London Business School.

Carlozzi, N. and Taylor, J. (1985) 'International Capital Mobility and the Coordination of Monetary Rules', in Bhandari, J. (ed.), *Exchange Rate Management under Uncertainty*, Cambridge, pp. 186–211.

Carraro, C., Laussel, D., Salmon, M. and Soubeyran, A. (eds.) (1991) *International Economic Policy Co-ordination*, Oxford/Cambridge: Blackwell.

Carraro, C., Giavazzi, F. (1991) 'Can International Policy Co-ordination really be Counterproductive?' in Carraro, C., Laussel, D., Salmon, M. and Soubeyran, A. (eds.) (1991) *International Economic Policy Coordination*, Oxford/Cambridge: Blackwell, pp. 184–198.

Castrén, O. (1998) 'Fiscal-Monetary Policy Coordination and Central Bank Independence', *Bank of Finland Studies E:12*.

Chang, R. (1997) 'Financial Integration With and Without International Policy Coordination', *International Economic Review* **38**(3), 547–564.

Christodoulakis, N., Garrat, A. and Currie, D. (1996) 'Target Zones and Alternative Proposals for G3 Policy Coordination: An Empirical Evaluation Using GEM', *Journal of Macroeconomics Winter* **18**(1), 49–68.

Cohen, D. (1997) *How will the Euro Behave? Seminar on EMU and the International Monetary System*, IMF Washington, D.C.

Cooper, R. (1968) *The Economics of Interdependence*, New York: McGraw-Hill.

Cooper, R. (1969) 'Macroeconomic Adjustment in Interdependent Economies', *Quarterly Journal of Economics 98*, November 1969, 1–24.

Cooper, R.N. (1985) 'Economic Interdependence and Coordination of Economic Policies', in *Jones/Kenen Handbook of International Economics Vol. II*, Amsterdam: North-Holland, pp. 1195–1235.

Cooper, R.N., Eichengreen, B., Henning, C.R., Holtham, G. and Putnam, R.D. (eds.) (1989) *Can Nations Agree? Issues in International Economic Cooperation*, The Brookings Institution Washington D.C.

Crockett, A. (1989) 'The Role of International Institutions in Surveillance and Policy Coordination', in Bryant, R.C., Currie, D.A., Frenkel, J.A., Masson, P.R., Portes, R. (eds.), *Macroeconomic Policies in an Interdependent World*, The Brookings Institution/CEPR/IMF, pp. 343–364.

Currie, D.A. and Levine, P. (1985) 'Macroeconomic Policy Design in an Interdependent World', in Buiter, W.H. et al. (eds.), *International Economic Policy Coordination*, Cambridge University Press, pp. 228–271.

Currie, D.A., Levine, P. and Vidalis, N. (1987) 'International Cooperation and Reputation in an Empirical Two-Bloc Model', in Bryant, R.C. and Portes, R. (eds.), *Global Macroeconomics.*
Policy Conflict and Cooperation, CEPR, Macmillan Press, pp. 75–121.

Currie, D.A., Holtham, G. and Hallett, A.H. (1989) 'The Theory and Practice of International Policy Coordination: Does Coordination Pay?' in Byrant, R.C. et al., *Macroeconomic Policies in an Interdependent World*, Brookings/CEPR/IMF, pp. 14–47.

Currie, D.A. and Wren-Lewis, S. (1989a) 'An Appraisal of Alternative Blueprints for International Policy Coordination', *European Economic Review* **33**, 1769–1785.

Currie, D.A. and Wren-Lewis, S. (1989b) 'Evaluating Blueprints for the Conduct of International Macro Policy', *American Economic Review Papers and Proceedings* **79**(2), 264–269.

Currie, D. and Wren-Lewis, S. (1990) 'Evaluating the Extended Target Zone Proposal for the G3', *The Economic Journal 100 (March 1990)*, pp. 105–123.

Currie, D.A. and Levine, P. (1991) 'The International Co-ordination of Monetary Policy: A Survey', in Green, C.J. and Llewellyn, D.T. (eds.), *Survey in Monetary Economics, Volume 1: Monetary Theory and Policy*, Cambridge/Oxford: Blackwell, pp. 379–417.

Currie, D.A. and Levine, P. (1993) *Rules, Reputation and Macroeconomic Policy Coordination*, Cambridge: Cambridge University Press.

Currie, D.A. (1993) 'International Cooperation in Monetary Policy: Has it a Future?' *The Economic Journal* **103**(416), 178–188.

Demertzis, M., Hughes Hallett, A.H. and Viegi, N. (1998) *Independently Blue? Accountability and Independence in the New European Central Bank*, CEPR Discussion Paper No. 1842.

Demertzis, M., Hughes Hallett, A.H. and Viegi, N. (1999) *Can the ECB be truly Independent? Should it be?* Paper for the VOWA workshop 1999-01-21.

Devereux, M.B. and Mansoorian, A. (1992) 'International Fiscal Policy Coordination and Economic Growth', *International Economic Review* **33**(2), 249–268.

Dobson, W. (1991) *Economic Policy Coordination: Requiem or Prologue.* Institute for International Economics. Washington D.C.

Dornbusch, R. and Frenkel, J. A. (eds.) (1979) *International Economic Policy. Theory and Evidence*, Baltimore and London: The Johns Hopkins University Press.

Eichengreen, B. (1985) 'International Policy Coordination in Historical Perspective: A View from the Interwar Years', in Buiter, W.H. et al., *International Economic Policy Coordination*, Cambridge: Cambridge University Press, pp. 139–184.

Eichengreen, B. (1989) 'Hegemonic Stability Theories of the International Monetary System', in Cooper, R.N. et al., *Can Nations Agree?. Issues in International Economic Cooperation*,The Brookings Institution, Washington D.C., pp. 255–299.

Eichengreen, B. (1996) *Globalizing Capital: A History of the International Monetary System*,New Jersey: Princeton University Press, Princeton.

Eichengreen, B. (1997) 'European Monetary Unification and International Monetary Cooperation', in Working Paper No. C97–091, Center for International and Development Economics Research, Berkely.

Fearon, J.D. (XXXX) 'Bargaining, Enforcement and International Cooperation', *International Organization*, **52**(2), 269–307.

Feldstein, M.S. (1988) 'Distinguished Lecture on Economics in Government: Thinking about International Economic Coordination', *Journal of Economic Perspectives* **2**(2), 3–13.

Fischer, S. (1988) 'Macroeconomic Policy', in Feldstein, M. (ed.), *International Economic Cooperation*, Chicago: University of Chicago Press.

Frankel, J.A. (1987) 'Obstacles to International Macroeconomic Policy Coordination', IMF Working Paper No. 87/28.

Frankel, J.A. and Rockett, K.E. (1988) 'International Macroeconomic Policy Coordination when Policymakers Do Not Agree on the True Model', *The American Economic Review* **78**(3), 318–340.

Frankel, J.A. (1988) 'Obstacles to International Macroeconomic Policy Coordination', in *Princeton Studies in International Finance No. 64*, Princeton.

Frankel, J.A. (1990a) 'International Nominal Targeting (INT): A Proposal for Monetary Policy Coordination in the 1990s', *The World Economy* **13**(2), 263–273.

Frankel, J.A. (1990b) 'Obstacles to Coordination, and a Consideration of Two Proposals to Overcome them: International Nominal Targeting and the Hosomi Fund', in Branson et al. (eds.), *International Policy Coordination and Exchange Rate Fluctuations*, A National Bureau of Economic Research Conference Report, The University of Chicago Press, pp. 109–145.

Fratianni, M. and von Hagen, J. (1992) *The European Monetary System and European Monetary Union*, Boulder, San Francisco, Oxford: Westview Press.

Fratianni, M.U. and Salvatore, D. (eds.) (1993) *Monetary Policy in Developed Economies. Studies in Comparative Economic Policies*, Amsterdam: North-Holland.

Frenkel, J.A., Goldstein, M. and Masson, P. (1988) *International Coordination of Economic Policies: Scope, Methods and Effects*, International Monetary Fund Working Paper WP/88/53.

Frenkel, J.A., Goldstein, M. and Masson, P.R. (1989) 'Simulating the Effects of Some Simple Co-ordinated Versus uncoordinated Policy Rules' in Byrant, R.C. et al., *Macroeconomic Policies in an Interdependent World*, Brookings/CEPR/IMF, pp. 203–240.

Frenkel, J.A., Goldstein, M. and Masson P.R. (1990) 'The Rationale for, and Effects of International Economic Policy Coordination', Branson et al. (eds.), *International Policy Coordination and Exchange Rate Fluctuations*, A National Bureau of Economic Research Conference Report, The University of Chicago Press, pp. 9–63.

Friedman, J.W. (ed.) (1994) 'Problems of Coordination', in *Economic Activity. Recent Economic Thought Series*, London.

Fudenberg, D. and Tirole, J. (1996) *Game Theory*, Cambridge. London: The MIT Press.

Gilpin, R. (1975) *U.S. Power and the Multinational Corporations*, Kehohe, P.J. (1991) New York.

Goldstein, M. (1984) The Exchange Rate System: Lessons of the Past and options for the Future. IMF Occasional Paper No. 30. Washington D.C.

Goldstein, M. (1994) 'Improving Economic Policy Coordination: Evaluating Some New and Some Not-So-New Proposals', in Kenen, P.B. and Papadia, F. and Saccomanni (eds.), *The International Monetary System. Proceedings of a Conference organized by the Banca d'Italia*, Cambridge, pp. 298–324.

Ghosh, A.R. and Masson, P.R. (1987) International Policy Coordination in a World with Model Uncertainty. International Monetary Fund Working Paper WP/87/81.

Ghosh, A.R. and Ghosh, S.R. (1991) 'Does Model Uncertainty Really Preclude International Policy Coordination', *Journal of International Economics* **31**(3/4), 325–340.

Ghosh, A.R. and Masson, P.R. (1991) 'Model Uncertainty, Learning, and the Gains from Coordination', *The American Economic Review*, 465–479.

Ghosh, A.R. and Masson, P.R. (1994) *Economic Cooperation in an Uncertain World*, Oxford.

Gourevitch, PA. (1996) 'Squaring the Circle: The Domestic Sources of International Cooperation', *International Organization* **50**(2), 349–373.

Green, C.J. and Llewellyn, D.T. (eds.) (1991) 'Survey in Monetary Economics', Vol. 1, *Monetary Theory and Policy*, Cambridge/Oxford: Blackwell.

Grieco, J.M. (1988) 'Anarchy and the Limits of Cooperation: A Realist Critique of the Newest Liberal Institutionalism', *International Organization* **42**(3), 485–507.

Guth (Moderator) (1988) *Economic Policy Coordination. Proceedings of an International Seminar held in Hamburg*, IMF/HWWA.

Haas, P. (1990) *Saving the Mediterranean: The Politics of International Environmental Cooperation*, Columbia University Press, New York.

Haas, P. (1992) 'Knowledge, Power and International Policy Coordination', *Special Issue of International Organization* **46**(1).

Hamada, K. (1974) 'Alternative Exchange Rate Systems and the Interdependence of Monetary Policies', in Aliber, R.Z. (ed.), *National Monetary Policies and the International Financial System*, Chicago: University of Chicago Press.

Hamada, K. (1976) 'A Strategic Analysis of Monetary Interdependence', *Journal of Political Economy* **84**(4), 677–701.

Hamada, K. (1979) 'Macroeconomic Strategy and Coordination under Alternative Exchange Rates', in Dornbusch, R. and Frenkel, J. A. (eds.), *International Economic Policy. Theory and Evidence*, Baltimore and London: The Johns Hopkins University Press, pp. 292–324.

Hamada, K. and Sakurai, M. (1978) 'International Transmission of Stagnation under Fixed and Flexible Exchange Rates', *Journal of Political Economy* **86**(5), 877–897.

Hamada, K. (1985) *The Political Economy of International Monetary Interdependence*, Cambridge and London: The MIT Press.

Hamada, K. and Kawai, M. (1997) 'International Economic Policy Coordination: Theory and Policy Implications', in Fratianni, M.U., Salvatore, D. and Hagen, J. (eds.), *Macroeconomic Policy in Open Economies*.

Holtham, G. and Hughes-Hallett, A. (1987) 'International Policy Coordination and Model Uncertainty', in Bryant, R. and Portes, R. (eds.), *Global Macroeconomics: Policy Conflict and Cooperation*, London, pp. 128–184.

Holtham, G. and Hughes-Hallett, A. (1992) International Macroeconomic Policy Coordination when Policymakers Do Not Agree on the True Model: Comment in *American Economic Review* **82**, pp. 1043–1051.

Horne, J. and Masson, P.R. (1988) Scope and Limits of International Economic Cooperation and Policy Coordination in IMF staff Papers 35 (June), pp. 259–296.

Hughes-Hallett, A.J. (1986a) Autonomy and the Choice of Policy in Asymmetrically Dependent Economies. An Investigation from International Policy Co-ordination in *Oxford Economic Papers* **38**, pp. 516–544.

Hughes-Hallett, A.J. (1986b) International Policy Design and the Sustainability of Policy Bargains in *Journal of Economic Dynamics and Control* **10**, pp. 467–494.

Hughes-Hallett, A.J. (1989) 'What are the Risks in Co-ordinating Economic Policies Internationally?' in MacDonald, R. and Taylor, M.P. (eds.), *Exchange Rates and Open Economy Macroeconomics*, Cambridge: Basil Blackwell, pp. 307–358.

Hughes-Hallett, A.J., Holtham, G. and Hutson, G. (1989) 'Exchange-rate Targetting as Surrogate International Cooperation', in Miller, M. et al., *Blueprints for Exchange-rate Management*, Academic Press: Centre for Economic Policy Research, pp. 239–278.

Hughes-Hallett, A.J. (1992a) 'Policy Collaboration and Information Exchanges with Risk Averse Policymakers: The Case for Making Strategic Model Choices', in Barrell, R. and Whitley, J. (eds.), *Macroeconomic Policy Coordination in Europe*, pp. 152–171.

Hughes Hallett, A.J. (1992b) 'Target Zones and International Policy Coordination. The Contrast between the Necessary and Sufficient Conditions for Success', *European Economic Review* **36**, 893–914.

Hughes Hallett, A.J. and Vines D. (1993) 'On the Possible Costs of European Monetary Union', *The Manchester School* **LXI**(1), 35–64.

Hughes-Hallett, A.J. (1994) 'On the Imperfect Substitutability of Policy Regimes: Exchange Rate Targeting vs Policy Coordination', *Economics Letters* **44**(1–2), 159–164.

Hughes-Hallett, A.J. and Yue Ma (1995) Economic Cooperation within Europe: Lessons from the Monetary Arrangements in the 1990s.

Johansen, L. (1982) 'A Note on the Possibility of an International Equilibrium with Low Levels of Activity', *Journal of International Economics* **13**, 257–265.

Jones, R.W. and Kenen, P.B. (eds.) (1985) 'Handbook of International Economics', Vol. II, *International Monetary Economics and Finance*, Amsterdam: North-Holland.

Kehohe, P.J. (1987) 'Coordination of Fiscal Policies in a World Economy', *Journal of Monetary Economics* **19**, 349–376.

Kehohe, P.J. (1991) 'Policy Co-operation among Benevolent Governments May be Undesirable: An Extension', in Carraro, C. et al. (eds.), *International Economic Policy Co-ordination*, Oxford/ Cambridge: Blackwell, pp. 166–183.

Kenen, P.B. (1987) Exchange rates and Policy Coordination in Brookings Discussion Papers on International Economics, No.61, Washington D.C.

Kenen, P.B. (1990) 'The Coordination of Macroeconomic Policies', in Branson, W.H., Frenkel, J.A. and Goldstein, M. (eds.), *International Policy Coordination and Exchange Rate Fluctuations. A National Bureau of Economic Research Conference Report*, The University of Chicago Press, pp. 63–102.

Kenen, P.B., Papadia, F. and Saccomanni, F. (eds.) (1994) The International Monetary System. Proceedings of a Conference organized by the Banca d'Italia. Cambridge: Cambridge University Press.

Kenen, P.B. (ed.) (1995) *Understanding Interdependence. The Macroeconomics of the Open Economy*, Princeton, New Jersey: Princeton University Press.

Keohane, R.O. (1984) *After Hegemony. Cooperation and Discord in the World Political Economy*, Princeton, New Jersey, Princeton University Press.

Kindleberger, C. (1973) *The World in Depression 1929–39*, Berkely: University of California Press.

Kindleberger, C. (1986) 'International Public Goods without International Government', *The American Economic Review* **76**(1), 1–13.

Krasner, S.D. (1976) 'State Power and the Structure of International Trade', *World Politics* **28**(3), 317–347.

Krasner, S. D. (1983) *International Regimes*, Ithaca, New York: Cornell University Press.

Krasner, S.D. (1991) 'Global Communications and National Power: Life on the Pareto Frontier', *World Politics* **43**, 336–366.

Krichel, T., Levine P., Pearlman, J. (1996) 'Fiscal and Monetary Policy in a Monetary Union: Credible Inflation Targets or Monetized Debt?', *Weltwirtschaftliches Archiv* **132**(1), 28–53.

Kydland, F.E. and Prescot, E.C. (1977) 'Rules rather than Discretion: The Inconsistency of Optimal Plans', *Journal of Political Economy* **85**, 473–491.

Levine, P. and Currie, D. (1987) 'Does International Macroeconomic Policy Coordination Pay and is it Sustainable: A Two Country Analysis', *Oxford Economic Papers* **39**, 38–74.

Levine, P., Currie, D.A. and Gaines, J. (1989) 'The Use of Simple Rules for International Policy Agreements', in Eichengreen et al. (eds.), *Blueprints for Exchange Rate Mangement*, London and New York.

MacDonald, R. and Taylor, M.P. (eds.) (1989) *Exchange Rates and Open Economy Macroeconomics*, Cambridge: Basil Blackwell.

Machlup, F., Fels, G. and Müller-Groeling, H. (eds.) (1981) 'Reflections on a Troubled World Economy', *Essays in Honour of Herbert Giersch*, London: Trade Policy Research Centre, Macmillan Press Ltd.

Martinez Oliva, J.C. (1991) 'One Remark on Spillover Effects and the Gains from Coordination', *Oxford Economic Papers* **43**, 172–176.

Masson, P.R. (1992) Portfolio Preference Uncertainty and Gains from Policy Coordination, International Monetary Fund Staff Papers 39 (March), pp. 101–120.

McCallum, B.T. (1997) 'Issues in the Design of Monetary Policy Rules', in NBER Working Paper No. 6016.

McKibbin, W.J. and Sachs, J.D. (1989) 'Implications of Policy Rules for the World Economy', in Byrant, R.C., Currie, D.A., Frenkel, J.A., Masson, P.R., and Portes, R. (eds.), *Macroeconomic Policies in an Interdependent World*, The Brookings Institution/CEPR/IMF, pp. 151–194.

McKibbin, W.J. and Sachs, J.D. (1991) *Global Linkages. Macroeconomic Interdependence and Cooperation in the World Economy*, Washington, D.C.: The Brookings Institution.

Meade, J.E. (1951) 'The Theory of International Economic Policy', Vol. 1, *The Balance of Payments*, London: Oxford University Press.

Miller, M. and Salmon, M. (1985) Policy Coordination and Dynamic Games in Buiter, W.H. et al. (eds.), *International Economic Policy Coordination*, Cambridge: Cambridge University Press, pp. 184–220.

Miller, M., Eichengreen, B. and Portes, R. (eds.) (1989) *Blueprints for Exchange-rate Management*, New York/Berkeley: Centre for Economic Policy Research. Academic Press.

Milner, H. (1992) 'International Theories of Cooperation among Nations: Strengths and Weaknesses in', *World Politics* **44**(3), 466–496.

Morales, A.J. and Padilla, A.J. (1995) Designing Institutions for International Monetary Policy Coordination. Center for Economic Policy Research Discussion Paper No. 1180 May 1995.

Motamen-Scobie, H. and Starck, C. (1992) *Economic Policy Coordination in an Integrating Europe*, Bank of Finland.

Moravcsik, A. (1993) 'Introduction: Integrating International and Domestic Theories of International Bargaining', in Evans, P.B., Jacobson, H.K. and Putnam, R.D., *Double-edged Diplomacy: International Bargaining and Domestic Politics*, Berkely.

Niou, E.M.S. and Ordeshook, P.C. (1994) 'Less Filling, Tastes Great: The Realist – Neoliberal Debate', *World Politics*, **46**(2), 209–235.

Nolan, C. and Schaling, E. (1996) 'International Monetary Policy Co-ordination: Some Lessons from the Literature', *Bank of England Quarterly Bulletin*, November 1996, 412–417.

Nordhaus, W.D. (1994) 'Policy Games: Coordination and Independence in Monetary and Fiscal Policies', in *Brookings Papers on Economic Activity* **2**, 139–216.

Oudiz, G. and Sachs, J.D. (1984) 'Macroeconomic Policy Coordination among the Industrial Economies', *Brookings Papers on Economic Activity* **1**, 1–76.

Oudiz, G. (1985) 'European Policy Coordination: An Evaluation', *Recherches Economiqie de Louvain* **51**, 301–309.

Oudiz, G. and Sachs, J.D. (1985) 'International Policy Coordination in Dynamic Macroeconomic Models', in Buiter, W.H. and Marston, R.C. (eds.), *International Economic Policy Coordination*, Cambridge University Press, pp. 274–318.

Oye, K.A. (1986) *Cooperation under Anarchy*, Princeton: Princeton University Press.

Persson, T. and Tabellini, G. (1995) 'Double-edged Incentives: Institutions and Policy Coordination', Centre for Economic Policy Research Discussion Paper No. 1141.

Persson, T. and Tabellini, G. (1996) 'Monetary Cohabitation in Europe', Centre for Economic Policy Research Discussion Paper No. 1380, May 1996.

Polak, J.J. (1991) 'International Policy Coordination and the Functioning of the International Monetary System – A Search for Realism', in Blommestein, H.J. (ed.), *The Reality of International Economic Policy Coordination. Contributions to Economic Analysis*, Amsterdam: North-Holland, pp. 151–172.

Power, S. and Rowe, N. (1998) 'Independent Central Banks: Coordination Problems and Budget Deficits', *Economic Issues* **3**(1), 69–75.

Putnam, R.D. and Bayne, N. (1987) *Hanging Together: Cooperation and Conflict in the Seven-Power Summits*, Cambridge: Havard University Press.

Putnam, R.D. (1988) 'Diplomacy and Domestic Politics: The logic of Two-level Games', *International Organization* **42**, 427–460.

Putnam, R.D. and Henning, C.R. (1989) 'The Bonn Summit of 1979: A Case Study in Coordination', in Cooper, R.N. et al., *Can Nations Agree?* Washington, D.C., pp. 12–140.

Rogoff, K. (1985) 'Can International Monetary Policy Cooperation be Counterproductive?', *Journal of International Economics* **18**, 199–217.

Sachs, J. and McKibbin, W. (1985) 'Macroeconomic Policies in the OECD and LDC External Adjustment', in NBER Working Paper No. 1534.

Salvatore, D. (1995) 'The Operation and Future of the International Monetary System', *Journal of Policy Modeling* **17**(5), 513–530.

Scharpf, F.W. (1994) 'Games Real Actors Could Play. Positive and Negative Coordination in Embedded Negotiations', *Journal of Theoretical Politics* **6**(1), 27–53.

Snidal, D. (1985) 'The Limits of Hegemonic Stability Theory', *International Organization* **394**, 579–614.

Solomon, R. (1991) 'Background Paper', in *Partners in Prosperity: The Report of the Twentieth Century Fund Task Force on the International Coordination of National Economic Policies*, New York: Priority Press Publications.

Tanzi, V. (1988) International Coordination of Fiscal Policies: A review of some major issues International Monetary Fund Working Paper WP/88/70.

Taylor, J.B. (1985) 'International Coordination in the Design of Macroeconomic Policy Rules', *European Economic Review* **28**, 53–81.

Taylor, M. (1987) *The Possibility of Cooperation*, Cambridge: Cambridge University Press.

Taylor, J.B. (1989) *Policy Analysis with a Multicountry Model*, in Byrant et al., *Macroeconomic Policies in an Interdependent World*, The Brookings Institution, Centre for Economic Policy Research and International Monetary Fund, pp. 122–142.

Tobin J. (1987) 'Agenda for International Coordination of Macroeconomic Policies', in *International Monetary Cooperation: Essays in Honor of Henry C. Wallich, Essays International Finance*, No. 169, Princeton University Press, pp. 61–69.

Turnovsky, S.J. and D'Orey, V. (1986) 'Monetary Policies in Interdependent Economies with Stochastic Disturbances: A Strategic Approach', *The Economic Journal* **96**, 696–721.

Turnovsky, S.J., Basar, T. and D'Orey, V. (1988) 'Dynamic Strategic Monetary Policies and Coordination in Interdependent Economies', *The American Economic Review* (June), 341–361.

Van der Ploeg, F. (1988) 'International Policy Coordination in Interdependent Monetary Economies', *Journal of International Economics* **25**, 15-XXX.

Van Lennep, E. (1991) 'Institutional Aspects of International Economic Policy Cooperation and Coordination', in Blommestein, H.J. (ed.), *The Reality of International Economic Policy Coordination. Contributions to Economic Analysis*, Amsterdam: North-Holland, pp. 61–74.

Vaubel, R. (1983) 'Coordination or Competition among National Macro-economic Policies', in Machlup, F. et al. (eds.), *Reflections on a Troubled World Economy. Essays in Honour of Herbert Giersch*, London: Trade Policy Research, pp. 3–28.

Wallich, H.C. (1984) 'Institutional Cooperation in the World Economy', in Frenkel, J.A. and Mussa, M.L. (eds.), *The World Economic System: Performance and Prospects*, Dover.

Webb, M.C. (1994) 'Understanding Patterns of Macroeconomic Policy Co-ordination in the Post-War Period', in Stubbs, R. and Underhill, G.R.D. (eds.), *Political Economy and the Changing Global Order*, pp. 176–189.

Webb, M.C. (1995) *The Political Economy of Policy Coordination. International Adjustment Since 1945*, Ithaca and London: Cornell University Press.

Williamson, J. and Miller, M.H. (1987) *Targets and Indicators: A Blueprint for International Co-ordination of Economic Policy. Policy Analyses in International Economics 22*, Washington, D.C.: Institute for International Economics.

5. The Euro and Internal Economic Policy Coordination

ALEXANDER ITALIANER*
European Commission, Wetstraat 200, B-1049 Brussels

> *"Though this be madness, yet there is method in't."*
> W. Shakespeare, *Hamlet*, Act II, scene 2

I. Introduction

Ever since the breakdown of the Bretton Woods system in 1973, economists and policy-makers alike have been confronted with the issue of international economic policy coordination. In the 1980s, the gathering of G7 Finance Ministers and Central Bank Governors emerged as the main international coordination forum, culminating in the Plaza and Louvre agreements of 1985 and 1987.[1] But recent events such as the Asian or Russian crises have underscored the limitations of what basically amounts to an informal coordination framework. Subsequently, the attention of policy-makers, as exemplified for instance in the action plan of the G7 leaders of October 1998,[2] is now turning towards the strengthening of institutions such as the IMF, the World Bank and the BIS.

Against this background of modest institutional developments at the international level, the steps taken towards economic and monetary integration in Europe over the last decade may at least be qualified as remarkable. In pre-1973 terms, the introduction of the euro that took place on 1 January 1999 may be characterised as going beyond the restoration, albeit at regional level, of the Bretton Woods system of fixed, but adjustable, parities.

This article will concentrate on the objectives, forms, scope, levels, implementation and challenges for internal economic policy coordination under Economic and Monetary Union (EMU) in Europe. It will not dwell on the arguments in favour of or against the euro,[3] nor on the particular institutional architecture which the Maastricht Treaty bestowed upon EMU, i.e., a single monetary policy entrusted to a completely independent, federal structure in the form of the European System of Central Banks (ESCB) and a decentralised economic policy that is relying on coordination mechanisms between the participating Member States.[4]

Three preliminary remarks are in order. First, we will emphasise the coordination issues for "economic" policies, be it on their own merit or in relation to monetary or exchange rate policy.[5] Secondly, we will mainly concentrate on the euro participants and the structures in place for them, thus disregarding the particular coordination issues between "ins" and "pre-ins" such as the new Exchange Rate Mechanism, and while realising that the "pre-ins" are already involved in these structures to a

A. H. Hallett et al. (eds), Challenges for Economic Policy Coordination with European Monetary Union, 91–104.

large extent. Finally, we will leave largely aside the external implications of the euro and the ensuing consequences for policy coordination at the international, global, level.

II. Why Coordination?

As stated above, the institutional set-up chosen for economic policy under the euro is that of a coordination mechanism between the participating Member States. Contrary to a supranational or purely federal structure with a top-down approach to economic policy based on a transfer of power and resources to a central institution, the coordination approach is one based on subsidiarity; in other words, Member States will only engage in coordination, and therefore implicitly pool some of their sovereignty, if this is necessary for the proper functioning of the euro and the internal market on which it is built.

The first major coordination issue is therefore that of the objectives which it should seek to realise. Following Currie et al. (1989), one can distinguish between absolute and relative coordination. *Absolute coordination* pertains to objectives to be realised at the level of the European Union (EU), while *relative coordination* refers to objectives at the national or even regional level.

At the *EU level*, it is obvious that the single monetary policy and exchange rate for the euro impact directly on the macro-economic performance of the participating Member States. It follows that they have an obvious interest to coordinate those national economic policies that interact with the single monetary policy, such as the aggregate budgetary policy stance. Moreover, aggregate wage/price developments and inflationary expectations also interact with monetary policy. The euro exchange rate is influenced, in turn, by the EU policy mix and macro-economic prospects.

Absolute coordination may also be required at the micro-economic level in view of the functioning of the internal market, for instance as regards the provision of indivisibilities such as trans-European infrastructure networks, R&D projects or development of risk-pooling instruments for the financing of investment.

Coordination objectives at *national/regional level* derive from a host of factors. First, they could serve to generate positive externalities, for instance in the area of budgetary policy or exchange of best practice, or combat negative externalities, such as beggar-thy-neighbour policies or wage demonstration effects. Second, given the stated EU objective of solidarity, they may serve to attain explicit redistribution objectives between countries or regions. Finally, such objectives may derive from an insurance perspective, for instance against asymmetric shocks. Some of these objectives are directly linked to the introduction of a single currency. Others, such as redistribution, may derive from the economic integration process more generally.

III. Forms of Coordination

There is no uniformly agreed definition of what "coordination" actually means.[6] In what follows, we develop six aspects of the coordination process that appear of relevance for EMU. These aspects, covering procedures, exchange of information, the analytical framework, monitoring, policy interactions and joint policies are neither exhaustive nor exclusive.[7]

PROCEDURAL FRAMEWORK

Although perhaps not the most relevant aspect of the coordination process in terms of substance, the procedural framework is certainly politically extremely important. Rules on participation, the degree of formality, the logistical, secretarial and analytical support as well as decision rules can keep politicians, and even more their officials, busy for hours.

At EU level, Member States coordinate their economic policies according to the Treaty in the Council (Ecofin), i.e., with the participation of ministers from all 15 Member States, the presence of the European Commission and, where necessary, the President of the European Central Bank (ECB). The relative formality of this body and the abundance of accompanying officials have, over the last years, tended to shift the focus of attention to the twice-yearly informal meetings of ministers of finance and central bank governors, which often managed to give decisive political impulses to the EMU process.

Based on this successful formula, and as a visible expression of the specific coordination needs among the participants in the euro, the European Council in Luxembourg agreed on the possibility of informal meetings for the relevant ministers and the European Commission, a forum that later became known as the Euro-11 Group. A specific feature of this group, which at times is enlarged to all 15 Member States and regularly invites the ECB President, is that it is always chaired by a minister of a participating Member State, also if the Member State holding the EU Presidency is not participating in the euro.[8]

Restrictive participation and *informality* are often deemed to be crucial factors for the effectiveness of groups such as the Euro-11 or the G7-Finance. However, there is a trade-off here between efficiency on the one hand, and accountability and transparency on the other. Indeed, the Plaza-Louvre agreements might not have worked in the way they did if their precise content had been rendered public. At EU level, a clear dividing line has been drawn by laying down that the Ecofin Council is the centre for coordination and the only body empowered to take formal decisions in the relevant areas.

In order to safeguard the effectiveness of informal groups, they have often been wary of creating separate underlying *secretarial support*. The G7-Finance has no Secretariat, although it relies on the IMF for analysis of the world economic situation. The Euro-11 Group receives logistic support from the Council Secretariat, and is prepared at the level of officials in the framework of the Economic and Financial Committee that has replaced the Monetary Committee as of 1 January 1999.

A drawback from informal coordination groups is that they generally function by *consensus*. Although this may seem of minor importance for groups in which no formal decisions are taken, it is a feature that underscores the intergovernmental nature of these bodies. This contrasts with the approach laid down in the Maastricht Treaty, according to which, for instance, specific recommendations can be addressed to a Member State on the basis of qualified majority voting. As observed at the level of G7-Finance and in particular its communiqués, an informality-based consensus rule could ultimately be an obstacle to addressing openly policy problems in a specific Member State.

EXCHANGE OF INFORMATION

Successful coordination by definition relies on exchange of information. The examples of the excessive deficit procedure, and the convergence criteria more generally under the Maastricht Treaty, have underscored the importance of working on the basis of the same *indicators* and accepted common *definitions*.

For instance, by laying down the relevant definitions in Protocols annexed to the Treaty, there was a basis for the many clarifications to be given by Eurostat, the Statistical Office of the European Communities, as regards the precise definitions of a public budget deficit, whereas it also allowed a harmonised index of consumer prices (HICP) to be put in place. It can be expected, as the coordination process evolves, that the need for indicators will widen (e.g., quarterly national accounts) and that further harmonisation of definitions will continue to take place.

Obviously, statistical requirements are also essential for the functioning of the *European Central Bank*, which not only has to be able to monitor and set monetary variables, but is also depending on a host of other indicators in order to get an appropriate picture of the economic environment in which it takes monetary policy decisions.[9]

The availability of indicators and common definitions are also relevant for coordination processes falling outside the strict EMU domain, such as the coordination of *employment policies* that was introduced through the Amsterdam Treaty and which took off at the European Council meeting in Luxembourg in November 1997. Similarly, the coordination of tax *policies* with a view to avoiding harmful tax competition that culminated in a Code of Conduct on business taxation agreed in December 1997 is referring to a common concept such as the "effective level of taxation".

ANALYTICAL FRAMEWORK

The exchange of information is but a first step on the road towards a successful coordination process. The next step is to have an analytical framework that is based as much as possible on the same premises. The Maastricht Treaty already contains many of the basic premises underlying the move towards a single currency: the principle of an open market economy with free competition, the primary objective of price stability for the ECB, the obligation to avoid excessive deficits and the need for sound public finances are the main features.

For purposes of actual coordination, it would be equally important to base each other's analysis of the economic situation on agreed elements such as common short-term economic forecasts or a common methodology for calculating cyclical variables (e.g., output gaps or cyclical elements of budget deficits), and to agree on the different spillover effects that may be at work.

As regards monetary policy, important analytical elements concern the monetary transmission mechanism and the relation between monetary policy and intermediary or final monetary targets more generally. At the level of the dialogue between the ECB and the economic policy "pole" (Ecofin or Euro-11 Group), a convergence of views on the desirable policy mix based on a shared analysis would also be a relevant factor.

MONITORING

Coordination that is exclusively focused on past performance would mainly be an academic exercise. Effective coordination therefore also requires a regular monitoring of the policy intentions of the participants in the coordination process. By bringing these two aspects together, an *early warning mechanism* can be developed.

Such an early warning mechanism is explicitly foreseen under the Stability and Growth Pact concluded at the European Council meeting in Amsterdam in June 1997. The euro participants set out their policy intentions in so-called Stability programmes (the "pre-ins" do the same in their convergence programmes). These programmes are updated yearly, and their execution is monitored in the context of the multilateral surveillance process and the excessive deficit procedure. In the area of employment, a similar procedure was installed under the Amsterdam Treaty according to which Member States put forward National Action Plans for their employment policies whose execution is also monitored yearly.

POLICY INTERACTIONS

As soon as participants in the policy coordination process take account, in their own policy determination process, of the interactions with the policies or performance of others, one may say that the actual purpose of coordination, i.e., the orientation of national policies towards the realisation of one or more of the objectives stated above, is in principle achieved. Taking account of such policy interactions can be a spontaneous and natural result of the coordination process. Member States participating in the euro, for instance, know that the primary policy objective of the ECB is price stability, and will take this into account when setting their budgetary policy.

Alternatively, an explicit expression of the *policy preferences* of the partners in the coordination process may be required, such as a country-specific recommendation under the multilateral surveillance process, or the threat of sanctions under the excessive deficit procedure.

JOINT POLICY DETERMINATION

As an ultimate step in the coordination process, participants could decide on a *joint determination* of economic policies. In the monetary policy area, the single monetary policy is the most far-reaching step in this regard, even although in institutional terms the existing competences of the European Commission for competition policy and some other common policies go further since they are exercised by a supranational rather than a federal institution.

Outside monetary policy, the single exchange rate policy is the most far-reaching form of a jointly determined policy, requiring coordination not only among the participating Member States; but also between them (through the Council) and the ECB. In practice, however, the euro exchange rate policy is more likely to be the subject of monitoring with the possibility for discretionary action, rather than of regular active coordination. Indeed, one may distinguish between *discretionary* and regular joint determination of economic policies.[10]

Regular exercises of joint determination of policies concern the Broad Guidelines for economic policies as well as the Guidelines for employment policies introduced by the Amsterdam Treaty.

IV. Scope of Coordination

Not all coordination mechanisms foreseen in the Maastricht Treaty, laid down in secondary legislation or applied in practice are the same. This is partly for institutional reasons, and partly due to the nature of the coordination issue at hand. In this section we briefly examine the latter for eight major areas of coordination.

For *monetary policy* we will not discuss the coordination issues that arise inside the ESCB due to its federal character, but rather the interaction of the single monetary policy with economic policies. Due to the independence of the ECB and its statutory primary objective of price stability, the role for monetary policy in the coordination process is clearly *asymmetric*, in the sense that the support for economic policies is only a secondary objective for the single monetary policy. That being said, the ECB has a clear incentive to engage in a dialogue with the economic pole in order to ensure that economic policies are as supportive for its objectives as possible.

For *budgetary policy*, the rationale for coordination is manifold. Sound budgetary policies, including for social security systems, and the avoidance of excessive deficits as laid down in the Stability and Growth Pact, contribute to safeguarding the price stability objective of the ECB, thereby putting less pressure on monetary policy than otherwise could be the case. Secondly, the aggregate budgetary stance of the euro zone could play an important role in the dialogue with the ECB on the policy mix. Finally, budgetary policy coordination could serve to avoid negative spillovers, for instance in the case of asymmetric shocks, or encourage positive spillovers such as positive network externalities from the exchange of best practice.

By definition, the euro has a single *exchange rate policy*, and coordination at different levels is required to give this policy substance. The main coordination issue is that between the ECB and the Council in the case of formal exchange rate agreements or general orientations for exchange rate policy. In both cases, the Council and the ECB have to enter into a dialogue, which should ensure in particular that the ECB's primary objective of price stability is safeguarded. In the case of formal *exchange rate regimes* with extra-EU currencies, the Council has the last word. In the case of general *orientations for exchange rate policy*,the ECB has to manage its reserves in accordance with these orientations but the latter have to be without prejudice to the primary objective of price stability. In some sense, this gives the ECB the last word. At the Luxembourg European Council in December 1997, it was however agreed that such general orientations would be issued only exceptionally, e.g., in the case of a clear misalignment.

There are two main dimensions to *labour market* coordination. The first is that wage evolutions in the euro zone are an important indicator for the ECB in setting its monetary policy. Coordination inside and between Member States involving the social partners may be important in arriving at aggregate *wage developments* that at the same time permit to safeguard price stability, enhance the profitability of job-creating investments and are consistent with the evolution of labour productivity.

The second dimension is that of the labour market as an *adjustment mechanism* in the case of asymmetric shocks. Although the functioning of the labour market, including its interaction with tax and benefit systems, is a more general policy issue, its adjustment function in the absence of national exchange rate and monetary policies is a prime rationale for coordination aiming at diffusion of best practices.

In the area of *taxation*, the free movement of capital that was introduced in stage 1 of the EMU process and the disappearance of exchange rate uncertainty as of the start of stage 3 will lead to increased mobility of production factors, in particular financial and physical capital. Coordination could aim to prevent this increased mobility given an additional incentive for beggar-thy-neighbour policies in the field of taxation, especially as regards the taxation of *income from capital* and *business* taxation.[11]

The need for adjustment to asymmetric shocks is not confined to labour markets. The functioning of *product markets* for goods and services may be deemed to be equally important. The *internal market*, and in particular the liberalisation of previously closed sectors such as telecommunications, energy or transport plays an important role in this respect. But experiences at the *national* level, such as the recent introduction of more competition and deregulation in the Netherlands, have set examples that could usefully be included in an exchange of best practices.

Finally, there is a three-fold incentive for coordination in the area of *capital markets*. Firstly, there is the *efficiency* argument that in order to derive the full benefits of the introduction of the euro, there should be a deep, liquid pan-European capital market allowing for an optimal allocation of capital. Especially in the area of the provision of risk capital, there are still many obstacles, in particular at national level, to the creation of such a pan-European market.[12] Secondly, the recent literature on *asymmetric shocks* in a monetary union has demonstrated that capital flows inside such a union can play an important role in adjusting to such shocks, provided capital can flow freely.[13] Finally, there is the issue of financial *stability* in the euro zone, requiring cooperation between regulators, central banks and supervisors in order to avoid systemic risk and, when necessary, to address the lender of last resort issue.

V. Levels of Coordination

The highest coordination level in the EU is that of the *Heads of State or Government*, in particular through the European Council (of which the President of the European Commission is also a member) that, in accordance with the Maastricht Treaty, meets in the presence of Ecofin Ministers when issues of relevance to EMU are discussed. Its role in the coordination process derives from the political impulses that it gives, as well as from the formal role that it has in the respective decision processes concerning the Broad Guidelines for economic policies and the Guidelines for employment policies. It can also point to cross-coordination issues, as it did for instance in Vienna in December 1998 when it asked for greater synergy between the two different sets of guidelines referred to above.

At the *Ministerial* level, the main co-ordinating bodies are the Council and the Euro-11 Group. For matters related to EMU and taxation, the most relevant *Council* formation is that of Economic and Finance Ministers (Ecofin), while for employment policies the Employment/Social Affairs Council takes the lead.

As stated above, the *Euro-11 Group*, in which national delegations are restricted to two persons (generally the Minister plus the relevant member of the Economic and Financial Committee) was installed as an informal coordination body among euro participants, and regularly meets with the ECB President (who is also invited to Ecofin meetings for issues of relevance to the competence of the ECB) and sometimes in enlarged composition when issues of relevance to all Member States are discussed.

The *European Commission* is present both at Council and Euro-11 meetings in order to be able to exercise its right of initiative, safeguard the respect of the treaties and provide reports on the basis of which multilateral surveillance takes place.

The *social partners*, finally, are involved in the coordination process at "ministerial" level through the participation of the main European employers' and employees' organisations in fora such as the Standing Committee on Employment or the Macro-economic dialogue. In the "European Social Dialogue", the European social partners also have the possibility to negotiate agreements which can be transformed into Council decisions.

Below the level of ministers, there is a host of fora in which *officials* are involved in the different coordination processes. In the strict EMU area, the most important body is the *Economic and Financial Committee* (since 1 January 1999 the successor of the Monetary Committee), that has advisory and preparatory functions regarding Council meetings. Its composition, consisting of bicephalous (administration, central bank) national representation and two Commission and ECB representatives each, also makes it the body for informal dialogue between officials from the economic and monetary poles. While the Economic and Financial Committee has a traditional orientation on macro-economic and financial issues, the *Economic Policy Committee*,[14] which generally mixes officials from Economic ministries with those from Finance ministries, is principally concerned with structural policies such as labour market and sectoral or horizontal economic policies.

As regards employment policies, the Amsterdam Treaty gives a similar function to the newly established *Employment Committee* (successor of the Employment and Labour Market Committee) as to the Economic and Financial Committee in the EMU area. In the financial area, the *Banking Advisory Committee* is a committee alongside the Commission on which national representatives in the field of credit institutions are sitting, and which plays an important role in preparing EU prudential regulation. In November 1998, the Ecofin Council agreed to the creation of a temporary high-level group in the area of financial services (*Financial Services Policy Group*) that should work on the remaining obstacles to the creation of a single financial area in the EU. The *Banking Supervision Committee* of the ECB, which gathers representatives from supervisory authorities and, if this is not the same, national central banks as well as a Commission observer is versed to play an important coordination role inside the EU in the area of prudential supervision on banks.

In the area of taxation, the main coordination body involved in avoiding harmful tax competition is the so-called *Code of Conduct Group on business taxation* installed under the UK Presidency in March 1997.

On the statistical side, finally, the Committee *for Monetary, Financial and Balance of Payments Statistics* (CMFB), which joins experts from National Statistical Institutes, Central Banks and the Commission, was set up in 1991 with the particular statistical requirements of EMU in mind.

VI. Coordination: Treaty Provisions

All the major elements of the coordination process under EMU derive directly from the Maastricht Treaty.[15]

Article 99 lays down the general principle that Member States should consider their economic policies as a matter of common concern and institutes the procedure for the Broad Guidelines on economic policies of the Community and the Member States involving the European Council. More broadly, it contains the framework for the multilateral surveillance procedure aimed at monitoring the consistency of economic policies with the Broad Guidelines and the functioning of EMU in general, including the possibility to address confidential or public recommendations to Member States whose performance or policies are not consistent with the Broad Guidelines or jeopardise the functioning of EMU.

Article 100 contains two paragraphs. The first, existing already in the Treaty of Rome, allows the Council to take measures in special circumstances, in particular the shortage of supply of certain products. The second provision, introduced through the Maastricht Treaty, allows the Council to decide on *financial assistance* in case of difficulties in a particular Member State, whether it participates in the euro or not. It may be regarded as a safety net in the case of asymmetric shocks falling outside the control of the national government, thus providing an insurance function.

Article 104 and the relevant Protocol contain the provisions as regards the excessive deficit procedure, which aims at avoiding excessive deficits through a monitoring exercise based on the well known "Maastricht" deficit and debt criteria and which could ultimately lead to financial sanctions. The Stability and Growth Pact consists for an important part secondary legislation that installs an early warning mechanism for budgetary policy under article 99 and a speeding up and clarification of the conditions under which the excessive deficit procedure is applied.

Article 111 provides the possibility for the Council to issue general orientations for exchange rate policy. The orientations must not prejudice the primary ESCB objective of price stability and must be issued after consulting the ECB (if the Council acts on a Commission recommendation) or on a recommendation from it.

The Treaty basis for the dialogue between the ECB and the Council is *Article 113*, which foresees in particular cross-participation of their respective Presidents in the meetings of the two institutions. Like the President of the Council, the Commission may participate in meetings of the ECB Governing Council without having the

Table 1. Coordination: Treaty provisions

Article	Description
99	Principle of coordination
	Broad guidelines for economic policies
	Multilateral surveillance (incl. recommendations)
100	Exceptional measures
	Financial assistance
104	Excessive deficit procedure – sanctions
111	Exchange rate policy
113	Dialogue Council – ECB
114	Economic and Financial Committee
124	Exchange rate policy pre-ins
	Amsterdam Treaty new provisions
43–45	Closer cooperation
125–130	Employment

right to vote. A little-noticed provision, inspired by the Bundesbank law, is that the President of the Council may submit a motion for deliberation to the Governing Council of the ECB. As already described above, the Economic and Financial Committee, whose tasks and composition are laid down in *Article 114*, brings together representatives of the Ecofin ministers, national central banks, the Commission and the ECB.

Finally, it should be noted that the Intergovernmental Conference leading to the Amsterdam Treaty took great care not to modify any of the carefully balanced EMU provisions in the Maastricht Treaty, but that it contains two Chapters that are of relevance to the coordination process in the EU.

The first concerns the new Articles 125–130,[16] which lay down a procedure in the area of *employment policies* that is very similar to the multilateral surveillance procedure of Article 99, and in some aspects goes even further, for instance as regards the possibility for the Council to adopt "incentive measures".

The second new chapter, whose practical importance is as yet unclear, contains the new articles 43–45 on *"closer cooperation"* allowing a group of Member States to use the Treaty framework to move ahead in certain areas for which they cannot achieve sufficient progress with all Member States. The latter could become relevant in areas, such as taxation, where the Amsterdam Treaty has not changed the rules of voting by unanimity.

VII. Coordination in Practice

At the European Council meeting in Vienna in December 1998, the Ecofin Council reported on the economic policy coordination framework as laid down in the European Council Resolution agreed in Luxembourg the year before.[17]

According to this report, the *Ecofin Council* and, informally and where relevant, the *Euro-11 Group* will concentrate their multilateral surveillance on macro-economic developments in the Union and in the Member States, national budgetary positions in the context of the Stability and Growth Pact, real and nominal wage developments, as well as structural policies in the context of the economic reform process started at the European Council in Cardiff. They will in addition monitor the evolution of the euro exchange rate, while the Ecofin Council will also examine the National Employment Action Plans, notably as regards their economic content. The *Employment/Social Affairs Council* takes the lead more generally in the multilateral surveillance process of employment policies.

Separately, the Ecofin Council is concerned with the coordination of taxation policies, including the Code of Conduct on business taxation and treatment of legislative texts. It is also in charge of coordination efforts, including possible legislation, in order to ensure a single financial area with free provision of financial services and pan-European access to risk capital.

The second coordination nexus is the *dialogue* between the *Council* and the *ECB*. The regular presence of the President of the ECB in the Euro-11 Group and/or Council meetings and the presence of both the President of the Council and a member of the Commission at meetings of the Governing Council of the ECB allow to exchange views on the economic situation and economic policies that are pursued in the Member States and in the Community, as well as a discussion on exchange rate developments. The Economic and Financial Committee, in which both sides are represented, provides a setting for a similar dialogue at the level of officials.

The third coordination nexus is that between the *Council* and the *European Social Partners*, which allows discussing the macro-economic situation, wage developments and employment policies. At the European Council in Cologne, this Macro-economic dialogue was formalised and extended to include the ECB.

Although the scope of coordination has been enlarged and the mechanisms have been strengthened only recently, a rolling agenda seems now to have been gradually established that lays down an *annual cycle* for the "mainstream" coordination process (see Table 2). The two focal points in the course of a year are the end-of-Presidency European Council meetings in June and December, at which the Broad Guidelines for economic policies and the Guidelines for employment policies, respectively, are adopted. In between, Member States provide their (updated) programmes in the respective areas, which are monitored with a view to their consistency with the Guidelines and Treaty requirements, and could possibly be the subject of recommendations, and, in the case of budgetary policy, could ultimately lead to financial sanctions.

VIII. Conclusion: Challenges for Coordination

From an historical and international perspective, the coordination process installed through the Maastricht and Amsterdam Treaties is unprecedented. Although most of the building blocks seem to have been put in place, it still remains to be seen how the process will evolve now that the euro has been launched. Viewed from the current perspective, a number of challenges that could arise can already be identified.

The first challenge is that of the interaction between the *Council and the ECB*, which is still largely uncharted territory. Different circumstances could be imagined under which the real value of their dialogue would need to be proven, such as a severe slowdown in economic growth, the case of exchange rate misalignments or

Table 2. Coordination – annual cycle

	Economic policy	Employment
Year end	• Progress reports Member States + Commission on product and capital markets	
Jan/Feb	• Annual Economic Report • Stability/convergence programmes: submission + Council opinion • Commission report on structural policies • Member States submit budget data	
Spring	• Broad discussion on basis of Annual Economic Report • Macro-economic dialogue • Commission presents draft Broad Guidelines + Forecasts	
May	Draft Broad Guidelines adopted by Ecofin	National Action Plans: implementation reports + update
June	European Council adopts conclusions on Broad Guidelines – Ecofin adopts	
July	Monitoring budget execution	
August	Member States submit budget data	Commission presents draft Joint Employment report + Guidelines
Autumn	• Commission presents forecasts • Macro-economic dialogue • Discuss next year's national budgets	Joint Employment report
Year end		Modification Employment Guidelines European Council – Council adopts

the appearance of factors jeopardising price stability. In this context, it is telling that when the ECB decreased its interest rates in April 1999, it urged those responsible for other policy areas to take the necessary steps to improve the long-term growth prospects for the euro area.

A second area, on which much of the theoretical literature on optimal currency areas has focused, concerns that of *country-specific events*. This concerns the appearance of asymmetric shocks, the related issue of budgetary stabilisation, the monetary policy transmission mechanism, the spillover issue and the use of ex-ante or ex-post coordination instruments.

The third issue that poses a challenge to coordination is that of *financial market integration*. On the one hand, there are still obstacles to the cross border provision of financial services such as pensions or access to risk capital. On the other hand, the integration of the banking sector in the euro-zone may, in the case of failures, pose a systemic risk to be addressed by supervisors, central banks and Finance ministries. In case of a liquidity risk, there is the issue of the lender of last resort. All these issues will, in the absence of an agreed EU-wide approach, have to rely on ad-hoc coordination, preferably along the lines of previously agreed procedures.

A fourth issue that may come up concerns the behaviour of social partners in respect of *wage bargaining*. In cases where EU-wide bargaining would take place for a particular sector, this could interact with national/regional productivity differences and therefore be the source of asymmetric shocks or lead to unwarranted general wage increases.[18] The macro-economic dialogue at the EU level between Social Partners, the economic pole and the ECB could gain in importance as a result.

Finally, there is the possibility, offered by the Amsterdam Treaty, of *closer cooperation* between sub-groups of Member States in areas where no progress can be made with all Member States together. Due to the unanimity requirements for voting in the Council, such a cooperation could take place, for instance, in the area of taxation. Whether this is useful in combating harmful taxation remains to be seen. Altogether, it seems that the introduction of the euro on 1 January 1999 marks only the beginning of a coordination process whose value-added is potentially present but still needs to undergo its baptism of fire. As this article has tried to demonstrate, there is however a "method" in the complex mechanisms that have been put in place.

Notes

* The views expressed in this paper do not necessarily reflect those of the European Commission. With many thanks to Odete da Cunha for her precious assistance and participants of the Workshop *Economic policy challenges within EMU* of the Austrian National Bank for a stimulating discussion.

1. E.g., Dobson (1991), Buiter and Marston (1985) or Bryant et al. (1989).
2. G7 Leaders' Statement on the World Economy, 30 October 1998.
3. Emerson et al. (1990), Buti and Sapir (1998).
4. At the extreme opposite, one could imagine the single monetary policy managed through full coordination of the existing national central banks, and economic policy in the hands of a supranational or fully federal structure. See van der Ploeg (1991).
5. See Allsop and Vines (1998) for a recent overview of the policy issues involved, including monetary policy.
6. See, for instance, Currie et al. (1989).
7. Huizinga and Nielsen (1998), for instance, show the welfare-improving effects of coordination of budgetary policies in the absence and presence of capital income tax coordination.
8. Accordingly, the first meeting of the Euro-11 Group in June 1998, during the UK Presidency, was chaired by the Austrian Minister of Finance, Austria being the following Member State to hold the EU Presidency.
9. See EMI (1996).
10. An older example of *discretionary* joint determination dates back to the first oil crisis when the Council decided, on the basis of still existing Treaty provisions, on a mechanism for intervening in the oil supply to Member States (which, however, was never activated). See Council Directive (73/238/EEC) of 24 July 1973 on measures to mitigate the effects of difficulties in the supply of crude oil and petroleum products, OJ L228 16.8.73.
11. At EU level and as regards business taxation, such policies are known as "harmful tax competition"; curbing such tax measures is aimed at the reduction of internal market distortions, prevention of tax revenue losses and making tax structures more employment-friendly.
12. See European Commission (1998).
13. See Obstfeld and Peri (1998).
14. The Economic Policy Committee was set up in 1974, taking over the tasks of three committees that had been established in the 1960s.

15. The numbers of the Articles concerning EMU referred to are those after the renumbering introduced by the Amsterdam Treaty.
16. Articles renumbered in accordance with the declaration on consolidation of the Treaties added to the Final Act of the Amsterdam Treaty.
17. Annex to Annex II of the Presidency Conclusions of the European Council in Vienna, 11–12 December 1998.
18. See Abraham and van Rompuy (1998) for a discussion of these issues in the Belgian context.

References

Abraham, F. and van Rompuy, J. (1998) 'Is Belgium Ready for EMU? A Look at National, Sectoral and Regional Developments', *CES Discussion Paper No. 9825*, Katholieke Universiteit Leuven.

Allsop, C. and Vines, D. (1998) 'The Assessment: Macroeconomic Policy After EMU', *Oxford Review of Economic Policy* **14**(3), 1–23.

Bryant, R.C., Curie, D.A., Frankel, J.A., Masson, P.R., and Portes, R. (1989), *Macroeconomic Policies in an Independent World*, Bookings Institution/CEPR/IMF.

Buiter, W.H. and Marston, R.C. (eds.) (1985) *International Economic Policy Coordination*,Cambridge University Press.

Buti, M. and Sapir, A. (eds.) (1998) *Economic Policy in EMU*, Oxford University Press.

Currie, D.A., Holtham, G., and Hallet, A. Hughes (1989) 'The Theory and Practice of International Policy Coordination: Does Coordination Pay?', in Bryant et al. (eds.), pp. 14–46.

Dobson, W. (1991) *Economic Policy Coordination: Requiem or Prologue?*, Institute for International Economics, Washington.

Emerson, M., Gros, D., Italianer, A., Pisani-Ferry, J., and Reichenbach, H. (1990) *One Market, One Money*, Oxford University Press.

European Commission (1998) *Risk Capital – A Key for Job Creation in the European Union*,SEC (1998) 552 Final.

European Monetary Institute (1996) *The Statistical Requirements for Monetary Union*, Frankfurt am Main.

Huizinga, H. and Nielsen, S.B. (1998) 'Is Coordination of Fiscal Deficits Necessary?', *CentER Discussion Paper No. 9861*, Tilburg University.

Obstfeld, M. and Peri, G. (1998) 'Regional Non-Adjustment and Fiscal Policy', *Economic Policy* **26**, 205–259.

Van der Ploeg, F. (1991) 'Macroeconomic Policy Coordination Issues During the Various Phases of Economic and Monetary Integration in Europe', *European Economy*, special edition no. 1, The Economics of EMU.

6. Can the ECB be Truly Independent? Should It Be?

MARIA DEMERTZIS, ANDREW HUGHES HALLETT and NICOLA VIEGI
Department of Economics, Curran Building, 100 Cathedral Street, Glasgow G4 OLN, Scotland

I. Introduction

This paper traces the link between the importance of adjusting the mix of policies correctly, and the need to resolve the accountability vs. independence debate which has grown up with the institutional changes in fiscal policy and the new Central Bank in Europe. We find that unfettered competition between independent policy makers with different preferences over the targets of economic policy, make it unlikely that policy makers will either be able to set the right policy mix (for their own targets, or for those of the economy as a whole); or to adjust it properly around the cycle. Such conflicts lead one policy to undermine the effectiveness of the other, in which case no one's targets are met. On the other hand, limiting either fiscal or monetary policy in order to get a more effective mix, is no more than a partial remedy. Independently negotiated coordination agreements (or performance contracts) between fiscal and monetary policy makers are a more appropriate solution.

II. Accountability and the Policy Mix in EMU: An Institutional View

Why might policy makers not choose the right policy mix, or not adjust it properly to meet the economy's performance targets? Essentially the issue is one of different priorities among policy makers. If one set of policy makers gets to dominate the policy setting process due to institutional or legal restrictions; or through the exercise of market or political power; or because it has a first mover advantage in the decision making process, then the policy mix will be chosen as far as possible to suit those policy makers. And to the extent that such an outcome does not suit other groups of policy makers, the latter will inevitably use their instruments to retaliate and move the policy mix back in their direction. In this way no-one gets what they want because of a lack of accountability for the damage caused to the targets of others in the independent pursuit of individual preferences. The problem therefore arises when there are differences in preferences and instruments among policy makers, and a lack of coordination between them.

Why might this be a problem in EMU? First, the statutes of the European Central Bank (ECB) state that price stability is the primary target of policy, and that output growth and employment can be pursued only if they do not prejudice that price stability. But governments and fiscal policy makers are likely to put a rather higher priority than that on growth and job creation; and if wide differences persist between these two sets of policy makers then the credibility and effectiveness of the ECB's (independent) monetary policy is likely to be undermined by the actions of fiscal policy. The extent to which that happens depends on the differences in preferences.

A. H. Hallett et al. (eds), Challenges for Economic Policy Coordination with European Monetary Union, 105–125.

This is not a question of the independent ECB not having output growth as a target, but simply that it will have a lower priority on that target since it is not charged with achieving it. Conversely, a little accountability for the consequences of actions for the targets to which it is not assigned would make the ECB more successful with the target to which it has been assigned. One way in which this may happen in practice, even with the best intentioned and most independent central bank, is shown by Woodford's (1995) model of "unpleasant fiscal arithmetic".

A tight monetary policy triggers unsustainable fiscal responses designed to save output and employment. Markets, anticipating a budget constraint failure at some point in the future, will expect, if not a build up of excess demand, then a liquidity injection to prevent a collapse of the capital markets. Either way consumption will boom and prices will adjust in advance – obviating the need to adjust liquidity, even in fact if the money supply never changes.[1]

It might be thought that this does not matter since the ECB is modelled on the Bundesbank, and the Bundesbank has always managed to balance two targets reasonably well by allowing suitable shifts in the policy mix. Why should the ECB not do the same? Partly because the ECB's constitutional position is quite different and partly because there is no obvious mechanism by which it can coordinate with the fiscal authorities (indeed, strictly speaking, such contacts are ruled out by the Maastricht treaty). By contrast the Bundesbank is quite conscious that its independence of action could be cancelled by a simple vote in the Bundestag.

The ECB's statutes however contain no such provision; and even if they did, the ECB is expressly forbidden to talk to the national governments and hence to exactly those people who are likely to complain about a lack of accountability, or to those who are legally in a position to amend the bank's statutes, targets or operating rules. That gives the ECB considerable protection from outside influences, as a support to its independence. Indeed it is the national governments who are the signatories to the treaty which governs the ECB's operations, not the European Parliament where the ECB might have to account for its actions. Thus the ECB can only be called to account by those who cannot change its statutes and procedures; and is forbidden to talk to those with whom it needs to coordinate its policies.

The Bundesbank by contrast can be called to account by those who can change its statutes and those with whom it has to coordinate. And, an examination of the transcripts of Bundesbank policy meetings over the years, shows that this has made a significant difference to its decisions (von Hagen, 1998). The Bundesbank appears to have learnt that if it did not take the targets of output growth and stability seriously, and explain its decisions carefully against that background, then no-one would understand or accept their policies – with the result that their policies then wouldn't work (Posen, 1997). In particular the Bank found that not accounting for output growth merely triggered compensatory fiscal and/or wage policies from both government and the unions which, in turn, undermined the Bank's inflation control policies. Lohmann (1998), for example, has shown that the Bundesbank has been more accommodating when both houses of the German Parliament were controlled by the same party, when popular opinion might force a revision of its statutes. In other words, the Bundesbank has coordinated with both government and unions in order to avoid policy conflicts (von Hagen, 1998). But there is no reason to suppose that the ECB, with a much more explicit commitment to independence, would find any incentive either to accept "voluntary accountability" or to enter any coordination arrangements.

Now one could also argue that none of this matters because Alesina and Summers (1993) and Alesina and Gatti (1995), among many others, have argued that there is really no conflict between the targets of inflation and output stability. They claim that countries with an independent central bank typically have lower inflation at no extra cost to output growth or output stability. But those studies are misleading in that they ignore fiscal policy. They argue that you get lower inflation without extra output volatility because the independent central bank is able to take out the politically motivated part of the cycle. What they don't show, but the algebra of their model clearly implies, is that the economically driven part of the cycle can easily become larger when greater attention is paid to inflation rather than output. If the increase in the economic cycle is larger than the decrease in the political part of the cycle, which it often is in their model (Hughes Hallett and Demertzis, 1999), then output volatility must rise overall.

The reason that we don't see this in practice is that fiscal policy (although not represented in these models) is still available and is being used to smooth output.

Indeed Melitz (1997) notes that fiscal and monetary policy interventions tend to move in opposite directions in the OECD countries, even in the countries with the most independent central banks (i.e., Germany and the US). Thus fiscal policy tends to ease the real effects of a tightening monetary policy (and vice versa). If this represents an informal coordination of fiscal and monetary policies, it also signals a desire to avoid open conflict between them. Similarly Campillo and Miron (1997) show that an independent Central Bank is not sufficient, in practice, to ensure low inflation without some cost.

Consequently the lesson from these studies is that fiscal policy doesn't go away with the independence of the Central Bank: in fact, granting the Central Bank full independence sets fiscal policy free at the same time. And since the fiscal authorities set their own objectives and priorities in the same way as the Central Bank, one can expect them to pursue their own interests independently of what that may mean for the targets of others – in the same way that an independent Central Bank would. That implies a return to noncooperative decision making. Hence the stability pact. Is that desirable and incentive compatible? The next sections show that it is not, unless some degree of accountability can be introduced to improve the coordination of monetary and fiscal policies.

III. The Costs of Being Unable to Adjust the Policy Mix Correctly

We can best illustrate how monetary and fiscal policies can be rendered quite ineffective by the uncoordinated actions of independent policies, through an example. To that end we have tested the performances of four different regimes in a two country monetary union within the world economy. In that context, we examine two different sets of preferences and either a temporary symmetric inflation shock[2] of 10% to Germany and France in period 1, or an asymmetric inflation shock of 0% and 20% in period 1. The model used to generate this example, and the regimes tested, are defined in the appendices. Tables 1–3 summarise the results showing the

Table 1. Symmetric inflation shock (10%, 10%) in period 1

Homogeneous preferences				
Policy regimes	Europe	Germany	France	ECB
Non coop.	160.58	160.58	160.58	376.89
Coop (1)	104.98	104.98	104.98	**318.10**
Infl. target	**70.42**	**70.42**	**70.42**	497.92
Non-homogeneous preferences				
Policy regimes	Europe	Germany	France	ECB
Non coop.	220.77	288.01	153.54	342.11
Coop (1)	**177.47**	**228.30**	126.64	**313.89**
Infl. Target	199.59	339.08	**60.09**	443.43

Table 2. Asymmetric inflation shock (0%, 20%) in period 1

Homogeneous preferences				
Policy regimes	Europe	Germany	France	ECB
Non coop.	359.86	**4.85**	714.88	376.89
Coop (1)	271.52	45.45	497.59	**318.10**
Infl. target	**142.20**	24.85	**259.54**	497.92
Non-homogeneous preferences				
Policy regimes	Europe	Germany	France	ECB
Non coop.	390.47	**22.18**	758.76	372.16
Coop (1)	314.64	58.16	571.11	**309.48**
Infl. Target	**210.14**	169.55	**250.74**	434.14

(a) Coop (1) refers to full Co operation between France, Germany and the ECB; see Equation (A6).
(b) Each figure is the objective function evaluation of the first 5 years, for the specified player, preference scheme and shocks.

welfare losses for each country, the ECB and for Europe on average. The figures in bold show each country's best choice of policy rule, and that for the ECB.

OVERALL PERFORMANCE

The critical result is that the ECB actually does worse, in terms of satisfying its own inflation objectives, when it is granted total independence compared to when accountability is imposed. That is shown by comparing the first line in each panel, with the second or third. It is true that too much accountability – inflation targeting in this case – may make things worse for the ECB. But going the other way, i.e., granting the ECB full target and instrument independence, does not give the ECB sufficient policy strength to regain its own inflation objectives either. Hence some accountability is always desirable, even for the ECB. But full independence is not.

How do these results arise? The explanation is straightforward. Since granting independence without accountability implies non-cooperative decision making, the ECB is free to make whatever policy decisions will bring it closest to its own targets, without concern for what that may do to other people's targets. And since the ECB's targets are primarily the elimination of inflation, this regime gives full rein to the

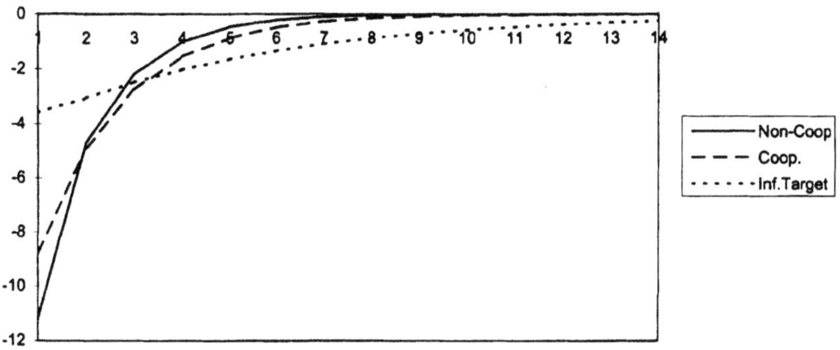

Figure 1. Output dynamics, Germany and France. Symmetric inflation shock – symmetric preferences.

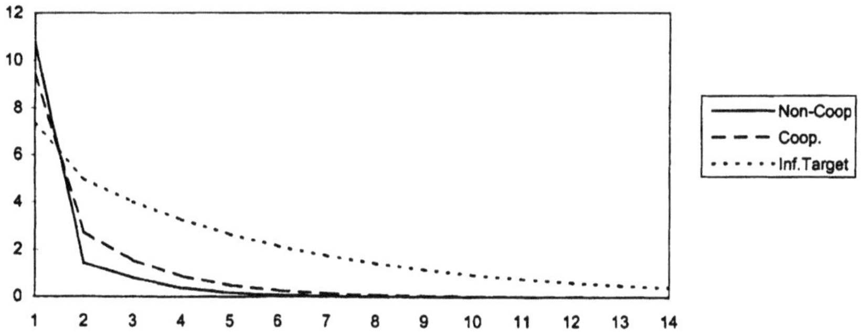

Figure 2. Inflation dynamics, Germany and France. Symmetric inflation shock – symmetric preferences.

idea of a fully independent central bank. The difficulty is that any central bank has to allow for the fact that there are others in this policy game; and if their reactions are strong enough they may overpower the central bank's policies with their own policies, even if the bank has correctly allowed for that. In this case, Germany and France can usually (but not always, depending on their own inflation aversion) do better for themselves the more they impose accountability on the ECB – and by most if they impose inflation targets on the ECB.

Moreover, it is clear that the ECB is being overpowered since Figures 1 and 2 show that the losses in inflation and output targets are of roughly equal size despite inflation having a penalty which is more than five times larger than that on output; and because it is the lower penalty output target which improves most when accountability is introduced. In other words, when improvements come they come in output; not in inflation as you would expect if the ECB were in control.

The next section explains in detail how this happens. But the key point is that the independence of the central bank is of no avail if other policy makers have the power and the incentive to neutralise it. The logic of wanting an independent central bank is as strong as ever, but it is of little value if you cannot use it.

Table 3. Capitulation solutions

Homogeneous preferences, symmetric inflation shocks				
Policy regimes	Europe	Germany	France	ECB
Monetary surrender	92.74	92.74	92.74	354.10
Fiscal surrender	115.91	115.91	115.91	309.97(BB)
Homogeneous preferences, asymmetric inflation shock				
Policy regimes	Europe	Germany	France	ECB
Monetary surrender	263.77	71.71	455.84	354.10
Fiscal surrender	269.23	27.60	510.87	309.97(BB)
Non-homogeneous preferences, symmetric inflation shocks				
Policy regimes	Europe	Germany	France	ECB
Monetary surrender	173.12	219.14	127.10	316.86
Fiscal surrender	209.43	302.95	115.91	309.97(BB)

BB = balanced budget imposed.

WHY DOES FISCAL POLICY DOMINATE DESPITE THE INDEPENDENCE OF THE CENTRAL BANK?

We can show how these inferior outcomes come from the conflicts between fiscal and monetary policy generated when a Central Bank acts independently, by considering the case where no fiscal interventions are allowed (g and g^*, of appendix 1, are constrained to zero). This is the fiscal surrender solution in Table 3. In that situation, we would expect the ECB simply to raise interest rates to counter the Europe-wide inflationary shock. And if the bank were acting alone, that would be all it would do, since it has little interest in (and a low priority on) preserving output levels. Consequently inflation would be steadily squeezed out, at some cost in terms of lower output.

And that is exactly what we find in Table 4. In fact, left to itself the independent central bank raises interest rates quite sharply in the aftermath of the inflation shock – in contrast to the results in Table 5 where governments are allowed to use their fiscal policies (albeit noncooperatively because the bank remains independent). The nominal exchange rate then depreciates as expected, but not by enough to prevent a real appreciation. Moreover there is no overshooting. As a result output, wealth, investment and the current accounts all deteriorate instead of improving. Consequently we get the traditional outcomes: inflation is disciplined away, but at the cost of losses in output and wealth (or investment) which are larger than in the case where fiscal policy is allowed (compare Table 5).

Consequently it is obvious that governments would have the incentive to try to recover output and wealth once they are let back into the game, and that fiscal policy will be their only means of doing so. Indeed Table 5 shows exactly that when the Central Bank is not acting alone.[3] In this case, interest rates actually fall; and both inflation and output losses, while large to start with, are reduced pretty rapidly and at fairly equal rates. Paradoxically fiscal policy is now strongly contractionary; and both nominal and real exchange rates depreciate instead of appreciating.

Why this apparently perverse behaviour? Table 5 shows it is the result of a conflict between the bank and the fiscal authorities. Faced with the bank's preference to raise interest rates and appreciate the currency in order to eliminate inflation, the fiscal

Table 4. Two country monetary union, the balanced budgets case. Time con-sistent policy rule – non-cooperative Nash equilibrium symmetric inflation shock (10%, 10%), homogeneous preferences

		1	2	3	4	5
German economy						
Output	%	−10.41	−4.96	−2.4	−1.16	−0.56
CPI inflation	D	9.53	1.45	0.72	0.35	0.17
Domestic price level	%	10.00	11.21	11.82	12.11	12.25
Wage level	%	1.68	10.37	11.39	11.91	12.15
Nominal interest rate	D	4.68	2.25	1.09	0.53	0.25
Real interest rate	D	3.47	1.65	0.8	0.38	0.19
Nominal exchange rate	%	2.88	7.8	10.17	11.32	11.87
Real exchange rate	%	−6.65	−3.19	−1.54	−0.74	−0.36
Fiscal stance	%	0	0	0	0	0
Wealth	%	−2.6	−3.84	−4.44	−4.73	−4.87
Investment	%	−2.17	−1.03	−0.5	−0.24	−0.12
Current account	%	−0.44	−0.21	−0.1	−0.05	−0.02
French economy						
Output	%	−10.41	−4.96	−2.4	−1.16	−0.56
CPI inflation	D	9.53	1.45	0.72	0.35	0.17
Domestic price level	%	10.00	11.21	11.82	12.11	12.25
Wage level	%	1.68	10.37	11.39	11.91	12.15
Nominal interest rate	D	4.68	2.25	1.09	0.53	0.25
Real interest rate	D	3.47	1.65	0.8	0.38	0.19
Nominal exchange rate	%	2.88	7.8	10.17	11.32	11.87
Real exchange rate	%	−6.65	−3.19	−1.54	−0.74	−0.36
Fiscal stance	%	0	0	0	0	0
Wealth	%	−2.6	−3.84	−4.44	−4.73	−4.87
Investment	%	−2.17	−1.03	−0.5	−0.24	−0.12
Current account	%	−0.44	−0.21	−0.1	−0.05	−0.02

% is percent deviation from unchanged baseline; D is change from unchanged baseline.
FAIR – TAYLOR Algorithm by Warwick McKibbin.

authorities have to respond to save output – their preferred target. They cannot do that by increasing net fiscal expenditures since that would simply add to the inflationary pressures, and hence slow down the correction of inflation and output losses even further. Instead the fiscal authorities have to do it by decreasing fiscal expenditures (or increasing taxation) since that will help reduce interest rates and depreciate the currency – albeit inefficiently – and hence restore aggregate demand at home and from abroad without immediately adding to inflation. And if they do this strongly enough, the fiscal contractions will eventually overcome the monetary tightening. In that way we end up with a net cut in interest rates (real and nominal) and a net depreciation in the exchange rate (real and nominal). This, in turn, leads to a fairly rapid and even handed elimination of both the inflation and output disturbances, instead of the elimination of inflation at the expense of output. Given that policy independence automatically puts us in a non-cooperative world, where policies are freely chosen to suit "private" objectives, and where one player favours inflation but the other output, we could not expect anything else.

Table 5. Two country monetary union. Time consistent policy rules – non-cooperative Nash equilibrium symmetric inflation shock (10%, 10%), homogeneous preferences

		1	2	3	4	5
German economy						
Output	%	−11.21	−4.71	−2.2	−1.01	−0.47
CPI inflation	D	10.77	1.43	0.81	0.37	0.17
Domestic price level	%	10.00	11.8	12.82	13.29	13.51
Nominal interest rate	D	−3.45	−2.07	−0.94	−0.43	−0.2
Real interest rate	D	−5.25	−3.1	−1.4	−0.65	−0.3
Nominal exchange rate	%	21.72	17.9	15.62	14.58	14.1
Real exchange rate	%	10.95	5.71	2.61	1.21	0.56
Fiscal stance	%	−8.78	−4.44	−2.04	−0.94	−0.44
Wealth	%	5.98	9.24	10.73	11.42	11.74
Investment	%	3.28	1.93	0.88	0.41	0.19
Current account	%	2.7	1.33	0.61	0.28	0.13
Debt	D	−8.78	−13.22	−15.26	−16.20	−16.64
French economy						
Output	%	−11.21	−4.71	−2.2	−1.01	−0.47
CPI inflation	D	10.77	1.43	0.81	0.37	0.17
Domestic price level	%	10.00	11.8	12.82	13.29	13.51
Wage level	%	1.03	11.4	12.48	13.14	13.44
Nominal interest rate	D	−3.45	−2.07	−0.94	−0.43	−0.2
Real interest rate	D	−5.25	−3.1	−1.4	−0.65	−0.3
Nominal exchange rate	%	21.72	17.9	15.62	14.58	14.1
Real exchange rate	%	10.95	5.71	2.61	1.21	0.56
Fiscal stance	%	−8.78	−4.44	−2.04	−0.94	−0.44
Wealth	%	5.98	9.24	10.73	11.42	11.74
Investment	%	3.28	1.93	0.88	0.41	0.19
Current account	%	2.7	1.33	0.61	0.28	0.13
Debt	D	−8.78	−13.22	−15.26	−16.20	−16.64

% is percent deviation from unchanged baseline; D is change from unchanged baseline.
FAIR – TAYLOR algorithm by Warwick McKibbin.

Nevertheless, because any attempts to boost demand through lower interest and exchange rates will eventually add to inflation, the final equilibrium must eventually restore interest rates to their original level and the currency depreciations must be brought to an end. Consequently, after the initial overshooting, both players have to allow the currency to appreciate back up – engineered now by removing the initial fiscal contractions and by tightening monetary policy. Consequently the exchange rate has to jump down and then appreciate back up if equilibrium is to be regained.

This sequence of lower interest rates and currency depreciations, together with a fiscal contraction followed by a currency appreciation and rising interest rates, shows that the fiscal authorities do initially overpower the central bank despite its independence.

ACCOUNTABILITY HELPS REDUCE FISCAL (OR MONETARY) DOMINANCE

To summarise: First, in a world of more than one fiscal authority but one central bank, the former may well try to dominate the latter's policies in order to preserve their own targets. So, even when independence is enforced, we cannot guarantee that it proves effective. Second, limiting fiscal interventions by the national governments by a stability pact is indeed a way of preserving the independence of the central bank and its policies, (Artis and Winkler, 1997). But that may mean rather little inflation control: each group of policy makers will simply aim to neutralise the policies of the others. In fact in our case, limiting fiscal interventions achieved little more than doing nothing at all. Far better, therefore, to introduce some accountability in the targets as a means of limiting the excesses of, and conflicts between, these independent policy making authorities.

The key result therefore is that policy independence generates policy conflicts which make it more difficult for either party to reach their own preferred targets, let alone the targets of other decision makers. We have demonstrated that with a simple numerical example. But it is important to stress that these same conflicts arise naturally in any of the standard theory models that we use to justify the independence of the central bank (Demertzis et al., 1999). So they are not a specific feature of our example. Indeed self-defeating conflicts which become more acute the more an independent central bank or governments press to recover their own targets, are an unavoidable feature of the problem. This we show in the next section and Figure 3, to complete the case for some accountability and coordination.

IV. Accountability Through Cooperation between Independent Players

FISCAL–MONETARY COORDINATION

These results need to be compared to the third option which is to impose some accountability (Table 6: the cooperative solution). Like the fiscal restrictions in Table 4, accountability also removes the inefficient policy assignments of Table 5. Indeed monetary policy is used to restrain inflation (as you would expect, and more strongly than in Table 4). Similarly Table 6 also shows some fiscal expansions in year 1 – but within the limits of the Stability Pact. That eliminates the output losses of that year. As a result the output and inflation losses are both smaller than with a fully independent central bank. And Table 7 (inflation targeting) shows exactly the same thing, but in more moderate form. Inflation targeting also produces better investment figures than cooperation, but at the cost of larger current account deficits.

In other words accountability rescues policy effectiveness by reinstating the more efficient policy assignments. That lowers the degree of self-defeating competition between policy makers with different objectives. That in turn allows instruments to be used mainly, but not exclusively, according to their comparative advantage – interest rates for inflation, fiscal policy for output – and without the unnecessary overshooting which has to be corrected again in later periods. As a result the extremes in inflation and output losses are avoided, even if the reduction of inflation is slightly slower between years 2 and 3. That delivers a Pareto improvement over full independence (Table 1) or monetary dominance (Table 3).

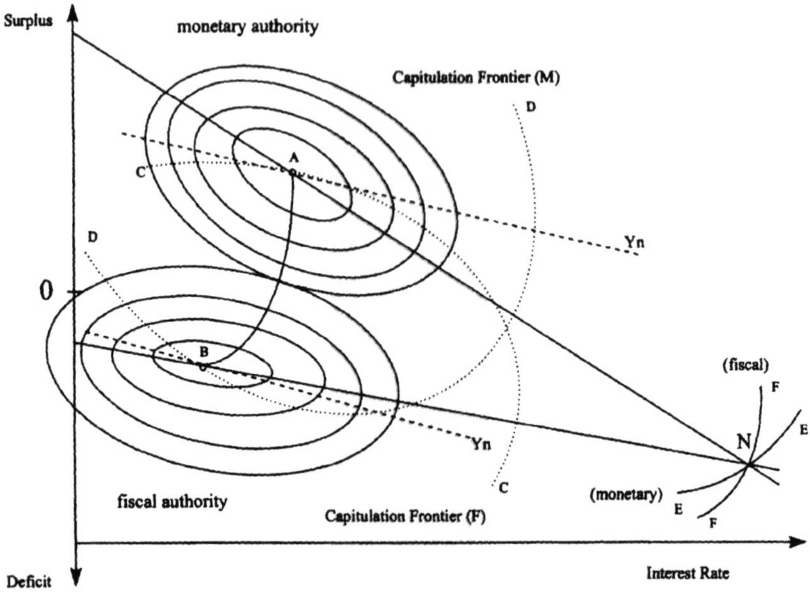

Figure 3. The incentive to remain independent.

Explanatory notes:
1. AB = contract curve for coordination. It provides the incentive compatibility constraint for cooperation, corresponding to the segment of the contract curve which strictly dominates N (the whole contract curve in this diagram). It has to lie within the intersection of the two utility contours marked EE and FF.
2. A and B = "bliss" points in constrained optimisation space; N = Nash (noncooperative) equilibrium.
3. CC and DD = the indifference contours (one for each player) which go through the other player's "bliss" point. They provide the incentive compatibility constraints for remaining independent, corresponding to those segments of the utility and reaction curves which lie inside the indifference contours marked "capitulation frontier". If N lies outside a players own capitulation frontier, then he has no incentive to act independently.

Moreover because cooperation necessarily delivers a pareto improvement over the best that can be done in a noncooperative setting, transparency and final responsibility are always involved. They are made explicit by virtue of the bargain struck by the participants. Thus accountability, over the best that one can do on ones own account, implies transparency. But transparency may not always imply accountability because the former does not necessarily imply any feedback from "society" to its policy institutions. Hence transparency may not always provide legitimacy.

CAPITULATION VS. THE INCENTIVE TO REMAIN INDEPENDENT

Nordhaus (1994) has pointed out that a given national income level can always be achieved with a variety of different combinations of interest rates and budget deficits. But these different combinations will have different implications for inflation, which means that the fiscal and monetary authorities would want to take different positions

Table 6. Two country monetary union cooperative equilibrium with identical weights as in (A6). Symmetric inflation shock (10%, 10%), homogeneous preferences

		1	2	3	4	5
German economy						
Output	%	−8.78	−4.91	−2.76	−1.55	−0.87
CPI inflation	D	9.43	2.74	1.55	0.87	0.49
Domestic price level	%	10	12.4	13.84	14.65	15.11
Wage level	%	2.98	11.11	13.11	14.24	14.88
Nominal interest rate	D	7.17	2.94	1.66	0.93	0.52
Real interest rate	D	4.77	1.5	0.85	0.48	0.27
Nominal exchange rate	%	1.22	8.73	11.77	13.49	14.45
Real exchange rate	%	−8.2	−3.43	−1.93	−1.09	−0.61
Fiscal stance	%	1.61	−0.03	−0.02	−0.01	−0.01
Wealth	%	−3.8	−4.99	−5.67	−6.05	−6.26
Investment	%	−2.98	−0.94	−0.53	−0.3	−0.17
Current account	%	−0.82	−0.26	−0.15	−0.08	−0.05
Debt	D	1.61	1.57	1.56	1.55	1.54
French economy						
Output	%	−8.78	−4.91	−2.76	−1.55	−0.87
CPI inflation	D	9.43	2.74	1.55	0.87	0.49
Domestic price level	%	10	12.4	13.84	14.65	15.11
Wage level	%	2.98	11.11	13.11	14.24	14.88
Nominal interest rate	D	7.17	2.94	1.66	0.93	0.52
Real interest rate	D	4.77	1.5	0.85	0.48	0.27
Nominal exchange rate	%	1.22	8.73	11.77	13.49	14.45
Real exchange rate	%	−8.2	−3.43	−1.93	−1.09	−0.61
Fiscal stance	%	1.61	−0.03	−0.02	−0.01	−0.01
Wealth	%	−3.8	−4.99	−5.67	−6.05	−6.26
Investment	%	−2.98	−0.94	−0.53	−0.3	−0.17
Current account	%	−0.82	−0.26	−0.15	−0.08	−0.05
Debt	D	1.61	1.57	1.56	1.55	1.54

% is percent deviation from unchanged baseline; D is change from unchanged baseline.
FAIR – TAYLOR algorithm by Warwick.

in the diagram showing the different interest rate – budget deficit combinations that could yield the same level of national income (Figure 3).[4]

In that case, if one player finds that, given full policy independence, the Nash noncooperative solution lies outside the indifference contour from his own utility function that goes through the other player's most preferred position [at the chosen level of national income], then it would pay the first player to give up and hand over control of his own instrument to the other player. At least he would get the other players preferred outcome, and hence a higher level in his own utility[5] – compared to fighting it out, and ending up at the Nash point which represents a lower level of utility for both of them.

Of course there is no guarantee that such a possibility actually exists in any given case; or that capitulation by the other party might not also benefit both of them. Both possibilities will have to be checked out on a case-by-case basis.

Table 7. Two country monetary union, inflation targeting. Non-cooperative Nash equilibrium, symmetric inflation shock (10%, 10%)

		1	2	3	4	5
German economy						
Output	%	−3.6	−3.06	−2.49	−2.03	−1.65
CPI inflation	D	7.32	4.97	4.01	3.26	2.65
Domestic price level	%	10	14.43	18.04	20.96	23.35
Wage level	%	7.12	13.06	16.96	20.09	22.64
Nominal interest rate	D	−3.3	−2.14	−1.72	−1.4	−1.14
Real interest rate	D	−7.73	−5.75	−4.65	−3.78	−3.07
Nominal exchange rate	%	−31.04	−18.33	−8.57	−0.66	5.77
Real exchange rate	%	−38.35	−30.62	−24.87	−20.21	−16.43
Fiscal stance	%	0.73	0.79	0.65	0.53	0.43
Wealth	%	−1.63	−3.18	−4.45	−5.48	−6.32
Investment	%	4.83	3.59	2.91	2.36	1.92
Current account	%	−6.46	−5.14	−4.18	−3.4	−2.76
French economy						
Output	%	−3.6	−3.06	−2.49	−2.03	−1.65
CPI inflation	D	7.32	4.97	4.01	3.26	2.65
Domestic price level	%	10	14.43	18.04	20.96	23.35
Wage level	%	7.12	13.06	16.96	20.09	22.64
Nominal interest rate	D	−3.3	−2.14	−1.72	−1.4	−1.14
Real interest rate	D	−7.73	−5.75	−4.65	−3.78	−3.07
Nominal exchange rate	%	−31.04	−18.33	−8.57	−0.66	5.77
Real exchange rate	%	−38.35	−30.62	−24.87	−20.21	−16.43
Fiscal stance	%	0.73	0.79	0.65	0.53	0.43
Wealth	%	−1.63	−3.18	−4.45	−5.48	−6.32
Investment	%	4.83	3.59	2.91	2.36	1.92
Current account	%	−6.46	−5.14	−4.18	−3.4	−2.76

% is percent deviation from unchanged baseline; D is change from unchanged baseline.
FAIR – TAYLOR Algorithm by Warwick McKibbin.

However it is obvious that capitulation is more likely if the constrained "bliss points" are similar in one dimension, but different in the other; if the players have very different priorities on the two targets; or that at least one of them has a high priority in the dimension in which their aspirations differ; or if they both accept a reasonable degree of substitution between instruments (e.g., governments will accept low deficits and less intervention, if the central banks agree to keep interest rates low on average). In other words, capitulation is all to do with differences in preferences and very little to do with the kind of model being used.[6]

V. Monetary Surrender (Fiscal Dominance)

In our case, national governments clearly make the greatest gains by imposing strong forms of accountability; e.g., inflation targeting (Tables 1 and 2). At least this is true when shocks are symmetric; and for the country suffering the shock, if not. But these gains come at the expense of the ECB, and those whose preferences are aligned with the ECB. Accountability can therefore go too far. But some degree of accountability is always desirable for everyone.

That result underlines the obvious attraction of allowing a fiscal coalition to take responsibility for the design of monetary policy (using Equation (A7) to define their preferences) in order to strengthen the ability of those governments to reach their own targets. Indeed the outcomes of a fiscal coalition are nearly as good as those from a three party partnership ("coop (1)"). [Compare the monetary surrender results in Table 3]. That illustrates the weakness of an independent ECB. A carefully controlled fiscal policy by France and Germany could deliver results that are almost as good. That is going to be important where there are asymmetries, and where the policy mix between g_F and g_G [Equation (A3)], needs to be adjusted to meet those asymmetries. Conversely asymmetries in the preferences and/or structures will cause a lot of damage if fiscal policy is somehow restricted under a single monetary policy.

The crucial point here is that a rational central bank would never want to insist on exercising its independence against the odds, when preferences are very different elsewhere. Instead it would *either* prefer to capitulate to the fiscal authorities and allow them to set interest rates according to their priorities – a relatively un-sophisticated response, of the kind we got in the 1970s and 1980s. *Or*, in a rather more sophisticated approach, it would actively seek accountability in order to enlist the support of the fiscal authorities. At least the central bank would be sure that its priorities would get to influence the outcomes that way. With full independence it could not be so sure. That's the gain in accepting voluntary accountability.

VI. Fiscal Surrender

The alternative and more relevant possibility for EMU, is a capitulation by the fiscal authorities. That would involve either a balanced budget amendment (the preferred choice in the US and what EMU is supposed to achieve),[7] or some version of the stability pact. Is there any incentive for such arrangements? The answer is yes.

The balanced budget results were discussed in Section 3 and Table 4. The overall evaluation is given in Table 3. Evidently fiscal surrender produces better outcomes, for all parties, than unrestricted monetary independence. So far so good: there is a significant incentive for the fiscal policymakers to surrender. However, both Germany and France could do even better for themselves if they could persuade the monetary authorities to surrender instead; and even better again if the ECB could be persuaded to accept an inflation target. That means that, politically, the issue is not yet resolved because it is not clear who will dominate in practice. Both sets of policy makers may realise that the economy would benefit if conflicts were avoided. But which one should exercise discretion and who should lead? Governments would naturally prefer a monetary surrender, and the ECB a fiscal surrender. Only cooperation, by minimising the (expected) losses of both were they to lose the struggle, offers a way out and an improvement over what will happen otherwise. Accountability, directed at obtaining the appropriate policy mix for the economy as a whole, is therefore in the interest of both parties.

VII. Concluding Observations

(a) We have made a distinction between three types of fiscal-monetary policy regimes: coordination; capitulation; or full (Central Bank) independence. The problem with the latter two is that they prevent the policy mix from adjusting to the level necessary to satisfy the targets of the economy as a whole. And if the policy mix is not able to adjust, then it will trigger policy conflicts which imply that either no-one achieves their objectives or only one party does.

(b) Practical ways of constructing a coordinated solution include creating a forum for negotiating adjustments to the policy mix between the relevant policy authorities; creating a form of inflation targeting regime; or obliging independent policy makers to follow some kind of joint "inflation and output growth" contract. Each of these schemes imposes some notion of accountability on the individual policy makers. The key ingredient is that, in each case, the policy maker remains an independent and freely contracting party to the arrangement. In other words, they retain full instrument independence, but accept certain limits on their degree of target independence.

(c) We found that an "inflation and growth targeting" contract approach allows free fiscal policy and an independent monetary policy making without violating the Stability Pact. It could be introduced in the form of the broad policy guidelines which article 103 of the Amsterdam Treaty specifies should be imposed on the policy makers – which in turn would allow "Euro-X" to become the coordinating forum for fiscal, monetary and labour market policies. Such an arrangement would introduce an important but subtle change in the currently proposed accountability framework. As things stand, the European Parliament can only criticise the ECB's past performance. That form of accountability is purely backward looking. By contrast some form of accountability would prevent a policy vacuum in which the ECB would inevitably be blamed for any failures.

(d) The current set up therefore looks more like a swap of one set of asymmetric restrictions (the fiscal dominance and monetary dependence of the 1970s) for another set (i.e., monetary dominance and fiscal surrender via the Stability Pact of the 1990s). Such extremes are seldom optimal because they represent the attempt by one of the parties to capture all the gains from policy for their own benefit.[8] Whether such a regime is actually better than allowing all policy makers full independence depends on the degree of asymmetry between different targets compared to the degree of asymmetry between different policy makers, and on the degree of asymmetry in the responses of a given target to each policy instrument. If those asymmetries are quite large, as in Figure 3, then restricting one policy maker to give the other a decisive lead in setting policies will remove many of the conflicts (inefficiencies) inherent in independent policy making.[9] But it will not remove them all; such capitulation solutions will remain inferior, perhaps significantly so, to the coordinated solution.

(e) It may be thought that such arguments are unimportant in Europe because there will be insufficient fiscal-to-fiscal coordination to mount a serious challenge to the effectiveness of monetary policy. That of course relates only to the independence solution; it has no bearing on the capitulation and coordination solutions. But if tax harmonisation, limits on fiscal policy and Frankel and Rose's (1998) notion of an endogenous coordination of national cycles are important elements of our monetary union, then countries will want more similar and closely coordinated fiscal policies.[10] In that case fiscal – monetary coordination becomes more important.

Acknowledgement

We would like to thank seminar participants at the National Bank of Austria, the Bank of England, the European Monetary Institute, the European Investment Bank, and the European Commission. The usual disclaimer naturally applies.

Appendix I: The Model Used in Sections III and IV

Like Oudiz and Sachs (1985), McKibbin and Sachs (1991) and Hughes Hallett and Vines (1993) before us, we use an adaptation of a Dornbusch model with forward looking financial markets and overlapping contracts. There are two regions 'Europe' and 'the United States'. Europe contains two countries: 'Germany, 'France' and a common European Central Bank. The distinction between the countries lies only in the asymmetry of shocks or preferences. Finally, the US – representing the rest of the world – is fixed exogenously in relation to Europe.

The model contains both forward looking behaviour and rigidities. First external exchange rates are determined according to uncovered interest parity, and exchange rate developments are perfectly anticipated with the exception of initial shocks.

By contrast, Europe's internal exchange rates are fixed (with no risk premium or possibility of time inconsistencies) in order to provide a single currency. Second, current wages and prices are jointly determined with expected future prices which themselves respond to lagged consumer price inflation and output, but not to expected future inflation rates. That puts some inertia into the system, to reflect the fact that contract wages cannot immediately adjust to market clearing levels but nonetheless retain some sensitivity to the economy's expected evolution. Hence, in the short run, the exchange rate disciplines inflation. But in the long run wages and prices are tied down by the assumption that agents expect equilibrium to be re-established eventually (a terminal condition). The long run Phillips curve is therefore vertical. Consumption, however, is not forward looking. We adopt this specification on the assumption – broadly in line with experience of the 1990s – that some consumers will be liquidity constrained and therefore unable to carry out the inter-temporal optimizations needed to smooth their consumption. A full model listing now follows:

The model is in levels, and all variables are expressed in deviations from their long run (equilibrium) growth paths. All US variables are exogenous, and are therefore suppressed. The European exchange rate is expressed in terms of the dollar.

Parameters have been chosen so as to correspond in a stylized fashion with reality:

(i) The Keynesian multiplier has a value of 2.0.
(ii) The marginal propensity to import is 0.25 in all countries.
(iii) At the margin (that is, in variations around the equilibrium growth paths), 72%

of European trade is between themselves. This means that the marginal propensity of each to import from the other is 18%, and 7% from elsewhere.

(iv) Trade elasticities are of a standard size: the sum of the price elasticities of demand for exports and imports is 2.5.

Equations (1) and (1*) show the determination of aggregate demands. The real exchange rate terms show the effects on the home country trade balance of home country and foreign country exchange rates. The y^* term shows the foreign demand for domestic exports, and vice versa in equation (1*). Equations (2) and (2*) are the Phillips curves, which contain effects on both the level of and change in output. Equations (3) and (3*) relate consumer prices to output and import prices (which are influenced by real exchange rates). Equations (4) and (4*) show current account evolution and Equations (5) and (5*) show investment. Equations (6) and (6*) and (10) show exchange rate determination between Europe and US under perfect capital mobility and model-consistent expectations, Finally Equations (7), (8) and (9) – also (7*), (8*) and (9*) – are recursive to the rest of the model and describe the evolution of money supplies, the debt ratio, and net wealth respectively.

THE MODEL

Equations (a '+1' subscript denotes a forward looking variable)

'German' Block

$$y = 1.25a - 0.90a^* - 0.90a^* + 0.36y^* + 2.0inv + 2.0g \quad (1)$$

$$p_{+1} = p + pc - p_{-1} + 0.5y + 0.3(y - y_{-1}) \quad (2)$$

$$pc = p + 0.25a - 0.18a^* \quad (3)$$

$$ca = 0.625a - 0.45a^* - 0.25y + 0.18y^* \quad (4)$$

$$inv = -0.625(r - p_{+1} + p) \quad (5)$$

$$a_{+1} = a + (r - p_{+1} + p) \quad (6)$$

$$m = ky + lr, \quad k > 0, \ l < 0 \quad (7)$$

$$d = (1 + r - \Delta y - \Delta p)d_{-1} + g \quad (8)$$

$$w = (1 + r)w_{-1} + inv + ca \quad (9)$$

'French Block'

$$y^* = 1.25a^* - 0.90a + 0.36y + 2.0inv^* + 2.0g^* \quad (1^*)$$

$$p_{+1} = p^* + pc^* - pc^*_{-1} + 0.5y^* + 0.3(y^* - y^*_{-1}) \quad (2^*)$$

$$pc^* = p^* + 0.25a^* - 0.18a \quad (3^*)$$

$$ca^* = 0.625a^* - 0.45a - 0.25y^* + 0.18y \quad (4^*)$$

$$inv^* = -0.625(r - p^*_{+1} + p^*) \quad (5^*)$$

$$a^*_{+1} = a^* + (r - p^*_{+1} + p^*) \quad (6^*)$$

$$m^* = ky^* + lr \quad (7^*)$$

$$d^* = (1 + r - \Delta y^* - \Delta p^*)d^*_{-1} + g \quad (8^*)$$

$$w^* = (1 + r)w_{-1} + inv + ca \quad (9^*)$$

'European Block'

$$n = (a + a^*) + (p + p^*) \tag{10}$$

A star denotes a 'French' variable; variables without stars are 'German' variables.

Endogenous Variables		*Policy Instruments*	
y:	output	*g*:	*net* fiscal expenditures
p:	output prices	*r*:	European nominal interest rate
pc:	consumer prices	*Recursive Variables*	
ca:	current balance	*m*:	money stock
inv:	investment	*d*:	debt to GNP ratio
a:	real exchange rate in $ terms	*w*:	national wealth
n:	nominal exchange rate (vs. $)		

Appendix II: The Regimes and Objective Functions Used in Sections III and IV

THE POLICY AUTHORITIES, TARGETS AND POLICY INSTRUMENTS

There are three policy players: the two national Fiscal Authorities, and the European Central Bank. While the two national fiscal authorities target national variables, the ECB targets European aggregates, defined here as the weighted average of the national aggregates. In the spirit of the Maastricht Treaty, we take price stability and the deviation of output from full capacity as the main objectives of policy.

For each of the scenarios studied below, we carry out time consistent policy optimizations over 100 periods (a 'long run'), in order to determine the best possible responses to shocks to the system. This grants the ECB full credibility, which is the principle benefit of having a fully independent central bank.

We take each policy variable to be measured as a deviation from its equilibrium or target path. The welfare functions then penalize squared deviations of each target and instrument from its equilibrium value in each period in order to generate a rapid return to equilibrium.

The simulations are based on the assumption that the ECB is at least as 'conservative' as the most conservative of the fiscal authorities, where 'being conservative' is defined as putting a higher weight on controlling inflation. This means that the ECB decides its policy by minimising the following objective function:

$$U_{\text{ECB}} = \frac{1}{2}\sum_t \left[y^2 + \beta n^2 + \delta r^2 + \gamma(\pi - \pi^*)^2\right], \tag{A1}$$

where $7\gamma = 5$ and $\delta = \beta = 0.5$; and where n is the nominal Euro exchange rate, r is the nominal interest rate, and $(\pi - \pi^*)$ is the difference between European inflation in period t and its target value (equal to zero in most of the simulations). Inflation and output are defined as European averages here.

The policy instrument in the hands of the ECB is the nominal interest rate. The use of interest rates as the monetary instrument, rather than the money stock, corresponds to actual practice and is not subject to the 'indeterminacy of the price level' problem because interest rates are endogenised in order to control inflation.

The two fiscal authorities on the other hand minimise their own objective functions

$$U_i = \frac{1}{2}\sum_t [y_i^2 + \varepsilon w_i^2 + \eta g_i^2 + \theta(\pi_i)^2] \quad i = F, G; \gamma > \theta, \tag{A2}$$

where w_i stands for wealth and g_i is the net fiscal stance, being the instrument in the hands of the fiscal authority. All the variables are defined in national terms: G for Germany and F for France. ε, η are defined in (A3)–(A5).

The choice of the parameter θ defines the two different preference schemes:

1. *Homogeneous preferences*: In the first scheme the two fiscal authorities have the same preferences, represented by a special case of (A2):

$$U_i = \frac{1}{2}\sum_t [y_i^2 + 0.1w_I^2 + 0.5g_i^2 + (\pi_i)^2] \quad \theta_F = \theta_G = 1, \quad \text{where } i = F, G. \tag{A3}$$

This objective function states that both fiscal authorities put the same weight on inflation control and output stabilisation. The combination of objective functions (A1) and (A2) defines a regime in which the ECB is significantly more 'conservative' than the national authorities, because $\gamma > \theta$.

2. *Non-Homogeneous preferences*: In the second scheme, German preferences are geared more towards controlling inflation than French preferences. The German fiscal authority therefore sets policies which minimise the objective function

$$U_G = \frac{1}{2}\sum_t [y_G^2 + 0.1w_G^2 + 0.5g_G^2 + 5(\pi_G)^2] \quad \theta_G = 5 \tag{A4}$$

but the French authorities minimise

$$U_F = \frac{1}{2}\sum_t [y_F^2 + 0.1w_F^2 + 0.5g_F^2 + \pi_F^2] \quad \theta_F = 1. \tag{A5}$$

This scenario defines a regime in which Germany shares the preferences of the more conservative ECB, but France does not.

THE POLICY REGIMES

1. A Non-Cooperative Nash Game (Full Independence)

The three policy authorities optimise simultaneously in their own interest. In this policy rule the ECB has both instrument and target independence. There is no accountability.

2. The Cooperative Game

The cooperative equilibrium was computed optimising an equally weighted aver-age of individual objective functions:

$$U = (1/3)U_G + (1/3)U_F + (1/3)U_{ECB}. \tag{A6}$$

For identically symmetric cases, this will deliver an optimal Nash bargain. This time the ECB has instrument independence; but its target independence is strictly circumscribed. Each policy maker is symmetrically accountable to the others.

3. Capitulation Solutions

Monetary surrender: This equilibrium was computed optimising a weighted average of the individual objective functions with a zero weight on the preferences of the ECB: i.e.

$$U = (1/2)U_G + (1/2)U_F + (0)U_{\text{ECB}}. \tag{A7}$$

The ECB's preferences therefore play no role in determining the optimal policies.

But since both fiscal authorities have low inflation among their targets, interest rates are now set by the less conservative fiscal authorities – instead of by the more conservative central bankers. In this case the ECB is fully accountable, and has no independence. To match this we have included a *fiscal surrender* solution, in which national governments are obliged to accept a fully independent monetary policy and a balanced budget. The outcomes are determined by monetary policy, rather than by fiscal intervention.

4. A Non-Cooperative Nash Game with Inflation Targeting

We consider one regime where the ECB has instrument independence but no target independence. The two fiscal authorities determine, simultaneously and noncooperatively, their fiscal policy and indicate to the ECB their preferred inflation target. The inflation target itself is determined by the optimisation of the two objective functions in (A2), using two 'instruments' – public expenditures (g) and an inflation target (π^*) – to do so. The ECB, meanwhile, has to maximize its own objective function (A1), as usual, in which the inflation target is defined as the weighted average of the optimal inflation targets of the two fiscal authorities (should they differ).

Notes

1. Leith and Wren-Lewis (1998) give a formal demonstration of this in a Blanchard–Yaari model with asset accumulation and intertemporal budget constraints. Another way that the same thing can happen is the Sargent and Wallace (1981) result that undisciplined fiscal authorities can put pressure (1982) on the Central Bank to monetise their debt.
2. We do not identify whether the origin of these shocks is on the demand side or the supply side. Were the shocks to be permanent, this distinction would determine the appropriate policy response. But they are transient, lasting just one period in a 100 period optimisation problem. So the best response is an open question. Moreover, all disturbances are deviations from the long run equilibrium path. So if supply shocks do alter the natural rate of output, but demand shocks do not, then we are trying to eliminate the deviations from that new natural rate, and from the original price level. The origin of the changes no longer matters. Indeed, in our model, the sign of dy/dp, is ambiguous so a positive price shock could represent either a demand or a supply shock.
3. Table 5 removes the balanced budget constraint and allows governments to use fiscal policy noncooperatively (to preserve the independence of the central bank), but freely, subject to the constraints implied by the penalties in their objective functions – Equation (A2) in the Appendix.
4. Moving along one y_n line in Figure 3 implies accepting different rates of inflation for that y_n

(the natural level of output in a neoclassical model). Moving to a different y_n implies a different way of getting to the same set of (y_n inflation) combinations: the fiscal authority prefers to manipulate the budget, the monetary authority interest rates. The difference between the y_n lines and the reaction curves is that the former ignore reactions by the other policy maker, whereas the reaction functions do not.

5. Were the Nash point inside that particular indifference contour, then it would pay the first player to fight it out in order to get the better outcomes in terms of his own preferences, even if it produces worse outcomes for the other player. Note that this is all happening in a constrained optimisation space.
6. Recall that these policy conflicts are an inevitable consequence of having independent policy authorities with differing policy priorities. They are not a specific feature of the model we have used.
7. Duisenberg (1997).
8. Because they correspond to the extreme points at each end of the cooperation curve, such outcomes actually represent "coalition" solutions in which one group of policy makers attempt to use their economic or political power to expropriate all the gains for their own targets, at the expense of the targets of others. This is unlikely to be a stable solution in a democratic and pluralist society, and any movement away from such a position is likely to be welfare improving for society as a whole. Adjustments to the policy mix would be the vehicle for such movements.
9. As argued by Rankin (1998).
10. See Allsopp et al. (1999) for further evidence.

References

Alesina, A. and Summers, L. (1993) 'Central Bank Independence and Macroeconomic Performance: Some Comparative Evidence', *Journal of Money, Banking and Credit* **25**, 151–62.

Alesina, A. and Gatti, R. (1995) 'Independent Central Banks: Low Inflation at No Cost', *American Economic Review* **85**, 196–200.

Allsopp, C., McKibben, W. and Vines, D. (1999) 'Fiscal Consolidation in Europe: Some Empirical Issues', in A. Hughes Hallett, M. Hutchison and S. E. H. Jensen (eds.), *Fiscal Aspects. of European Monetary Integration*, Cambridge University Press, Cambridge.

Artis, M. and Winkler, B. (1997) 'The Stability Pact: Safeguarding the Credibility of the European Central Bank', Discussion Paper 1688, Centre for Economic Policy Research, London.

Campillo, M and Miron, J. A. (1997) 'Why Does Inflation Differ across Countries?', in C. Romer and D. Romer (eds.), *Reducing Inflation: Motivation and Strategy*, University of Chicago Press, Chicago.

Demertzis, M., Hughes Hallett, A. and Viegi, N. (1998) 'Independently Blue? Accountability and Independence in the New European Central Bank', Discussion Paper 1842, Centre for Economic Policy Research, London.

Demertzis, M, Hughes Hallett, A. and Veigi, N. (1999) 'An Independent Central Bank faced with Elected Governments', Discussion Paper 2219, Centre for Economic Policy Research, London.

Duisenberg, W. (1997) 'Monetary Policy and Competitiveness', Speech to the European Meeting of the Trilateral Commission, Den Haag, 25 October 1997.

Frankel, J. and Rose, A. (1998) 'The Endogeneity of Optimum Currency Area Criteria', *Economic Journal* **108**, 1009–25.

Hughes Hallett, A. and Vines, D. (1993) 'On the Possible Costs of Monetary Union in Europe', *Manchester School* **61**, 35–64.

Hughes Hallett, A. and Demertzis, M. (1999) 'When Can a Central Bank Offer Loners Inflation at No Cost? A Political Economy Analysis', Department of Economics, University of Strathclyde, Glasgow.

Leith, C. and Wren Lewis, S. (1998) 'Interactions between Monetary and Fiscal Policy Rules', Discussion Paper, University of Exeter, Department of Economics.

Lohmann, S. (1998) 'Federalism and Central Bank Independence: the Politics of German Monetary Policy 1957–92', *World Politics* **50**, 410–466.

McKibbin, W. and Sachs, J. (1991) 'Macroeconomic Interdependence and Cooperation in the World Economy', Brookings Institution, Washington DC.

Melitz, J. (1997) 'Some Cross-Country Evidence about Debt, Deficits and the Behaviour of Monetary and Fiscal Authorities', CEPR Discussion Paper No. 1653.

Nordhaus, W. (1994) 'Policy Games: Coordination and Independence in Monetary and Fiscal Policies', *Brookings Papers on Economic Activity* **25**(2), 139–216.

Oudiz, G. and Sachs, J. (1985) 'International Policy Coordination in Dynamic Macroeconomic Models', in W. Buiter and R. Masson (eds.), *International Economic Policy Coordination*, Cambridge University Press, Cambridge.

Posen, A. (1997) 'Lessons from the Bundesbank on the Occasion of its 40th (and second to last?) Birthday', Discussion Paper 97–4, Institute for International Economics, Washington.

Rankin, N. (1998) 'Is Delegating Half of Demand Management Sensible?', *International Review of Applied Economics* **12**, 439–46.

Sargent, T. and Wallace, N. (1981) 'Some Unpleasant Monetarist Arithmetic', *Federal Reserve Bank of Minneapolis Quarterly Review* **8**, 1–17.

von Hagen, J. (1998) 'Money Growth Targeting', Centre for European Integration Studies, University of Bonn, May 1998.

Woodford, M. (1995) 'Price Level Determinacy with Control of a Monetary Aggregate', Carnegie-Rochester Conference Series, 43.

7. The Stability and Growth Pact: A Delicate Balance or an Albatross?*

MATTHEW B. CANZONERI and BEHZAD T. DIBA
Department of Economics, Georgetown University, Washington, DC 20057-1036, USA

The Stability and Growth Pact of 1997 tried to strike a delicate balance.[1] On the one hand, it imposed the constraints on national fiscal policy that were deemed necessary to protect the new European Central Bank (ECB) from outside pressures, especially during the period in which it tried to establish credibility.[2] At the same time, the Pact allowed some flexibility for a counter-cyclical fiscal policy. This too was deemed necessary in EMU: a stable ECB policy might be expected to create stable macroeconomic conditions for the Euro-zone as a whole, but it could not be expected to iron out regional cyclical imbalances. Did the Pact strike a workable balance? Or is the Pact an unnecessary albatross that could seriously hamper the whole EMU project?

To answer these questions, one needs to analyze the flexibility that is embedded in the Pact, and one needs a well articulated explanation of the credibility problem that the Pact is supposed to address. Official institutions – the EU Commission, the OECD, the IMF – have provided the former, but the official community has not really done the latter. The academic literature provides a number of possible ex-planations, but it is not clear which, if any, of the explanations capture the concerns of the official community.

First, we review the official institutions' studies of the flexibility embedded in the Pact and find a rather strong consensus: the Pact seems likely to constrain counter-cyclical fiscal efforts in the years ahead, or at least until EU governments make one last fiscal retrenchment to bring their structural deficits roughly into balance. Then, we review conventional academic arguments that suggest a new central bank might need to be protected from external pressures,[3] and we ask if the constraints that were actually written into the Pact are likely to be helpful in this regard. We may as well give our bottom line at the top: we think the Pact is closer to an albatross than a delicately balanced package of necessary fiscal priorities.

I. The Stability and Growth Pact of 1997: Is It Flexible Enough for Stabilization?

The Stability and Growth Pact has several key elements:[4] (1) EU countries have committed themselves to "medium-term" budgets that are "close to balance or in

*This paper was prepared for the Austrian National Bank's Workshop on "Challenges for Economic Policy Coordination within EMU", January 22nd, 1999. We would like to thank, without implicating, Eduard Hochreiter and other Workshop participants for their helpful comments.

A. H. Hallett et al. (eds), Challenges for Economic Policy Coordination with European Monetary Union, 127–142.

surplus". (2) EU countries have to submit annual programs specifying medium term budgetary objectives; so, there will be a track record for the Council or the public to examine when assessing a country's compliance with the terms in the Pact (or the "convergence criteria" in the case of those who are not in the Euro-zone). (3) EU countries in the Euro-zone that run "excessive deficits" will be subject to financial penalties and public approbation; we think that the punishment for "excessive deficits" will be sufficient to affect government behavior.[5] (4) Deficits are "excessive" if they exceed 3% of GDP, unless they occur under "exceptional" circumstances. An annual decline in real output of more than 2% of GDP would be considered "exceptional"; a decline of 0.75% of GDP might be deemed "exceptional" if there is additional supporting evidence.

It is not clear how strictly the Council will interpret these provisions in practice. The EU has a history of exerting its discretion in the final analysis. For example, the "reference value" for debt (60% of GDP) that was written into the Maastricht Treaty played little role in the final decisions on which countries qualified to participate in EMU, and in fact debt limits are notably absent in the procedures outlined in the Pact; on the other hand, debt levels do continue to play a role in the annual stability programs that each government has to submit for approval, and debt levels may end up affecting how strictly the Council interprets the deficit provisions that are in the Pact. In this paper, we will ask whether the lack of emphasis on debt levels was a mistake, and more generally whether the Pact should be interpreted with considerable discretion.

Research coming from the European Commission, the OECD and the IMF suggests that the Pact will be flexible enough to accommodate the automatic counter-cyclical component of national fiscal policies *if member states bring their structural (or cyclically adjusted) deficits close to balance*.[6] (If one interprets the Pact's "medium-term" budget to mean the structural deficit, then member states are already committed to doing this.) The basic line of reasoning is as follows. In a typical EU country, the deficit rises by about 0.5% of GDP when output falls by 1%, and the output gap (the amount by which actual GDP falls short of potential) in a typical recession is about 3%. Suppose the structural deficit of the same typical EU country is reduced to say 1.5% of GDP. If the deficit to GDP to ratio is 1.5% when the gap is zero, then it will only rise to 3% ($= 1.5 + 0.5 \times 3$) during a typical recession; the constraint in the Pact will not be binding. Of course, the country may be risk averse and wish to plan for recessions that are worse than average; moreover, the country may wish to pursue a more active counter-cyclical policy after EMU, when national monetary policies are no longer an option, than it did before EMU. In either case, the country should aim for a lower structural deficit, perhaps something "close to balance or in surplus" as suggested by the Pact.

Looked at in this way, structural deficit targets are likely to vary from country to country. The cyclical sensitivity of budget deficits varies across countries, as presumably does the attitude toward risk. We have however seen estimates suggesting that structural deficits in the EU need on average to come down by about 1% of GDP. Until this final investment in fiscal austerity is made, the Pact seems likely to become an ongoing constraint on national counter-cyclical fiscal policies.

Will the final investment be made? EU deficits have already come down dramatically, from (on average) 6.1% of GDP in 1993 to 2.4% in 1997; Eichengreen and

Wyplosz (1998) suggest that "electorates lack the appetite for further spending cuts". If they are correct, then the Pact will likely be a binding constraint for the indefinite future.

What about the immediate future? Output gaps in the EU countries have been closing, but growth estimates have been revised downward. The *OECD Economic Outlook* for December, 1997, reports two simulations (of the INTERLINK model) for the deficit to GDP ratio: one for a "reference scenario" involving 2.5% GDP growth, and a second for a "slower growth scenario" with a growth slowdown in 1999 and 2000 to around 1.5% (see Figure 1). The "slower growth scenario" simulation suggests that France, Italy, Austria, Belgium and Spain would all violate the 3% constraint in the Pact; Germany, the Netherlands and Portugal would come close. These simulations suggest that the Pact may well be a constraint on counter-cyclical fiscal policy in the short run, even if member states do ultimately make the final investment in fiscal austerity and the Pact is not binding in the steady state.

Figure 1 illustrates a situation in which the Pact may have a particularly perverse effect. The Pact makes a huge distinction between a deficit that is 3.1% of GDP and a deficit that is 2.9% of GDP. In the first case, the country is in big trouble; in the second, it escapes unnoticed. In the "slower growth scenario" of Figure 1, eight of the eleven countries are in the neighborhood of the magical 3% mark. We suspect that in a situation like this there would be incredible political pressure on the ECB to lower debt finance costs enough to allow these countries to come in under the 3% mark. This is of course just the opposite of what the Pact was designed to do.

In summary, the consensus seems to be that the Pact will become a permanent impediment to counter-cyclical fiscal policy unless a final investment is made in bringing structural deficits down another 1% of GDP, and that in any case the Pact is likely to be a problem in the beginning years of EMU if there is a pronounced growth slowdown. This raises the question of whether the terms of the Pact can be interpreted loosely in the initial years, or whether the Pact should be rewritten altogether. What would be the consequences for the credibility of monetary policy?

II. Interest Rate Pressures on a Central Bank

It is extremely rare for a government to pressure its central bank directly to inflate. A sound currency is an unquestioned icon of national pride. Instead, the pressures to inflate generally take the form of complaints about interest rates. Both the Reagan Administration and the Clinton Administration complained about what they regarded as high interest rates coming from the Federal Reserve; both administrations claimed that the high interest rates were a drag on the "pro growth" policies that they had an electoral mandate to institute. Paul Volker responded that the high interest rates were caused by the Reagan Administration's borrowing to finance its deficits.[7] In Europe, much of the political concern in recent years has been that heavy refinance costs in high debt countries would prohibit them from achieving the 3% deficit to GDP ratio required for participation in EMU. As the discussion in the last section indicates, this concern is likely to live on in the Stability and Growth Pact until EU countries lower their structural deficits another 1% of GDP.

Moreover, political concerns about labor market conditions have led some politicians in France and Germany to focus attention on the level of the Euro-Dollar exchange rate, and of course an argument for a "competitive" exchange rate is a thinly disguised argument for a low interest rate. The Maastricht Treaty forbids national governments from putting direct pressure on the ECB to lower its interest rate, but the Treaty does give Ecofin (the Council of Ministers, meeting as finance ministers) some say about the general orientation of exchange rate policy. Thus, we may well see political pressures for lower interest rates and "competitive" exchange rates framed as proposals for formal agreements with the US and Japan about exchange rate target zones.

Strong political pressures to keep interest rates low may undermine the credibility of any central bank's mandate for price stability. Following Barro and Gordon (1983), a vast literature argues that these pressures are even more perverse than they might at first seem.[8] The essential insight of this literature is that farsighted actors in the private sector will anticipate the inflationary consequences of such pressures, and they will demand higher nominal interest rates and higher nominal wage rates to compensate for the expected inflation. The central bank will then be faced with the unhappy choice of accommodating these inflationary expectations or ending up with real interest rates and real wage rates that are abnormally high (or higher than what they would be in an equilibrium with full information). If the central bank sticks to its mandated inflation objectives, then the high real interest rates and the high real wages will have unintended implications for employment and output growth; moreover, the government's fiscal situation may worsen, leading to even more pressure to decrease interest rates in the future. The literature argues that the central bank will compromise in such a situation between its inflation goals and its fear of the consequences of not accommodating the private sector's inflationary expectations, and the inflation rate will be higher than desired. As long as the pressure for lower interest rates persists, so the argument goes, there will be a credibility problem and an inflation bias.

Suppose this reasoning captures the concerns that led to the fiscal criteria in the Maastricht Treaty and live on in the Stability and Growth Pact. We can now ask how effective the provisions in the Pact will be at easing the pressures, what the consequences would be of relaxing some of the provisions, and more generally whether other measures would be more effective.

First and perhaps foremost, it should be noted that much if not most of the political pressure for low interest rates may have nothing to do with government debt or deficits. New and more liberal governments have come to power in France and Germany, and unemployment seems to have replaced inflation as the major focus of political attention throughout most of the EU. It is difficult for us to see how the Pact will do anything to alleviate concerns for unemployment and growth; indeed, the Pact is more likely to aggravate them, as governments are required to curb their spending levels even further. Here again, the Pact may have perverse effects. It may actually increase pressure for low interest rates and make the ECB appear to be an institution designed to fight the last decade's war.[9]

What about political pressures that do come from difficulties in financing the debt. We have little doubt that these pressures exist. However, the point to be made here is that this is an argument for debt limits, not deficit limits. A country with little or no debt to finance (like Luxembourg) could be running rather large deficits, but its government would not have much incentive to pressure its central bank until the debt grew to a significant level. On the other hand, a country with a lot of debt (like Italy) can only limit its deficit to, say, 2.9% of GDP by running huge primary surpluses. Its government may well have an incentive to lobby for a lower interest rate; even a modest drop in the interest rate would allow it to run much smaller primary surpluses and still stay under the 3% cap specified in the Pact. The Pact does give a high debt country an incentive to lower its debt level over time; so, the Pact would seem to have some bite. However, the Pact's total focus on deficits, to the exclusion of the level of the debt, does seem misplaced, especially if interest rate pressures are thought to be the main concern.[10]

What is the cost of loosening the parameters of the Pact, or giving the Pact a rather loose interpretation? As discussed in the last section, this might be particularly appealing in the years just ahead, as EU countries look for an opportune moment to lower their structural deficits another 1% of GDP. To the extent that the Pact is actually limiting the political pressure for lower interest rates, any loosening of the constraints would presumably increase those pressures, and the theory suggests that this would intensify the credibility problem and increase the associated inflation bias. That bias increases in proportion with the political pressure.[11] Increasing political pressures at the same time as the new ECB is trying to establish its credibility would not seem to make sense. Those who think the Pact is necessary, and have in mind the reasoning outlined in this section, would probably be inclined to take a hard line on the Pact's interpretation in the next few years.

The discussion so far could apply equally well to the United States; and indeed, we have already made several references to US experience. The Federal Reserve seems to have managed its interactions with the US government rather well, and without the help of anything like a Stability and Growth Pact (or for that matter anything like the degree of legal and political independence that has been granted to the ECB). Does US history obviate the need for a Stability and Growth Pact in Europe? Before jumping to such a conclusion, we should note that there are at least two ways in which the situation in Europe is different from that in the US. First, the Federal Reserve has a track record that many would argue has established its credibility; the ECB is a new institution with no track record. One might question the necessity of something permanent, like the Pact, to address what is presumably a transitional issue, but we do agree that the lack of any track record may be a genuine concern. Second, and perhaps more important in the long run, the EU is characterized by a weak federal government, and a minuscule federal budget. For the most part, fiscal decisions are being made at the national level, and this situation is unlikely to change in the foreseeable future. Does the fact that the ECB will have to interact with several fiscal authorities make its situation fundamentally different than that of the Federal Reserve? We turn to this issue next.

III. Multiple Fiscal Authorities

A large literature on policy coordination suggests that the multiplicity of governments – or more precisely the multiplicity of fiscal authorities – adds two strategic dimensions to our discussion. First, increasing the number of fiscal authorities erodes the strategic position of any one authority vis à vis the central bank; each authority's incentive to manipulate the central bank is reduced. This suggests that the ECB may have less need of protection than say the Federal Reserve. Second, each individual authority may fail to internalize the adverse effects of its policies on the other fiscal authorities; as we will see, this may create a bias towards excessive government expenditure and/or borrowing, and this may in turn put pressure on the central bank to provide inflationary finance.[12] This suggests that the ECB may have more need of protection that the Federal Reserve. We begin with the issue of the number of players.

Beetsma and Bovenberg (1998) extend the Barro–Gordon analysis to demonstrate the erosion of strategic positions as the number of fiscal authorities increases; in particular, they show that the inflation bias described in the last section decreases as new, equally important, countries are added to a monetary union. The Euro-zone however consists of three big countries (four, if the UK joins) and a periphery.

Adding more countries to the periphery would not seem to diminish the influence of the big three significantly. However, the very fact that there are three large fiscal authorities instead of one does seem to make the ECB's situation different from the Federal Reserves':[13] the ECB may need less protection from fiscal authorities.

Institutional considerations also suggest that the decentralized political structure of the EU makes the ECB less susceptible to political pressure than the Federal Reserve. The Federal Reserve System is the creation of the US Congress, and Congress can change the way in which the Federal Reserve operates by simply passing a bill.[14] The European System of Central Banks is a creation of the EU, and its operation can only be changed by an amendment to the Maestricht Treaty. This is clearly a much more cumbersome process than passing a bill in Congress, and it gives the ECB more leeway to act in ways that might be deemed politically incorrect.

We turn next to the question of whether individual fiscal authorities pay enough attention to the adverse effects their policies may have on other members of the union, and how a common central bank may interact with this fiscal coordination problem. The policy coordination literature suggests that a coordination failure may lead to an expenditure bias through the effect of national fiscal policy on real interest rates, and the expenditure bias may in turn lead to pressure on the central bank to inflate.[15]

In Canzoneri and Diba (1991), we present a model in which government purchases in any one country raise real interest rates and crowd out investment community wide. The national fiscal authorities are assumed to care only about the welfare of their own citizens. Each fiscal authority weighs the costs and benefits for its own citizens of an increase in spending, and it ultimately decides to spend too much, since it ignores the adverse effects of higher interest rates and crowding out on welfare in the rest of the community. So, there is a government spending bias, due essentially to the fact that fiscal authorities have access to community wide capital markets.

Once this excessive government spending is set in place, it may induce a well meaning central bank to produce an inflation bias. Our model assumes that the common central bank cares about community wide welfare. Excessive spending ultimately means excessive taxation (which in our model is costly), but the central bank can decrease the tax burden by providing seigniorage. The central bank ends up setting inflation too high, relative to an equilibrium in which government spending is optimally coordinated across countries.

In fact, in our stylized model, the common central bank ends up choosing the same inflation rate that the fiscal authorities would have selected if they controlled monetary policy directly. This fact is not really surprising because once the level of government purchases is set, the inflation rate chosen by any welfare maximizing entity (the central bank or the fiscal authorities) is the solution to a standard Ramsey–Phelps public finance problem. The bottom line is that, in our model any-way, an independent central bank, charged only with maximizing community wide welfare, will not do anything to curb the excesses of the national fiscal authorities. Only a community wide constraint on national government spending would do that.

Does this line of reasoning provide a cogent argument for the Stability and Growth Pact? Its focus on community interest rates and access to community wide savings is reminiscent of discussions we have heard in the policy community. However, the characterization of these concerns given by our model, and others like it, seems somewhat dubious in Europe today. The logic of these models may be impeccable, but empirical questions can be raised about its importance in practice.

The first, and perhaps most important, problem with this line of reasoning is that seigniorage revenues are a small fraction of total tax revenues in Europe today. Will fiscal authorities bother to try to manipulate the ECB if the best they can expect is seigniorage revenues on the order of half a percent of GDP? Will the ECB bother to take account of how its transfers may reduce the welfare loss from distortionary direct taxes? We strongly suspect that the answer to both questions is no, at least in normal times. In certain abnormal circumstances, however, seigniorage revenues of even this magnitude may become a relevant political consideration. We have already noted that the Stability and Growth Pact incorporates a rather unfortunate feature: a deficit that is 2.9% of GDP goes unnoticed, while a deficit that is 3.1% of GDP may trigger major political difficulties. For a fiscal authority whose deficit is hovering around the magical 3% mark, transfers from the ECB may make the difference between meeting or exceeding the 3% limit. Moreover, a slight easing of monetary policy may be expected to lower the deficit by decreasing debt payments (in high debt countries anyway) or stimulating growth. These are clearly not arguments in favor the Pact; indeed, they suggest the Pact may create political pressures on the ECB where none existed before.

There may be a second problem with this line of reasoning that was outlined above. Given the global nature of today's capital markets, and the financial deregulation that has occurred within the EU in the last decade, Eichengreen and Wyplosz (1998) reject the notion that the actions of national fiscal authorities affect community real interest rates, and they present empirical evidence in support of that view. We think this is still an open empirical question deserving serious investigation. However, the basic notion that the actions of multiple fiscal authorities can pressure a common central bank to inflate does not require an interest rate channel to work through; indeed, it does not require any direct channel by which the actions of one fiscal authority affect welfare in another country.

Chari and Kehoe (1997) describe a fiscal externality that arises even though the monetary and fiscal policies of the countries involved have no effect on world real interest rates. The externality they highlight is clearly illustrated in a simple two period model.[16] In period 1, fiscal authorities undertake expenditures and borrow from the residents of other countries outside of the Euro-zone. The real interest rate on these loans is fixed at a world equilibrium level, but the nominal interest rate depends on expected inflation. In period 2, the ECB selects an inflation rate that maximizes the welfare of countries within the Euro-zone. The ECB's choice trades off the welfare loss from inflation (modeled here as a reduction in output) against the welfare gain from higher consumption (as inflation erodes the real value of the nominal debt issued to foreigners). When each fiscal authority decides on the amount of debt to issue, it takes into account the fact that the central bank will inflate away part of that debt in period 2, and it also understands that inflation will be higher the more debt that it issues, lowering home output; however, the fiscal authority has no interest in the fact that higher inflation will also lower output in other Euro-zone countries. Therefore, each fiscal authority issues too much debt in period 1, and the ECB ends up setting the inflation rate too high in period 2. In equilibrium, world lenders rationally anticipate the high rate of inflation and demand a commensurately high nominal interest rate on bonds denominated in Euro.

Does the Chari–Kehoe reasoning provide a more compelling rationale for the Stability and Growth Pact? We doubt it. The externality they describe, unlike the one considered by Canzoneri and Diba (1991), does not hinge on fiscal authorities being able to affect real interest rates. It does, however, hinge on the assumption that government bonds are held by investors living outside the Euro-zone, investors whose welfare is of no consequence to the ECB. To the extent that the bonds are held within the Euro-zone, the ECB would not be tempted to impose this inflation tax. This fact may limit the practical importance of the Chari–Kehoe argument.

Moreover, the Pact's constraint on deficits seems to miss the mark. In the Chari–Kehoe argument, the inflation bias is created by the central bank's temptation to tax foreign lenders; so, the appropriate remedy would be a constraint on the holding of government debt by investors who live outside of the Euro-zone. (This kind of targeted capital control would probably be difficult to implement in practice.) A constraint that restricts all government borrowing seems inefficient; it would, for example, preclude consumption smoothing between Euro-zone countries, which would lower welfare in (extensions of) the Chari–Kehoe model. A better – and probably more workable – remedy may be to require high debt countries to issue inflation indexed bonds.[17]

Finally, we might note that the arguments in this section and the last have at least one thing in common. Whatever the relevant constraint might be, all of the arguments suggest that relaxing the constraint will lead directly to an increase in the pressures on the central bank to inflate, or in what we have called the inflation bias. If the Council decides to interpret the provisions in the Pact more leniently in the initial phase, then we would expect a proportionate increase in the pressures on the ECB. The arguments we turn to next do not have this property; if they are the true source of concern, then the constraints in the Pact might be loosened considerably without detracting from their effect.

IV. Functional Independence: Who Actually Sets Prices? Who Pays the Bills?

Michael Woodford and Christopher Sims have popularized a new theory that emphasizes fiscal aspects of price determination.[18] This fiscal theory of price determination

(FTPD) suggests a different way of thinking about central bank independence; we call it a "functional" notion of independence. While we know that the policy community did not have this theory in mind when it drafted the Stability and Growth Pact, we think that this theory may provide a better rationale for constraints on deficits than the arguments that were given in the last two sections.

The FTPD has its roots in a much earlier literature associated with Thomas Sargent and Neil Wallace.[19] Sargent and Wallace emphasized the fact that a present value budget constraint must hold if the government is to be solvent. This constraint states that the real value of existing government debt must equal the expected present value of future primary surpluses inclusive of seigniorage revenues. Sargent and Wallace treated the real value of existing debt as given and focused on how the primary surpluses generated by the fiscal authority and the seigniorage revenues of the monetary authority must be expected to add up over time, to satisfy the present value budget constraint.

This adding up requirement raises the possibility that either the fiscal authority or the central bank may have to yield and allow their policies to be governed by the needs of fiscal solvency. Suppose the government's fiscal policy is firmly set in place, in the sense that the present value of primary surpluses is some fixed number. Then, the central bank has no choice but to deliver the seigniorage required to satisfy the budget constraint. In this case, Sargent and Wallace argued that the options open to the central bank are rather limited. It can keep inflation and seigniorage low for a while, but eventually it has to provide the seigniorage necessary to satisfy the budget constraint. Alternatively, suppose instead that the central bank's policy is firmly set in place, in the sense that the present value of seigniorage is a fixed number. Then, fiscal policy has no choice but to conform.

Absent from the Sargent and Wallace literature is much of any discussion about how either the central bank or the fiscal authority go about setting their policies firmly in place.[20] Nor does this literature address the question of what happens if neither the central bank nor the fiscal authority are willing to yield to the requirements of fiscal solvency. An important contribution of the new FTPD is to answer this question for the realistic case where the government issues nominal debt. In this case, if fiscal and monetary policy do not actively establish fiscal solvency, the government's budget constraint gets satisfied through changes in the price level, which adjust the real value of outstanding debt.[21]

More precisely, the present value budget constraint for year t is:

$$\frac{M_t + B_t}{p_t} = E_t \sum_{j=t}^{+\infty} \left(\frac{T_j - G_j}{p_j} \right) + E_t \sum_{j=t}^{+\infty} d_j \left(\frac{M_j}{p_j} \right), \tag{1}$$

where M_t is the money base at the beginning of year t, B_t is the face value of the debt that was inherited from past government borrowing, p_t is the price level, d_j is a discount factor (involving real interest rates), $T_j - G_j$ is the primary surplus in year j, and $M_{j+1} i_j$ is the central bank's transfer to the government (or seigniorage) in year j.[22] So, (1) says that the real value of total government liabilities must be equal to the present discounted value of present and future real primary surpluses plus the present discounted value of present and future real seigniorage; the expectation symbol, E_t, indicates that the right hand side of (1) is really the market's perception of these present values.

Suppose now that the fiscal authority and the central bank ignore the needs of solvency and have their policies firmly set in place, so that the right hand side of (1) adds up to some fixed number.[23] The budget constraint can still be satisfied if the price level, p_t, moves in equilibrium to make the real value of debt come in line. One way of understanding this point is to use the following analogy with a standard asset valuation equation.

The left hand side of (1) is the real value of total government liabilities, and the right hand side is the present value of expected payments on these liabilities. The two sides must be equal in equilibrium. If, for example, expected primary surpluses suddenly fall at date t, expected payments go down and the equilibrium value of liabilities is reduced via an increase in the price level. Although this way of thinking about the price level may be unfamiliar, it is not hard to grasp once we observe that the inverse of the price of goods represents the price of nominal liabilities in terms of goods.

For our discussion below, it will be convenient to rewrite (1) slightly to express liabilities, revenues and expenditures in terms of their ratios to GDP (since the provisions in the Pact are expressed in those terms). The budget constraint for year t can be expressed as:[24]

$$\frac{M_t - B_t}{p_t y_t} = E_t \sum_{j=t}^{+\infty} \delta_j \left(\frac{T_j - G_j}{p_j y_j}\right) + E_t \sum_{j=t}^{+\infty} \delta_j \left(\frac{M_{j+1}}{p_j y_j}\right) i, \tag{2}$$

where $p_j y_j$ is nominal GDP, and the discount factor δ_j now involves ratios of output growth to real interest rates. The interpretation of Equation (2) is the same as the interpretation of Equation (1), except that real liabilities, primary surpluses and seigniorage are measured per unit of output.

Once again we can think of a fiscal-monetary regime in which the fiscal authority and the central bank do not actively pursue fiscal solvency, and thus the ratios of the primary surplus and seigniorage to GDP evolve exogenously over time. In such a regime, nominal GDP.($p_t y_t$) must move in equilibrium to satisfy Equation (2). And we have a fiscal theory of nominal income determination: nominal income moves in equilibrium to assure fiscal solvency.[25] We will refer to a policy regime with exogenous primary surpluses (inclusive of seigniorage) as a Fiscal Dominant (FD) regime.

We can also think of a regime in which fiscal policy actively pursues solvency. In this case, given the left hand side of Equation (2), the fiscal authority is expected to adjust the ratio of its primary surpluses to GDP over time, to satisfy Equation (2). In this case, the needs of fiscal solvency do not pin down nominal GDP. Thus, nominal GDP can be determined in a more conventional way by monetary policy. We call such a regime money dominant (MD).

The possibility of a FD regime motivates our notion of the "functional independence" of a central bank. In this regime, even if the central bank enjoys legal and political independence in setting monetary policy, it can still lose control of nominal GDP and the price level. For the central bank to be functionally independent of the fiscal authorities, it must be the case that fiscal policy actively pursues solvency, and puts the economy in the MD regime.

Either one of the fiscal criteria written into the Maastricht Treaty would suffice, in theory, to guarantee that the Euro-zone is in a MD regime and to make the ECB functionally independent of fiscal policy. A cap on the debt to GDP ratio would make the fiscal authority responsible for solvency, and put the Euro-zone in a MD regime. But, it also turns out that a cap on the deficit to GDP ratio is a sufficient condition for a MD regime.

To see the latter point, consider any fiscal reaction function that makes the ratio of the primary surplus to GDP depend positively on the debt to GDP ratio:

$$\frac{T_j - G_j}{p_j y_j} = \alpha_j \left[\frac{B_j}{p_j y_j}\right] + x_j, \quad \alpha_j > 0, \tag{3}$$

where x_j is a bounded random variable. Equation (3) says that the ratio of the primary surplus to GDP may fluctuate over time due to changes in cyclical, political and other conditions reflected in x_j, but it also has a systematic tendency to rise with the debt to GDP ratio (because the coefficients α_j are assumed to be positive). Such a reaction function implies that as the debt to GDP ratio grows, the fiscal authority has to run larger and larger primary surpluses (relative to GDP). The larger surpluses will eventually curb the growth of debt and assure fiscal solvency.[26]

The Maastricht Treaty's 3% cap on the ratio of the deficit inclusive of interest payments to GDP requires that

$$\left[\frac{G_j - T_j}{p_j y_j}\right] + i_j \left[\frac{B_j}{p_j y_j}\right] \le 0.03, \tag{4}$$

where i_j is the nominal interest rate on debt. Since the nominal interest rate is positive, it serves as the coefficient α_j in Equation (3).[27] That is, as the debt to GDP ratio increases so does the interest obligation on debt. Thus, the primary surplus must rise to satisfy the 3% target for the deficit to GDP ratio. And this fiscal reaction assures a MD regime.

Although the fiscal criteria of the Maastricht treaty are sufficient to assure the functional independence of the ECB, much weaker fiscal restrictions would also suffice, at least in theory, for Equation (3) to hold. The cap on the deficit to GDP ratio could be (say) 5% instead of 3%. Or, the fiscal rule could require the sum of the primary surplus and (say) half the interest payments on debt to remain below (say) 3%.[28] Either of these options would assure the functional independence of the ECB and at the same time loosen the fiscal restriction on countries that currently have high debt to GDP ratios.

Our statement that looser fiscal constraints would work in theory is subject to the important qualification that such constraints must also be credible in practice. The right hand side of Equation (2) involves the private sector's expectations of how fiscal and monetary policy will behave in the future. So, putting a 10% cap on the deficit to GDP ratio would not assure a MD regime if the private sector does not expect the cap to be enforced once the deficit to GDP ratios of some countries have risen to the 10% level. From this perspective, the fact that some countries had to make a genuine and painful effort to meet the 3% target set by the Maastricht Treaty was probably a useful investment in making the target credible.

Note that the relevant notion of credibility here is not the credibility of the ECB but the credibility of fiscal rules. From this perspective the best fiscal rules would be ones that are manageable (not too stringent), transparent (easily verified) and irrevocable (thus, fully credible). How does the Stability Pact's treatment of fiscal constraints score along these dimensions?

First, the fact that the Pact emphasizes deficit caps and not debt limits is not problematic. Either type of constraint would suffice by itself to establish a MD regime. Second the deficit constraint could have been modified by the Pact to a constraint on the structural (i.e., full employment) deficit. For example, the Pact could have said that the structural deficit should not exceed (say) 2% of GDP. Such a constraint would have the advantage of alleviating the concerns (discussed in Section I above) about what the cyclical elasticity of deficits or the severity of future recessions may turn out to be. But to be transparent and credible, such a restriction would probably have to pin down how structural deficits are measured, and to make sure that the measurements are not subject to accounting gimmicks or manipulation by national fiscal authorities.

V. What Conclusions Do We Reach?

So, what do we finally conclude: Do the constraints on national fiscal deficits agreed in the Stability and Growth Pact strike a workable balance between the discipline needed to protect the ECB's credibility and the flexibility required for counter-cyclical stabilization? Or is the Pact an unnecessary albatross that could hamper the entire EMU effort? When we began our assessment of this issue, we had some sympathy for the Pact; perhaps our view was colored by our previous work in the area.[29] However, after reviewing all aspects of the question, we have moved considerably in the direction of thinking that the Pact may be an albatross.

In Section I, we reviewed studies done at official institutions – the Commission, the OECD and the IMF – on the flexibility of the constraints in the Pact. While the studies differ in detail, a general consensus does seem to emerge: in the long run – after governments have reduced structural deficits by another 1% or so of GDP – the deficit limits set in the Pact should not constrain normal counter-cyclical efforts; in the short run however, the lower growth rates now being projected may push a number of countries into violation of the Pact's limits, and hamper fiscal efforts to stimulate the EU economy. This would leave all of the onus on the ECB, at precisely the time in which it is trying to establish its anti-inflation credibility. The Pact may also hamper efforts at international policy coordination. It is no secret that US policymakers have been frustrated by the lack of fiscal stimulus coming from both Europe and Japan. So, in the immediate future, the Pact may hamper counter-cyclical policy at the national level, coordination of monetary and fiscal policy at the EC level, and international policy coordination at the G-3 level.

What does the Stability and Growth Pact buy at this price? Does it give the ECB needed protection as it tries to achieve credibility? In Sections II, III and IV, we reviewed arguments that have been made in the academic literature. Some of the arguments based on seigniorage seemed unlikely to be of much practical importance, and in any case we generally found that, once the argument was made clear, deficit constraints were weak or inappropriate instruments to address the problem at hand. In several cases, the appropriate constraint was on the level of debt, but the Pact focuses exclusively on deficits. And the main reasons why one might expect the newly elected governments of France and Germany to lobby for lower interest rates – high unemployment, low capital formation – have nothing to do with budget deficits; indeed, if the effect of the Pact is to constrain social spending, then the Pact might increase the pressures for a monetary expansion. Perhaps the best argument for some kind of deficit constraint came in Section IV, where a new theory of price determination suggested that national fiscal authorities have to take responsibility for paying their bills if the central bank is to have the "functional" independence to control its price level. However, we also argued that the Pact's constraint on deficits was probably stronger than necessary to achieve functional independence for the ECB. If this argument captures the main concern, then the provisions in the pact can be interpreted rather liberally in the next few years; all that matters is that the private sector must be convinced that fiscal authorities will eventually pay their bills.

Generally speaking, we found the case for the Pact to be weaker in the EU than it would be in the US, where experience suggests that it is probably not necessary. Arguments in the literature suggest that a multiplicity of fiscal authorities, instead of one federal authority, dilutes the pressures on a central bank. Moreover, the legal independence of the ECB seems much stronger than the Federal Reserve's; for example, political tampering with the ESCB legislation would require an amendment to the Maastricht Treaty, while tampering with the Federal Reserve System legislation would only require an act of Congress. One big difference remains: the Federal Reserve already has a proven track record, while the ECB is just starting out. But, establishing permanent constraints on fiscal policy seems a heavy handed way of addressing what is presumably a transitional problem.

The Maastricht Treaty's debt and deficit constraints seem to have forced a number of high debt countries to reform their fiscal policies, and many would argue that these reforms were needed for reasons that have nothing to do with monetary policy per se. Those same people may worry that the reforms will be short lived, and they may be happy to see some of the constraints live on in the Stability and Growth Pact, whether or not they have anything to do with monetary stability.

In this paper, we have only considered the merits of the Pact from the point of view of assuring monetary stability. From this narrow point of view, we would recommend that the Pact be interpreted loosely during the period in which the ECB is gaining credibility, especially if a growth slowdown materializes. In the longer run, the Pact may not be needed for monetary stability, but it may also not be binding if structural deficits are brought into balance.[30] If structural deficits do not come into balance, then the provisions in the Pact may have to be rethought in the longer run.

Notes

1. The Stability and Growth Pact consists of a Resolution adopted by the European Council in June of 1997, and two Council Regulations adopted in July of 1997. The Pact clarifies the "excessive deficits" procedure and penalties that were agreed in the Maastricht Treaty. Buti, Franco and Ongena (1998) outline the basic features of the Pact and discuss the negotiations that led to it.
2. There is a tension – some might call it a logical inconsistency – in both the Delors Report and

the Maastricht Treaty. If it were actually possible, and desirable, to create a completely independent central bank, dedicated solely to price stability, then why were constraints on fiscal policy thought to be necessary. Our interpretation is that the central bankers who wrote the Delors Report knew that it was impossible to make the ECB totally immune from external pressures (no matter what their official documents might have asserted), and that they therefore insisted upon the constraints. This paper is written from that perspective.

3. There is a vast literature, and we have made no attempt to provide a comprehensive survey. We focus on a few articles that clearly articulate arguments we want to investigate. Our choice will be viewed as self-serving by some, in that it may (incorrectly) suggest that we have been the major contributors to this literature.
4. See Buti, Franco and Ongena (1998).
5. This is of course debatable. To avoid financial penalties altogether, the member state would have to bring its deficit back to within 3% of GDP one year after the "excessive deficit" is detected, or in other words, two years after it first occurs. If this does not happen, the member state has to make an interest free deposit of 0.2% of GDP, plus 0.1% of the amount by which its deficit to GDP ratio exceeded 3%; the maximum deposit would be capped at 0.5% of GDP. The deposit if forfeited after two years if the "excessive deficit" persists. We estimate that the foregone interest in the first year of sanctions would be in the range of 250–500 million euros for one of the larger member states. Forfeiture of the deposit would of course be much more costly, but it would only occur if the "excessive deficit" persisted for five years. We doubt that the financial penalties alone would be sufficient to deter "excessive deficits"; however, we suspect that the public approbation that goes along with them will be politically embarrassing enough to get the attention of governments.
6. See Buti and Sapir (1998) for the Commission Services' analysis; see also *OECD Economic Outlook*, December 1997, and the IMF's *World Economic Outlook*, May 1998.
7. If fact, some speculate that Volker's switch to monetarism (which de-emphasized the FED's direct setting of short term interest rates) was designed to allow him to make this claim, and assert that interest rates were set by the market and not the FED.
8. Most of this literature is concerned with a central bank's incentives to keep unemployment below its natural rate. However, the general logic can easily be applied to political pressure for a real interest rate below its natural (or flexible price equilibrium) rate; see Canzoneri, Nolan and Yates (1997).
9. Eichengreen and Wyplosz (1998) carry this argument further. They note that governments have a finite amount political capital to spend on institutional reform, and they worry that if governments expend the capital necessary to lower structural deficits further (as required by the Pact), there will not be enough capital left for the product and labor market reform that would address the unemployment and growth issues.
10. A more sophisticated argument for deficit limits might be constructed along the following lines: Large deficits might raise the natural (or full information equilibrium) real rate of interest. This could in turn increase the gap between the rate interest desired by politicians and the equilibrium rate. In Canzoneri, Nolan and Yates (1997) modeling of the problem, this would increase the inflation bias.
11. See Canzoneri, Nolan and Yates (1997).
12. Aizenman (1992) presents a model where multiple government agencies can print money and shows that an inflation bias emerges. Our discussion below will focus on models that are more directly motivated by the institutional setting of EMU – where fiscal authorities cannot create money.
13. The US does have a large number of state fiscal authorities, and indeed about half of the total public spending is decided at the state or local level. However, Elmendorf and Mankiw (1998) note that "Most state governments hold positive net assets, because they are prohibited from running deficits in their operating budgets, and because the assets they accumulate to fund employee pensions exceed the debt they issue to finance capital projects".

14. An example of the political leverage this affords occurred at the beginning of the Clinton Administration. Much of the independence of Federal Reserve System enjoys comes from its de-politicized selection process for the District Bank presidents, who have a vote on the policy making Federal Open Market Committee (FOMC). Congress held hearings on proposals to either politicize the appointment of District Bank presidents or take away their vote on the FOMC. In the end, these proposals were put on hold, but a prominent Democrat suggested that the issues might be revisited in six months time, and he reminded the assembled District Bank presidents that the new administration had a pro growth agenda that required low interest rates.
15. Coordination failures need not imply that government spending is too high. Chari and Kehoe (1990) model externalities involving the terms of trade effects of government purchases. These externalities may lead to government expenditures that are suboptimally large *or* small, depending on whether the country is a net exporter or a net importer of the good whose relative price increases with government purchases. Similarly, in stabilization models, government expenditures can be suboptimally low, in the sense that they do not do enough to help neighboring countries out of their recessions.
16. Chari and Kehoe also present a dynamic general equilibrium model of this externality.
17. This alternative may not be cost free. It has been argued, for example, that nominal debt provides investors with a hedge against fluctuations in aggregate income. The constraint on government lending to foreigners appears to be the first best solution.
18. Canzoneri and Diba (1998) present a policy oriented introduction to this theory, and explain the notion of "functional independence" in more detail. There has been an explosion of papers on this topic in the last few years. Recent papers that have a European focus include Woodford (1996), Sims (1998), and Bergin (1998).
19. This literature often goes under the heading of "Unpleasant Monetarist Arithmetic". See Sargent and Wallace (1981).
20. Wallace argued at the time that Paul Volcker and Ronald Reagan set policies in place that were mutually inconsistent with the budget constraint. He noted that in such a situation something has to give, but he did not speculate whether the government or the central bank would give in. He would presumably argue today, almost twenty years later, that US fiscal policy finally came into line with the low inflation policy set by the Federal Reserve. [See Sargent (1987), page 176].
21. There is of course a large empirical literature that asks *whether* the budget constraint is satisfied, or whether the current policy of a particular government is sustainable. By contrast, the new theory of price determination argues that the constraint is implied by the optimizing behavior of the private sector [see, for example, Woodford (1995)]. As such, the constraint will always be satisfied in equilibrium; the only question is *how* it gets satisfied.
22. In the simple accounting framework used here, the central bank issues money in exchange for government debt; so, M_{j+1} is equal to the central bank's bond holdings at the end of year j. At the end of each year, central bank's profits (that is, the interest it collects on its bond holdings) are transferred back to the government's treasury; this is usually referred to as "seigniorage".
23. Real money demand (M/p) depends on interest rates and output. So, once the path of i_j has been specified, the present value of seigniorage is determined.
24. See Canzoneri and Diba (1998) or Canzoneri, Cumby and Diba (1998) for a more detailed discussion of the budget accounting framework.
25. A further advantage of focusing on Equation (2) instead of Equation (1) is that we can discuss nominal GDP movements without taking a stand on how they are split into real GDP and price movements in the short run.
26. See Canzoneri, Cumby and Diba (1998) for a formal proof.
27. The variable x_j in Equation (3) captures the numerical 3% cap and the fluctuations of the actual deficit to GDP ratio, on the left hand side of Equation (4), below the cap.
28. That is, the constraint could be on the primary surplus plus any fixed fraction of interest

payments. Note, however, that a constraint on the primary surplus alone would not establish the positive linkage between debt and surpluses, and would therefore not guarantee that Equation (3) holds.

29. See Canzoneri and Diba (1991 and 1998) and Canzoneri, Nolan and Yates (1997).
30. It may not be possible to discard the Pact altogether, since the Maastricht Treaty provides for something like it.

References

Barro, Robert J. and Gordon, David B. (1983) 'Rules, Discretion and Reputation in a Model of Monetary Policy', *Journal of Monetary Economics* **12**, 101–121.

Beetsma, Roel M.W.J. and Bovenberg, A. Lans (1998) 'Monetary Union without Fiscal Coordination May Discipline Policymakers', *Journal of International Economics* **45**, 239–258.

Bergin, Paul (1998) 'Fiscal Solvency and Price Level Determination in a Monetary Union', mimeo, University College, Davis.

Buti, Marco, Franco, Daniele, and Ongena, Hedwig (1998) 'Fiscal Discipline and Flexibility in EMU: The Implementation of the Stability and Growth Pact', *Oxford Review of Economic Policy* **14**, 81–97.

Buti, Marco and Andre Sapir (1998), *Economic Policy in EMU: A Study by the European Commission Services*, Clarendon Press, Oxford.

Canzoneri, Matthew, Cumby, Robert, and Diba, Behzad (1998) 'Is the Price Level Determined by the Needs of Fiscal Solvency', NBER Working Paper #6471.

Canzoneri, Matthew and Diba, Behzad (1998) 'Fiscal Constraints on Central Bank Independence and Price Stability', in Malo de Molina, Vinals and Gutierrez (eds.), *Monetary Policy and Inflation in Spain*, St. Martin's Press, New York.

Canzoneri, Matthew, Nolan, Charles, and Yates, Anthony (1997) 'Mechanisms for Achieving Monetary Stability: Inflation Targeting vs the ERM', *Journal of Money, Credit and Banking* **29**, 46–60.

Canzoneri, Matthew and Diba, Behzad (1991) 'Fiscal Deficits, Financial Integration, and a Central Bank for Europe', *Journal of the Japanese and International Economies* **5**, 381–403.

Chari, V.V. and Kehoe, Patrick (1997) 'On the Need for Fiscal Constraints in a Monetary Union', mimeo.

Elmendorf, Douglas and Mankiw, N. Gregory (1998) 'Government Debt', NBER Working Paper # 6470.

Eichengreen, Barry and Wyplosz, Charles (1998) 'The Stability Pact: More Than a Minor Nuisance?', *Economic Policy* **26**, 65–114.

Sargent, Thomas (1987) *Dynamic Macroeconomic Theory*, Harvard University Press, Cambridge.

Sargent, Thomas and Wallace, Neil (1981) 'Some Unpleasant Monetarist Arithmetic', *Quarterly Review of the Minneapolis Federal Reserve Bank* **5**, 1–17.

Sims, Christopher (1998) 'The Precarious Fiscal Foundations of EMU', mimeo.

Woodford, Michael (1996) 'Control of the Public Debt: A Requirement for Price Stability?', NBER Working Paper #5684.

8. Economic Policy Coordination in the EMU: Implications for the Stability and Growth Pact

FRITZ BREUSS* and ANDREA WEBER†
*Austrian Institute of Economic Research (Wifo) and University of Economics and Business Administration (Research Institute for European Affairs), Vienna
†Austrian Institute of Economic Research (Wifo), Vienna

I. Introduction

The new policy regime of EMU justifies to raise the old question whether policy coordination makes countries better off. On the one hand the Maastricht Treaty demands economic policy coordination in Article 99.[1] On the other hand the division of responsibility of economic policy making in EMU is unique. An independent European Central Bank (ECB) is responsible for the monetary policy for Euroland, whereas the EMU member countries still are the indivudal actors of the fiscal policy. However, the Stability and Growth Pact (SGP) limits fiscal expansion. These specific rules of the policy game imply different combinations for possible cooperations: either the EMU member countries cooperate in pursuing their fiscal policy and/or they cooperate with each other and with the ECB. So far, however, due to the strong independence position of the ECB it refused to cooperate with the national governments. The primary target for the ECB is to maintain price stability. Presently the most urgent target for the EMU member countries is full employment. However, reading the Articles of the TEC concerning coordination and those of the SGP (in particular Council Regulation (EC) No 1466/97 of 7 July 1997 on the strengthening of the surveillance of budgetary positions and the surveillance and "coordination" of economic policies) one gets the impression that coordination in the EMU primarily has a negative or passive connotation (medium-term objective of "sound budgetary positions close to balance or in surplus"). Normally, economic policy coordination aims at improving the economic position of a group of countries (positive or active connotation).

Several authors have already dealt with economic policy cooperation in EMU. However, most of them either used theoretically calibrated models (Krichel–Levine–Pearlman, 1996) or heavily stylized models (Demertis–Hughes Hallet–Viegi, 1999). In each case two countries are combined with one ECB. Huizinga–Nielsen (1998) ask whether policy coordination of fiscal deficits is necessary at all and under which theoretical conditions it may make sense. Karner (1999) analyses within a game-theoretic model with three countries and one ECB the outcome of the maximization of intertemporal utilities of countries and of the ECB (the latter also maximizes the levels of debt of the EMU countries?). Van Aarle–Engwerda–Plasmans–Weeren (1999) calibrate a two-country EMU with one ECB in the style of a New Keynesian disequilibrium model with unemployment. Rolf (1996) analyses game-theoretically the different aspects of cooperation within a fiscal solidarity union ("fiscal federalism")

A. H. Hallett et al. (eds), Challenges for Economic Policy Coordination with European Monetary Union, 143–167.

in the EMU. Non-cooperation would lead to higher optimal debts. Levine (1997) studies theoretically the possible interactions of EMU-"ins" and "outs" and the consequences of the delegation of monetary policy to an independent central bank. The empirical evidence on international economic policy coordination is generally neither overwhelmingly positive, nor are the gains very high (see for a recent survey Mooslechner–Schürz (1999). McKibbin (1997) in his review mentions gains from 0.5 to 1 percent of GDP at most.

We deal with the possible outcome of coordinating economic policy in the EMU. This means on the one hand (the theoretical case of) full coordination of fiscal and monetary policy between the EMU member states and the ECB and on the other hand only fiscal policy coordination among the EMU member states. The special problem of the policy interaction of the "ins" of EMU and the "pre-ins" is not addressed here. In order to derive welfare gains from policy cooperation in EMU, we apply a large-scale econometric model (Oxford Economic Forecasting – OEF – World model; OEF, 1999). This allows us to quantify welfare gains with real-world data and leads therefore to realistic policy conclusions. In doing so, we follow the classic approach by Oudiz–Sachs (1984). They did this exercise with two world models for three countries (USA, Japan and Germany). We do it with one world model for the specific policy constellation of EMU (11 countries plus the ECB).

After describing the framework of economic policy in EMU (chapter 2) we present evidence on policy multipliers of fiscal and monetary policy in EMU member countries. This gives an idea of the economic interdependencies in EMU (chapter 3). In chapter 4 we describe the strategy to measure welfare gains from cooperation. With the help of the large-scale econometric world model the concrete welfare gains of cooperation are derived under different scenarios: full cooperation (EMU countries plus ECB) and only cooperation among the EMU countries.

II. The New Policy Responsibility in EMU and Rules of Cooperation[2]

Compared to the benchmark country USA one has the impression that the European Union seems to have planned to create an EMU with an asymmetric economic policy framework. Whereas in the USA both, monetary and fiscal policy are centralised and they dispose of an inter-state transfer mechanism (fiscal federalism) which seems to be appropriate to cushion asymmetric or idiosyncratic shocks, the coming EMU is build upon an asymmetric architecture concerning economic policy.

According to the ideal architecture of economic policy laid down in the Treaty establishing the European Community (TEC) the EMU framework combines a centralised monetary policy (under the responsibility of the ECB) with decentralised fiscal or budgetary policies (under the responsibility of national governments, subject to Community rules on budgetary discipline, as the Stability and Growth Pact) and decentralised structural policies and wage setting (see Table 1).

This ideal Euro world implies a simple and clear assignment of policies: the single monetary policy would, given the primary objective of preserving price stability, be able to provide a common response to aggregate economic development (see *European Commission*, 1997B), whereas decentralised budgetary policies and other national economic policy instruments would be available for responding to country-specific circumstances (or shocks).

Table 1. The framework of economic policy in EMU with "ins" and "pre-ins"

Monetary Policy	Fiscal (Budgetary) policy	Incomes and wage policy
	11 Euro-"ins"	
centralised	decentralised	decentralised
(ESCB and ECB are responsible)	(governments of the Member States are responsible)	(Social Partners in the Member States are responsible)
Art. 105 and Protocol 18, Art. 2: ESCB and ECB: Primary objective: price stability; support of the general economic policies with a view of the objectives of the Community (Art. 2)	restricted by the *Stability and Growth Pact*: Deficit <3% of GDP (clarification of the excessive deficit procedure of Art. 104 in Reg. (EC) 1467/97); *no Fiscal Federalism* in the EU *no bail-out* (Art. 103(1)) (and declaration by the ECOFIN Council, Point 6, May 1, 1998) Economic policy coordination ("economic policies as a matter of common concern": Art. 99) *Multilateral surveillance* (Art. 99(3) and (4) and Reg. (EC) 1466/97): *Stability programmes* before March 1, 1999, thereafter annually	Resolution of the European Council on growth and employment 97/C 236/02) and the Commission's Recommendation for Broad Guidelines of the Economic Policies of the Member States and the Community (II/144/98, 13.5.98) suggest a "productivity oriented wage policy" which is enough "flexible" to make the labour markets more efficient (Mundell's precondition for an optimum currency area – OCA)
	Euro-"pre-ins"	
decentralised	decentralised	decentralised
(National central banks – NCB – are responsible) new *exchange-rate mechanism* in stage III of EMU – *ERM2* ("hub and spokes" model): Euro is the anchor – standard fluctuation band ±15% against the Euro (participation in ERM2 is voluntary: Resolution of the European Council 97/C 236/03)	(Member States are responsible) obligation to avoid excessive deficits (Art. 104 and Art. 116(4); each EU member is obliged to a stability oriented economic policy and to economic policy *coordination* ("economic policies as a matter of common concern": Art. 99) *Multilateral surveillance* (Art. 99(3) and (4) and Reg. (EC) 1466/97): *Convergence programmes* before March 1, 1999, thereafter annually.	(Social Partners in the Member States are responsible)

The Articles refer to the Treaty establishing the European Community (TEC) à la Amsterdam

After the Decision of the Council of the European Union, meeting in the composition of Heads of States or Government of May 3, 1998, the EMU started on January 1, 1999 with eleven countries. Based on Article 99(2) of the TEC the *European Commission* (1998, p. 4) has put forward "Broad Guidelines of the Economic Policies of the Member States and the Community" for the "ins" and the "pre-ins" of the EMU, which were confirmed by the Council Recommendation 98/454/EC of 6 July 1998. In its "growth and stability-oriented macroeconomic policy mix" scenario the Commission stresses that the overall macroeconomic *policy mix at the euro-zone level* (for the "ins") will result from the interaction of the common monetary policy on the one hand and with the average budgetary development and wage trends in the participating countries, on the other. According to this script for an ideal economic world in Euroland of 11 EU Member States, in the framework of the Treaty, supplemented by the Stability and Growth Pact and the Amsterdam European Council resolution on "Growth and Employment", the responsibilities are allocated as follows:

- *The single monetary policy* in the euro-area will be under the responsibility of the independent ECB and ESCB. In conformity with Article 105(1), the primary objective of monetary policy will be to maintain price stability and, subject thereto, to support the economic objectives of the Union, including, in particular, sustained, non-inflationary, growth and high level of employment, as laid down in Article 2 of the Treaty.
- *Budgetary policy* will remain in the responsibility of national governments but will be subject to the rules of the Treaty (Article 101 to 104) and the Stability and Growth Pact, which emphasises the need to have a budgetary position close to balance or in surplus in normal economic conditions and clarifies the key Treaty provisions on budgetary policy. National governments will have to coordinate their budgetary policies in the framework of the Broad Economic Policy Guidelines (Art. 99).
- *Wage setting* will remain in the responsibility of the social partners at the national, regional, sectoral or even at a more decentralised level following their respective traditions. As underlined in the Amsterdam Resolution on "Growth and employment" (97/C 236/02), the social partners are responsible for reconciling high employment with appropriate wage settlements and for setting up a suitable framework for the wage formation process. Since they have an important bearing on the overall macroeconomic policy mix, aggregate wage developments are of general interest." (European Commission, 1998, p. 4).

For the countries not participating initially in the euro-zone (the "pre-ins") the *European Commission* (1998, p. 5) stresses that "the need for stability-oriented and convergent macroeconomic policies will be equally strong, especially if they participate in the ERM2, as countries with a derogation are expected to. The strong economic and monetary interdependence between the euro-area countries and the Member States not as yet adopting the euro and the need to ensure further convergence and a smooth functioning of the single market, will require that all Member States are included in the co-ordination of economic policies."

The EU in general and the EMU in particular bases its *procedure of policy coordination* on a set of principles (layed down in the Treaty and in the SGP):

monitoring and controlling which results in a rolling agenda establishing an annual cycle for the "mainstream" coordination process (see *Italianer*, 1999, p. 213). There are several forms of coordination: (a) procedural framework (participation in the Council (Ecofin) of 15 Member States, the Commission and the president of the ECB); Euro-11 group only on the "ins" of EMU, formality, assistance, decision rules), (b) exchange of information (indicators, definitions), (c) common analytical framework (models, policy impact, forecasts), (d) monitoring (performance, policy intentions, early warning, multilateral surveillance), (e) take account of policy interactions with others (expression of preferences) and (f) joint determination of policies (regularly, discretionary; see *Italianer*, 1999, pp. 203–206).

The provisions concerning economic policy coordination are ruled in the TEC in general and in the Stability and Growth Pact (SGP)[3] for stage three of the EMU in particular. Article 99(1) says that the "Member States shall regard their economic policies as a matter of common concern and shall *coordinate* them within the Council ...". "The Council shall, acting by a qualified majority on a recommendation from the Commission, formulate a draft for the *broad guidelines* of the eocnomic policies of the Member States and the Community, and shall report its finding to the European Council." (Article 99(2)). Article 99(3) rules the monitoring procedure for closer cooperation of economic policies and sustained convergence of the economic performance of the Member States with a system of *multilateral surveillance.* The SGP (Council Regulation (EC) No 1466/97) then sets out the rules covering the content, the submission, the examination and the monitoring of *stability programmes* (for the "ins" of EMU) and the *convergence programmes* (for the "pre-ins" of EMU) – to be submitted to the Commission annually for a medium-term period of three years – "as part of the multilateral surveillance by the Council so as to prevent, at an early stage, the occurrence of excessive general deficits and to promote the surveillance and coordination of economic policies."

The *scope of coordination* in EMU – according to *Italianer* (1999, p.207) – can comprise monetary policy, fiscal or budgetary policy, exchange rate policy, labour markets (wage setting, structural aspects, active policies), tax policies, social security systems, product markets (goods, services), capital marktes. The coordination of economic policy in the EMU is already a very complex undertaking. It involves several processes: "Luxembourg process" (guidelines for employment policy), "Cardiff process" (structural policy targets), "Cologne process" (macro-policy dialogue within the European employment pact), "Lisbon process" (new open method to coordinate – lastly on the level of the European Council by the Heads of State and Government (see *Breuss*, 2000b). We restrict our analysis to the two major policy insruments, namely monetary and fiscal policy.

The next question concerns the *levels of coordination* in EMU. *Italianer* (1999, pp. 208-210) identifies three EU levels for coordination: (1) The highest coordination level in the EU is that of the Heads of State and Government, in particular through the European Council (of which the president of the European Commission is also a member) that meets in presence of Ecofin Ministers when issues of relevance to EMU are discussed. (2) At the Ministerial level, the main co-ordinating bodies are the Council and the Euro-11 group. For matters related to EMU and taxation, the most relevant Council formation is that of Economic and Finance Ministers (Ecofin), while for employment policies the Employment/Social Affairs Council takes the lead.

The ECB president is invited to the Ecofin and also to the more informal Euro-11 group. In the latter national delegations are restricted to two persons (the Minister plus the relevant member of the Economic and Financial Committee). The European Commission is present both at the Council (Ecofin) and the Euro-11 meetings. The social partners are involved in the coordination process at Ministerial level through the participation of the main European employers' and employees' organisations in the so-called European Social Dialogue. (3) The Senior officials level consists of several committees. In the EMU area, the most important is the Economic and Financial Committee (since January 1, 1999 the sucessor of the Monetary Committee, according to Article 114(2) TEC), which has advisory and preparatory functions in preparing the Council meetings. It is composed of two representatives of each EMU member state (one from the administration – finance ministry, one from the national central bank) and two Commission and ECB representatives each. So it is a body for informal dialogue between officials from the economic and moneatry poles. In addition there are other committees for different purposes (the Economic Policy Committee, the Employment Committee, the Banking Advisory Committe, the Banking Supervision Committee, the Code of Conduct Group business taxation, the Committee on Monetary, Financial and Balance of Payments Statistics).

The Treaty and the SGP always speak of economic policy "coordination". This is the more rigorous form of economic cooperation, involving a complicated procedure of mutually agreed guidelines and commitments how to conduct monetary and fiscal policies, as layed down in the Treaty. A narrower form of interaction, often used in game theory, is the notion of economic "cooperation" in contrast to non-cooperation. In a game-theory context this latter notion is more adequate, also it does not cover the more complicated form of coordination as those of the EMU.[4] Athough we aim at studying the implications of different scenarios of cooperation in EMU, technically speaking we have to restrict our calculations to the more narrow form of economic policy cooperation.

III. Economic Interdependencies in EMU

The first way to evaluate the macroeconomic interdependencies is to study the evidence on policy multipliers. For this purpose we apply a large-scale world macromodel (OEF, 1999). It encompasses 10 EMU countries (only Luxembourg is left out), as well as the major OECD countries. For the purpose of studying policy multipliers we only look at interdependencies within the EMU area. The simulation horizon is 1999–2001. Euroland is already modeled insofar as the 10 EU countries participating in the EMU have fixed bilateral exchange rates starting with 1Q1999 according to the conversion rates fixed on December 31, 1998. In addition, the ECB is emulated by assuming the same short-interest rate levels in Euroland. And the Euro is already anticipated and calculated against third country currencies, like the US-Dollar (USD) or the British Pound (GBP). So when simulating shocks one already anticipates the monetary behaviour of the European Central Bank (ECB). Its monetary policy reaction function follows something like a Taylor rule: the short-term interest rate adjusts in response both to the gap between a target for the stock of money and its actual value and to the gap between potential output and actual output.

We compare a fiscal policy stimulus with a monetary policy expansion. Fiscal policy expansion is measured by an increase of real goverment spending of one percent of GDP, executed individually by each of the 10 EMU member countries (Luxemburg excluded). Monetary expansion (done for the whole EMU area by the ECB) is measured by a one percentage-point decrease of short-term interest rate (uniform in all EMU countries).

As expected from a Mundell-Fleming type world macro model the own policy multipliers after a fiscal shock are large compared to the spill-overs to partner countries. The latter are mostly positive in sign. The two-years short-term GDP multipliers range from 0.3 (in Belgium) to 1.0 (in Italy). Inflation goes up, unemployment decreases (see Table 2). The budget deficit increases, as well as public debt. The current account deteriorates (see Table 3). Monetary policy (done centrally by the ECB for the whole EMU area) has a positive impact on real GDP and inflation, and reduces unemployment (see Table 2). However, the impact on budget deficit and public debt is positive. The results as far as the current account is concerned are mixed (see Table 3). As in the theoretical Mundell-Fleming model, fiscal policy expansion leads to an appreciation of the Euro agains the US-Dollar. Accordingly, the monetary expansion results in a depreciation of the Euro (see Table 3).

The fact that the size of the fiscal policy multipliers varies within the EMU from country to country is of course the consequence of a still not fully harmonized economic performance of the EMU members. Neither is the business cycle of all EMU members synchronized, nor are the responses of the economies similar to identical policy shocks. Differences in policy multipliers may also add to the catalogue of conditions which identify an optimum currency area (OCA). In addition to labour market flexibility (Mundell's criterium), a similar impact of policy impulses in a group of countries indicates that these countries would belong to an OCA rather than countries which react differently. But even within the so-called DM core, consisting of countries whose currencies more or less moved alongside the DM in the last decade, namely Austria, Belgium, France, the Netherlands and of course Germany, policy responses are not as similar as one would expect (see Table 2).

IV. Coordination of Fiscal and Monetary Policy in EMU

In following Oudiz-Sachs (1984), our strategy for measuring the gains from coordination is to compare two equilibria: one in which each country plus the ECB pursues optimal policies taking as given the action of the others ("noncooperative" or "Nash" equilibrium; in our empirical example the baseline is identified as the "Nash" equilibrium), and one in which the authorities "bargain" over a coordinated package of policies ("bargaining" or "cooperative" equilibrium).

A MODEL FOR THE NASH EQUILIBRIUM

For the empirical evaluation of the gains from cooperation we use the classic Tinbergen targets- and-instruments framework (see Oudiz-Sachs, 1984, pp. 59 ff.). We consider a static model, where the economy is represented by a set of multipliers.

Table 2. Policy Multipliers for Output, Inflation, and Unemployment in Euroland (EMU)[a]

Country acting, and policy	Belgium (B)			Germany (D)			Spain (E)			France (F)			Ireland (IRL)		
	y	p	u	y	p	u	y	p	u	y	p	u	y	p	u
I. Fiscal Policy[b]															
Belgium (B)	**0.26**	**0.77**	−**0.10**	0.02	0.01	−0.01	0.00	0.00	0.00	0.02	0.01	0.00	0.03	0.02	−0.01
Germany (D)	0.05	0.05	−0.02	**0.81**	**0.30**	−**0.50**	−0.08	−0.04	0.02	−0.02	−0.04	0.01	0.04	0.02	−0.02
Spain (E)	0.01	−0.01	0.00	0.00	−0.02	0.00	**0.78**	**0.18**	−**0.23**	0.03	−0.01	0.00	0.01	0.00	0.00
France (F)	0.07	0.12	−0.02	0.03	−0.01	−0.02	0.03	−0.01	−0.01	**0.79**	**0.41**	−**0.07**	0.06	0.02	−0.03
Ireland (IRL)	0.00	0.00	0.00	0.00	0.00	0.00	0.00	0.00	0.00	0.00	0.00	0.00	**0.52**	**0.11**	−**0.20**
Italy (I)	−0.01	−0.08	0.01	−0.03	−0.03	0.01	−0.07	−0.03	0.02	−0.01	−0.03	0.01	−0.06	−0.01	0.02
Netherlands (NL)	0.01	−0.02	−0.01	−0.01	−0.01	0.01	−0.02	−0.01	0.01	−0.02	−0.02	0.00	−0.01	0.00	0.01
Austria (A)	0.00	0.00	0.00	0.02	0.01	−0.01	−0.01	−0.01	0.00	0.00	−0.01	0.00	−0.01	0.00	0.00
Portugal (P)	0.01	0.01	0.00	0.01	0.00	0.00	0.03	0.01	−0.01	0.01	0.01	0.00	0.01	0.00	0.00
Finland (FIN)	0.00	0.00	0.00	0.00	0.00	0.00	−0.01	0.00	0.00	0.00	0.00	0.00	0.00	0.00	0.00
II. Monetary policy[c]															
European Central Bank (ECB)	0.44	1.38	−0.16	0.53	0.36	−0.30	0.63	0.28	−0.17	0.47	0.42	−0.07	0.81	0.27	−0.29

Country acting, and policy	*Italy (I)*			Netherlands (NL)			Austria (A)			Portugal (P)			Finland (FIN)		
	y	**p**	**u**	**y**	**p**	**u**	**y**	**p**	**u**	**y**	**p**	**u**	**y**	**p**	**u**
I. Fiscal Policy[b]															
Belgium (B)	0.01	0.00	0.00	0.04	0.02	−0.01	0.01	0.01	0.00	0.00	0.01	0.00	0.01	0.01	0.00
Germany (D)	0.03	−0.03	−0.01	0.07	0.03	−0.02	0.14	0.00	−0.05	−0.07	−0.03	0.03	−0.03	−0.01	0.01
Spain (E)	0.01	−0.01	0.00	0.00	−0.01	0.00	0.00	−0.01	0.01	0.06	0.03	−0.03	−0.01	−0.01	0.00
France (F)	0.04	−0.02	−0.01	0.03	0.01	−0.01	−0.01	−0.02	0.00	−0.01	0.01	0.01	−0.05	0.00	0.01
Ireland (IRL)	0.00	0.00	0.00	0.00	0.00	0.00	0.00	0.00	0.00	0.00	0.00	0.00	0.00	0.00	0.00
Italy (I)	**1.03**	**0.61**	**−0.31**	−0.03	−0.01	0.01	0.00	−0.02	0.00	−0.12	−0.07	0.05	−0.07	−0.03	0.02
Netherlands (NL)	−0.02	−0.02	0.01	**0.87**	**0.34**	**−0.20**	−0.01	−0.01	0.00	−0.03	−0.02	0.01	−0.02	−0.01	0.01
Austria (A)	0.01	0.00	0.00	0.01	0.00	0.00	**0.46**	**0.10**	**−0.16**	−0.01	−0.01	0.00	−0.01	0.00	0.00
Portugal (P)	0.01	0.00	0.00	0.01	0.00	0.00	0.00	0.00	0.00	**0.71**	**0.67**	**−0.31**	0.01	0.00	0.00
Finland (FIN)	0.00	0.00	0.00	0.00	0.00	0.00	0.00	0.00	−0.01	0.00	0.00	0.00	**0.71**	**0.24**	**−0.21**
II. Monetary policy[c]															
European Central Bank (ECB)	0.44	0.46	−0.12	0.54	0.23	−0.11	0.51	0.27	−0.13	0.78	0.60	−0.32	0.61	0.32	−0.17

Source: Own calculations with the Oxford Economic Forecasting Model (OEF model: Emerging Market Model, December 1998).

a. The table gives multipliers averaged over two years (1999–2000); y = real GDP (measured as a percentage deviation from a baseline); p = inflation rate (measured as a percentage-point deviation from a baseline);

u = unemploymente rate (measured as a percentage-point deviation from a baseline).

b. Fiscal policy (responsibility rests on the EMU member states) is measured by the increase of real government spending of one percent of real GDP.

c. Monetary policy (responsibility rests on the ECB) is measured by a one percentage-point decrease of short-term interest rate (uniform in all EMU countries).

EMU = Economic and Monetary Union.

Table 3. Policy Multipliers for Government Budget, Gross Public Debt, and Current Balance in Euroland (EMU)[a] (Implication for the US-Dollar/Euro Exchange Rate)

Country acting, and policy	Belgium (B)			Germany (D)			Spain (E)			France (F)			Ireland (IRL)		
	d	b	cb	d	b	cb	d	b	cb	d	b	cb	d	b	cb
I. Fiscal Policy[b]															
Belgium (B)	**−1.01**	**0.39**	**−0.28**	0.01	−0.02	0.02	0.00	0.00	0.01	0.00	−0.02	0.02	−0.01	−0.01	0.02
Germany (D)	−0.02	−0.08	0.18	**−0.71**	**0.09**	**−0.45**	−0.05	0.09	0.09	−0.05	0.05	0.09	−0.13	0.10	0.13
Spain (E)	−0.01	0.01	0.03	−0.01	0.01	0.02	**−0.87**	**0.30**	**−0.55**	0.00	−0.01	0.03	−0.02	0.03	0.04
France (F)	0.00	−0.14	0.17	−0.01	−0.01	0.07	−0.01	−0.02	0.08	**−0.55**	**−0.01**	**−0.55**	−0.07	−0.04	0.10
Ireland (IRL)	0.00	−0.01	0.00	0.00	0.00	0.00	0.00	0.00	0.00	0.00	0.00	0.00	**−1.02**	**0.77**	**−0.54**
Italy (I)	−0.03	0.06	0.01	−0.03	0.05	0.06	−0.03	0.07	0.07	−0.04	0.04	0.05	−0.09	0.10	0.07
Netherlands (NL)	0.00	−0.01	0.03	−0.01	0.02	0.01	−0.01	0.03	0.02	−0.02	0.03	0.03	−0.02	0.03	0.01
Austria (A)	0.00	0.00	0.01	0.01	−0.02	0.01	0.00	0.01	0.01	0.00	0.01	0.01	−0.01	0.01	0.01
Portugal (P)	0.00	−0.02	0.02	0.00	−0.01	0.01	0.00	−0.03	0.01	0.00	−0.01	0.00	0.00	0.00	0.01
Finland (FIN)	0.00	0.01	0.00	0.00	0.00	0.00	0.00	0.01	0.00	0.00	0.01	0.00	0.00	0.01	0.01
II. Monetary policy[c]															
European Central Bank (ECB)	0.22	−1.32	0.50	0.29	−0.74	−0.06	0.19	−0.67	−0.25	0.28	−0.65	−0.11	0.34	−0.83	−0.11

Country acting, and policy	Italy (I)			Netherlands (NL)			Austria (A)			Portugal (P)			Finland (FIN)			US-$/ Euro
	d	b	cb	d	b	cb	d	b	cb	d	b	cb	d	b	cb	
I. Fiscal Policy [b]																
Belgium (B)	−0.01	0.00	−0.01	0.04	−0.07	0.02	0.00	−0.01	−0.01	−0.02	0.01	0.01	0.00	0.00	0.02	**0.06**
Germany (D)	−0.13	0.08	−0.04	0.07	−0.16	0.13	0.03	−0.13	0.15	−0.20	0.24	0.15	−0.03	0.03	0.10	0.50
Spain (E)	−0.03	0.02	−0.01	0.01	−0.01	0.02	−0.01	0.01	0.02	0.01	−0.05	0.09	−0.01	0.02	0.02	0.16
France (F)	−0.08	0.02	−0.02	0.04	−0.08	0.05	−0.03	0.03	0.04	−0.09	0.09	0.11	−0.02	0.04	0.07	0.45
Ireland (IRL)	0.00	0.00	0.00	0.00	−0.01	0.00	0.00	0.00	0.00	0.00	−0.01	0.00	0.00	0.00	0.00	0.00
Italy (I)	**−0.92**	**−0.89**	**−0.68**	−0.02	0.01	0.04	−0.02	0.01	0.07	−0.17	0.25	0.07	−0.04	0.06	0.04	0.43
Netherlands (NL)	−0.02	0.05	−0.01	**−0.26**	**−0.45**	**−0.34**	−0.01	0.02	0.02	−0.04	0.07	0.02	−0.01	0.01	0.01	0.11
Austria (A)	−0.01	0.00	0.00	0.00	−0.01	0.01	**−1.00**	**0.74**	**−0.50**	−0.02	0.02	0.01	0.00	0.01	0.01	0.05
Portugal (P)	0.00	−0.01	0.00	0.01	−0.01	0.01	0.00	0.00	0.00	**−0.59**	**−0.16**	**−0.46**	0.00	0.00	0.01	0.02
Finland (FIN)	−0.01	0.01	0.00	0.00	0.00	0.01	0.00	0.00	0.01	−0.01	0.01	0.01	**−0.86**	**0.52**	**−0.73**	**−0.73**
II. Monetary policy [c]																
European Central Bank (ECB)	0.39	−1.21	0.14	0.43	−0.78	−0.05	0.27	−0.63	−0.24	0.82	−1.58	−0.18	0.25	−0.55	−0.02	−2.19

Source: Own calculations with the Oxford Economic Forecasting Model (OEF model: version Emerging Market Model, December 1998).

a. The table gives multipliers averaged over two years (1999 – 2000); d = government budget ratio (measured as an absolute deviation from a baseline in percent of GDP);

b = gross public debt ratio (measured as an absolute deviation from a baseline in percent of GDP);

cb = current account ratio (measured as an absolute deviation from a baseline of the current account balance as a percent of GDP).

b. Fiscal policy (responsibility rests on the EMU member states) is measured by the increase of real government spending of one percent of real GDP.

c. Monetary policy (responsibility rests on the ECB) is measured by a one percentage-point decrease of short-term interest rate (uniform in all EMU countries).

EMU = Economic and Monetary Union.

These multipliers link various "targets" of each country to policy instruments. The multipliers are taken from the OEF world model for the period 1999–2001.

The strategy is as follows: In a n-country world $T^i = (T^i_1, \ldots, T^i_m)$ is the vector of country i's targets. The baseline or "central variant" projection of T^i, T^{Bi} is taken from a simulation of the OEF world model. The policy controls for country i are the elements of vector $C^i = (C^i_1, \ldots, C^i_1)$. The authorities in country i maximize a welfare function $U^i(T^i)$.

The matrix Γ containes the multipliers linking the overall vector of controls $C = (C^1, C^2, \ldots, C^n)$ to the overall vector of targets $T = (T^1, T^2, \ldots, T^n)$, so that

$$T = C\Gamma + T^B. \tag{1}$$

When $C = 0$ then $T = T^B$, the baseline corresponds to the situation where no additional policy actions are taken.

Next we assume that the baseline is a Nash equilibrium for the n countries. The optimal policy for each country i, given the actions of the others, is $C^i = 0$ and consequently $T^i = T^{B^i}$. This assumption allows us to identify the key parameters of each country's utility function. Finally we find the cooperative equilibrium as the solution to a bargaining problem. A common utility function, which is given by the weighted sum of the coutries' utility functions, is optimised.

We adopt this framework to model the EMU. In the monetary union policy instruments are split between the ECB who is in charge of monetary policy for the union as a whole and the EMU member countries who control their own fiscal policy.

We consider $n = 10$ EMU countries, who's targets T^i are the value of the output gap (Q^i_t) and inflation as a deviation from target (π^i_t) over the years 1999 to 2001. Their only policy instrument is fiscal policy. *Fiscal policy* is measured by an increase in real government spending of one percent of real GDP sustained over the period 1999 to 2001. We write this as

$$T^i = (Q^i_{1999}, Q^i_{2000}, Q^i_{2001}, \pi^i_{1999}, \pi^i_{2000}, \pi^i_{2001}), \quad i = 1, \ldots, 10 \tag{2}$$

$$C^i = G^i \tag{3}$$

The ECB is modelled in our empirical analysis as a synthetic 11th EMU "country". This means that the targets of the ECB are the GDP-weighted averages of those of the 10 EMU countries. *Monetary policy* is pursued centralized by the ECB

$$T^{\text{ECB}} = (Q^{\text{ECB}}_{1999}, Q^{\text{ECB}}_{2000}, Q^{\text{ECB}}_{2001}, \pi^{\text{ECB}}_{1999}, {}^{\text{ECB}}_{2000}, \pi^{\text{ECB}}_{2001}) \tag{4}$$

$$C^{\text{ECB}} = M^{\text{ECB}} \tag{5}$$

The target variables are GDP-weighted sums of the same variables of the 10 EMU member countries:

$$Q^{\text{ECB}} = \sum_{i=1}^{10} g_i Q^i \quad \text{and} \quad \pi^{\text{ECB}} = \sum_{i=1}^{10} g_i \pi^i$$

with g_i = GDP weights.

Monetary policy is measured by a one percentage-point decrease of the short-term interest rate uniform in all countries, sustained over three years.

DERIVATION OF THE UTILITY FUNCTION PARAMETERS

The assumption that the baseline is a Nash equilibrium gives us a first oder condition on the utility function for every country: $(\partial U^i/\partial G^i) = 0$ and for the ECB: $(\partial U^{ECB}/\partial M^{ECB}) = 0$. The derivatives can be calculated by

$$\frac{\partial U^i}{\partial C^i} = u_1^i \left(\frac{\partial Q^i}{\partial C^i}\right) + u_2^i \left(\frac{\partial \pi^i}{\partial C^i}\right) = 0, \quad i = 1, \ldots, 11 \tag{6}$$

From now on the notation is identical fro the EMU member countries and the ECB ($i = 11 = \text{ECB}$).

The policy multipliers (such as $\partial Q^i/\partial C^i$ and $\partial \pi^i/\partial C^i$) are taken from the OEF model, the marginal utilities with respect to output and inflation u_1^i and u_2^i remain to be determined. The utility functions can be normalized by setting $u_1^i = 1$ for all $i = 1, \ldots, 11$, so that we are left with one equation for every unknown u_2^i. As output and inflation are targeted over a period of three years (see equation (2)), we have to assume a parametric specification af the utility function.

We specify the *utility functions* for the i EMU member countries as discounted sums of annual quadratic utilities,[5] with a fixed time discount factor, $\delta = 0.1$:

$$U^i = -\sum_{t=1999}^{2001} \frac{1}{2}(1+\delta)^{(1999-t)}[\mu_i(Q_t^i)^2 + \phi_i(\pi_t^i)^2], \quad i = 1, \ldots, 11 \tag{7}$$

In matrix notation the utility can be written as

$$U^i = -\frac{1}{2} T^i R_i T^{iT}, \tag{8}$$

where R_i is a diagonal matrix containig the country specific parameters:

$$R_i = \begin{bmatrix} \mu_i & 0 & 0 & 0 & 0 & 0 \\ 0 & (1+\delta)^{-1}\mu_i & 0 & 0 & 0 & 0 \\ 0 & 0 & (1+\delta)^{-2}\mu_i & 0 & 0 & 0 \\ 0 & 0 & 0 & \phi_i & 0 & 0 \\ 0 & 0 & 0 & 0 & (1+\delta)^{-1}\phi_i & 0 \\ 0 & 0 & 0 & 0 & 0 & (1+\delta)^{-2}\phi_i \end{bmatrix} \tag{9}$$

Now the parameters μ_i and ϕ_i are determined by the normalizing condition and the first order condition in equation (6):

$$\frac{\partial U^i}{\partial Q^i} = u_1^i = -\sum_{t=1999}^{2001} (1+\delta)^{(1999-t)} \mu_i Q_t^i = 1 \tag{10}$$

$$\frac{\partial U^i}{\partial C^i} = -\sum_{t=1999}^{2001} (1+\delta)^{(1999-t)} \mu_i Q_t^i \frac{\partial Q_t^i}{\partial C^i} - \sum_{t=1999}^{2001} (1+\delta)^{(1999-t)} \phi_i \pi_t^i \frac{\partial \pi_t^i}{\partial C^i} = 0. \tag{11}$$

The results of the derivatives of the national utility functions at the Nash equilibrium (u_1^i, u_2^i), as well as the derived utility function parameters (μ_i, ϕ_i) are presented in

Table 4. Partial derivatives of national utility functions at Nash equilibrium (u_1, u_2) and utility function parameters (μ_i, ϕ_i)

Country		Output u_1	Inflation u_2	Output μ_i	Inflation ϕ_i
Belgium	B	1	−0.264	0.424	0.056
Germany	D	1	−1.126	0.136	0.229
Spain	E	1	−2.288	0.036	0.408
France	F	1	−1.093	0.069	0.276
Ireland	IRL	1	−2.474	0.181	0.264
Italy	I	1	−0.953	0.036	0.175
Netherlands	NL	1	−1.032	0.358	0.184
Austria	A	1	−1.739	0.140	0.375
Portugal	P	1	−0.309	0.177	0.030
Finland	FIN	1	−1.683	0.145	0.302
ECB[a]	ECB	1	−0.687	0.074	0.137

[a] ECB is the "11th EMU member country". The respective parameters are derived from a weighted utility function with GDP weights of the EMU member countries.

Table 4. A high value of μ_i signifies that the country has a priority for the output target in its utility function, which is the case for Belgium, Ireland and the Neatherlands. The inflation target is more important (indicated by high values of ϕ_i) for Germany, Austria, Finland, Spain and of course for the ECB.

One has, however, to keep in minde that the parameters of the utility functions are dependent both on the baseline and the policy tradeoffs the countries are confronted with. And of course, the parameter are time-dependend. In our case we use the period 1999–2001. In an other period or business-cycle phase they could be different.

By setting $u_1^i = 1$ we normalized the marginal utility of a GDP increase (relative to the baseline) sutained for three years to equal 1. So u_2^i measures the welfare cost, in GDP equivalents, of a one percentage point increase in inflation held for three years. A value of $u_2^i = -2$, for example, means that on the margin, policy makers are indifferent between a one percentage point rise in inflation and a sustained GDP loss of two percent relative to baseline. In the empirical analysis the values of u_2^i for many countries is about 1. Small rises in inflation are equivalent to a one percent GDP loss for Belgium, Portugal and the ECB ($u_2^i < 1$).

Having these marginal weights, one can examine the scope for policy coordination. In a first step, we consider the effect on utility of country i of a rise in G in country j. By assumption, the own-effects of policy actions are zero at the Nash equilibrium. Then we get the *cross-country gains from fiscal and monetary expansion at the baseline* (at *Nash equilibrium*). Formally, the utility of country i is influenced by policy action of country j by:

$$\frac{\partial U^i}{\partial C^j} = -T^{Bi} R_i \Gamma_{ji}^T, \tag{12}$$

where Γ_{ji} is the block matrix of Γ which contains the multipliers of country i's targets with respect to country j's controls. The results are presented in Table 5. The cross-country gains (spill-over effects) are very low, in some cases even negative.

Table 5. Cross-country gains from fiscal and monetary expansion at Nash equilibrium ($\partial U^i/\partial C^j$)[a]

i = rows j = columns	B	D	E	F	IRL	I
B	0	0.010	0.004	0.006	0.002	0.015
D	0.001	0	0.024	0.046	0.000	0.062
E	0.001	0.055	0	0.052	0.000	0.059
F	0.005	0.049	0.026	0	0.000	0.054
IRL	−0.024	−0.100	−0.007	−0.059	0	−0.100
I	0.007	0.046	0.018	0.041	0.000	0
NL	−0.007	−0.032	−0.010	−0.038	0.006	−0.073
A	−0.005	0.072	0.024	0.042	0.000	0.045
P	−0.012	−0.085	0.017	−0.051	0.005	−0.155
FIN	−0.020	−0.049	0.002	−0.044	0.003	−0.043
ECB[b]	−0.007	0.124	0.063	0.084	0.004	0.041

= rows j = columns	NL	A	P	FIN	ECB
B	0.0040	0.000	0.001	0.002	−0.077
D	0.011	−0.001	0.004	0.005	−0.429
E	0.018	0.011	0.008	0.003	−0.502
F	0.018	0.008	0.002	0.002	−0.355
IRL	−0.020	−0.008	0.002	−0.004	−0.100
I	0.009	0.005	0.002	0.003	−0.252
NL	0	−0.003	0.001	−0.006	0.150
A	0.008	0	0.002	0.000	−0.432
P	−0.008	−0.007	0	−0.005	0.431
FIN	−0.004	−0.007	0.007	0	−0.124
ECB[b]	0.021	0.012	0.003	0.011	0

[a] The policy actions of the countries in the columns (C^j, fiscal and monetary policies) have an impact on the utility of the countries in the rows (U^i). Fiscal policy is independently executed by each of the 10 EMU countries. Monetary policy in the EMU is centrally executed by the ECB for the whole EMU area.
[b] The utility of the ECB (U^{ECB}) is measured by a weighted utility function with GDP weights of the EMU member countries.

EVALUATION OF THE COOPERATIVE EQUILIBRIUM

We remember that in the Nash equilibrium the maximization problem for country i was given by

$$\max_{C_i} U^i(T^i) \tag{13}$$

$$\text{s.t.} \quad T^i = (C^1, \ldots, C^{10}, C^{\mathrm{ECB}})\Gamma_i + T^{Bi} \tag{14}$$

where Γ_i is the block matrix of Γ which contains the policy multipliers of country i's targets with respect to policy actions of all countries and the ECB. By construction the optimal solution of the maximisation is given by $C^N = (0, \ldots, 0)$ and $T^N = (T^{B1}, \ldots, T^{B\,\mathrm{ECB}})$.

A *cooperative equilibrium* corresponds to the case where all the countries act jointly so as to maximize a collective utility function. This collective utility function is assumed to be a weighted average of each country's own utility function.

$$U^C(w^1, w^2, \ldots, w^{11}) = \sum_{i=1}^{11} w^i U^i \tag{15}$$

The weights granted to each country in the cooperative process are denoted by $w^1, w^2, \ldots, w^{11}$. For the practical process of cooperation the question arises which are the correct weights. Remembering the complicated framework of coordination described in chapter 2, one must conclude that the final level of coordination in EMU is the Council (the Ecofin). In the Council for a qualified majority the votes are weighted according to Article 205(2) TEC. That means the large countries have 10 votes, the medium-sized countries 5 votes and the small countries have votes from 2 to 4 votes. In total there are 87 votes. For most of the measures taken under the cooperation procedure a qualified majority is needed. That means the most plausible weighting scheme for a EMU-wide utility function is those according to the voting power of the EMU member countries in the Ecofin. Taking ECB as a large country an re-weighting on the basis of the 10 EMU member countries we get our weighting scheme for the EMU-wide utility function.

Equation (15) can be expressed alternatively in matrix notation as:

$$U^C(w^1, w^2, \ldots, w^{11}) = -\frac{1}{2} TR_C(w^1, w^2, \ldots, w^{11})T^T \tag{16}$$

with

$$R_C(w^1, w^2, \ldots, w^{11}) = \begin{bmatrix} w^1 R_1 & & & 0 \\ & w^2 R_2 & & \\ & & \ddots & \\ 0 & & & w^{11} R_{11} \end{bmatrix} \tag{17}$$

The *cooperative equilibrium* is thus the solution of the following optimisation problem:

$$\max_C U^C(w^1, w^2, \ldots, w^{11}) = -\frac{1}{2} TR_C(w^1, w^2, \ldots, w^{11})T^T \tag{18}$$

$$\text{s.t.} \quad T = C\Gamma + T^B \tag{19}$$

The solution to this problem (if there are no constraints or if they are not binding) can be derived analytically and is given by

$$C^C = -T^B R_C \Gamma^T (\Gamma R_C \Gamma^T)^{-1} \tag{20}$$

$$T^C = C^C \Gamma + T^B \tag{21}$$

And the *welfare gain from cooperation* (or coordination) is defined by

$$U^C - U^N = -\frac{1}{2} T^C R_C T^{CT} + \frac{1}{2} T^B R_C T^{BT}. \tag{22}$$

The argument for coordination can be demonstrated by a two-country example in a simple diagram (see Oudiz-Sachs, 1984, p. 27). In Figure 1 the indifference curves

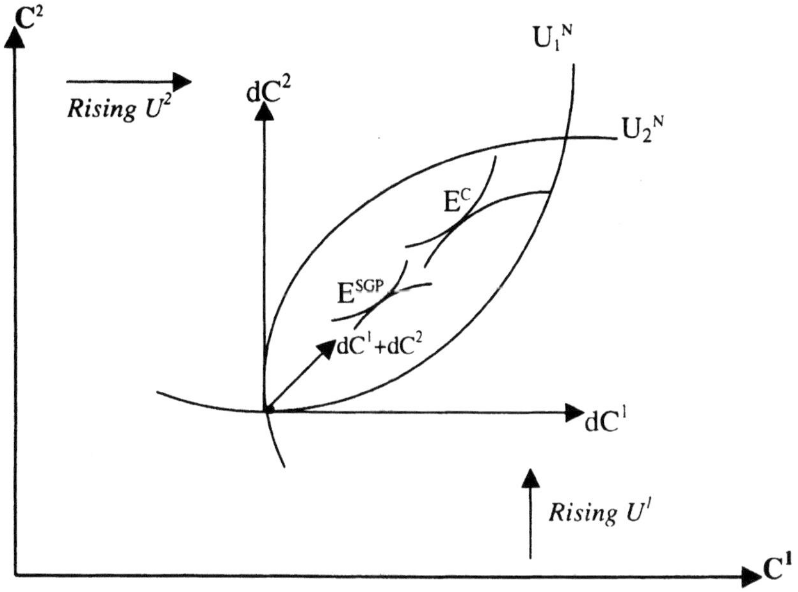

Figure 1. The Geometry of Policy Coordination in EMU

Two-country case: C^1 = (fiscal) policy of country 1; C^2 = (fiscal) policy of country 2. U_1^N and U_2^N are the indifference (utility) curves of country 1 and country 2 respectively. E^C = equilibrium with unrestraint cooperation. E^{SGP} = equilibrium with cooperation under the constraint of the stability and growth pact (SGP).

Source: Oudiz-Sachs (1984, p. 27) with own adjustments.

for countries $GRAPHIC$ and $GRAPHIC$ are drawn in (C^1, C^2) space. It is assumed that $\partial U^1/\partial C^2$ and $\partial U^2/\partial C^1$ are both positive. That means that the influence of the other country's policy action exerts a positive impact on the home country. At the Nash equilibrium, N, C^1 is chosen to maximize U^1 given C^{2N}, so that the indifference curve for 1 is horizontal at N (that is, $\partial U^1/\partial C^1 = 0$); similarly the indifference curve for 2 is vertical at N. Now, when C^1 is changed in the direction $\bar{\omega}(\partial U^2/\partial C^1)$ the domestic control is moved by the vector dC^1 ($\bar{\omega}$ is a positive small positive number). For small changes, $dU^1 \approx 0$ and $dU^2 > 0$ (actually, U^1 falls by a second-order term, while U^2 rises by a first-order term). The vertical vector in Figure 1 represents dC^2. By the same argument, a small rise in C^2 leads to $dU^1 > 0$ and $dU^2 \approx 0$. A cooperative equilibrium would be given by a sum of vectors dC^1 and dC^2, shown as the upward-sloping vector at point N. It clearly moves into a region of joint welfare improvement.

The region between the two indifference curves U_1^N and U_2^N describes the entire set of policy moves that are Pareto improving vis-a-vis N. In a non-EMU world, where each country has control over all policy instruments, at point E^C, the indifference curves of countries 1 and 2 are tangent. When no movement of C^1 and C^2 from E^C can be Pareto improving, E^C is an efficient policy equilibrium. The equilibrium E^C would be the optimal solution in a normal two-country world, where each country has full control over all policy instruments. However, in EMU – as described in chapter 2 – the framework is different. Even if point E^C might be the Pareto efficient coordination equilibrium, the Stability and Growth Pact (SGP) with its limitations of the government budget deficit to 3 percent of GDP as an upper limit and the medium term target of close to balance acts as a constraint for an unrestricted coordination equilibrium. Under the restrictive regime of the SGP the policy coordination outcome might result in an second-best equilibrium at point E^{SGP} (see Figure 1). As our results show, this is exactly the case. The SGP is binding for an optimal policy coordination outcome. These arguments can easily be generalized to a n – country world.

GAINS FROM COOPERATION

Based on the optimization procedure for cooperation described in the equations (19) and (20) we can calculate optimization gains for two scenarios, for (1) a "full cooperation" (all EMU countries coordinate their fiscal policy with the monetary policy of the ECB) and, (2) for a "partial cooperation" (where only the EMU countries coordinate their fiscal policy and the ECB stays aside). In both scenarios, firstly the unconstrained results are reported. Then restrictions to guarantee Pareto improvement are introduced and constraints by the SGP have to be taken into account. The numerical optimization are carried out with GAMS (General Algebraic Modeling System).

Gains from Full Fiscal and Monetary Policy Cooperation

Unconstrained cooperative equilibrium In a first step the cooperative equilibrium is calculated according to the optimization problem of the equations (18) and (19). This gives the unconstrained results for the optimal policy vector C^C of equation (20) (see Table 6) and hence the policy targets at cooperation T^C according to equation (21) (see Tables 7 and 8).

Using the weighting according to the votes in the Council, total utility in the EMU at cooperative equilibrium is higher by 0.56% of GDP[6] than in the case of the Nash equilibrium (or in the baseline; see Table 6). This implies an optimal fiscal policy impulse (increase of real public expenditures) in the EMU member states by 2 1/4 percent of GDP in the Netherlands and Italy to 7.2 percent of GDP in Ireland. As an optimal monetary policy the ECB would have to decrease the short-term interest rate y 3.5 percentage points. These high policy shocks leading to an optimal cooperative solution are also partly due to the weighting scheme we have chosen.[7] Again one must stress that the case of a broad joint cooperation of fiscal and monetary policy is not realistic in EMU practice but has more the character of an hypothetical exercise. As ECB president Duisenberg made it clear in the European Parliament when presenting the annual report a cooperation between the monetary and fiscal policy is not foreseen by the independent ECB!

Although in our unconstraint optimization solution total EMU utility would increase, in some EMU member states cooperation would lead to a welfare loss compared to the baseline situation (or non-cooperation). This is not an Pareto optimal solution for all EMU members.

Due to the high fiscal and monetary policy impulses implying full economic policy

Table 6. Optimal Fiscal and Monetary Policy with Cooperation and Welfare Gains from Cooperation in the EMU

	Optimal Policy C^C	Utility at Nash Equilibrium U^N	Utility at Cooperative Equilibrium U^C	Welfare gain[a] $(U^C - U^N)$
I. Fiscal Policy[b]				
Belgium (B)	6.223	−0.707	−1.098	−0.391
Germany (D)	3.799	−3.045	−1.419	1.626
Spain (E)	5.913	−8.183	−5.964	2.219
France (F)	4.165	−3.661	−2.133	1.528
Ireland (IRL)	7.217	−5.475	−7.154	−1.679
Italy (I)	2.302	−6.288	−4.934	1.354
Netherlands (NL)	2.220	−1.724	−5.037	−3.313
Austria (A)	6.258	−2.962	−1.295	1.667
Portugal (P)	4.437	−2.206	−5.777	−3.571
Finland (FIN)	5.360	−2.995	−3.814	−0.819
II. Monetary policy[c]				
European Central Bank (ECB)[d]	−3.549	−3.402	−2.156	1.246
Total[e]	—	−3.985	−3.425	0.560

[a] The unit of welfare gain is equivalent to a percentage change in GDP, averaged over three years (1999–2001).
[b] The unit of fiscal policy is a sustained increase of government spending equal x percent of GDP.
[c] The unit of monetary policy is a sustained decrease of EMU's short-term interest rate of x percent.
[d] Welfare of the ECB is calculated from a welfare function with GDP weighted target variables: output and inflation.
[e] Weighted average of the national utility levels (weights according to council votes; ECB is a large country).
Weighted total utility of EMU is maximized.

cooperation one can expect an improvement in the targets (output and inflation) in most countries compared to the baseline solution in the three years (1999–2001) under examination (see Table 7). The most unpleasant result, however, concerns the fiscal targets of the Stability and Growth Pact (SGP), namely the budget deficits (upper bound of 3% of GDP) and the public debt to GDP ratio (60%). In practically all EMU member countries the full policy coordination scenario would lead to a violation of the SGP targets (see Table 8).

Whereas in the baseline[8] all EMU member states exhibit already a fiscal balance below the 3% of GDP deficit target of the SGP, after the massive fiscal impulse, as the optimization solution for cooperation would imply this target would be violated by all countries (except the Netherlands) not only at the end of the three year period but already in 1999.

Confronted with this violation of the vital EMU fiscal policy targets one has to question the room for manoeuvre for fiscal and monetary policy coordination in EMU. In the next step we look therefore for the degree of welfare gains from cooperation, given the constraints of a Pareto optimal solution concerning utilities for all EMU countries (they should all be positive) and the objective that the fiscal targets (budget deficits and public debt) are not violated.

Table 7. Outcome of Fiscal and Monetary Policy Optimization with Cooperation: Output and Inflation in the EMU, 1999–2001

	Deviations from target values[a]					
	1999		2000		2001	
	T^C	T^B	T^C	T^B	T^C	T^B
I. Output						
B	−0.72	−1.08	−0.20	−0.97	**−1.83**	−0.48
D	−2.63	−4.64	−1.60	−2.51	**−1.26**	−0.52
E	−11.22	−15.01	−8.64	−8.93	−5.62	−5.95
F	−4.29	−6.84	−4.06	−5.16	**−3.80**	−3.60
IRL	1.48	−0.90	−2.15	−2.43	**−5.02**	−2.92
I	−11.77	−12.89	−8.62	−9.92	−6.67	−6.82
NL	1.51	−0.66	**−1.46**	−0.65	**−4.74**	−1.87
A	−1.63	−3.49	−1.21	−2.55	**−2.34**	−1.60
P	1.47	−0.09	**−4.05**	−2.69	**−6.97**	−3.78
FIN	−0.12	−2.28	−2.66	−2.66	**−5.02**	−2.65
ECB[b]	−4.82	−6.88	−3.88	−4.71	**−3.45**	−2.88
II. Inflation						
B	**3.76**	1.31	0.12	1.89	−0.09	2.08
D	0.57	0.85	2.05	2.28	1.55	2.42
E	1.50	1.88	2.15	2.16	2.08	2.13
F	0.87	0.98	**1.64**	1.58	1.06	1.87
IRL	2.78	2.96	**4.06**	3.73	**3.93**	3.64
I	1.65	1.98	1.35	1.96	1.42	2.05
NL	1.87	1.89	**2.32**	2.01	1.54	2.27
A	0.84	1.26	1.21	1.73	1.43	2.18
P	**3.90**	3.50	**5.04**	3.92	3.44	3.85
FIN	**1.95**	1.83	**2.34**	2.29	**2.02**	2.01
ECB[b]	1.24	1.37	1.81	2.04	1.46	2.19

[a] Target values are as follows: output gap, zero (full employment); inflation, zero.
T^C = target values at cooperative equilibrium; T^B = target values at baseline (Nash equilibrium).

[b] The outcome for the ECB is equivalent to the GDP weighted average of those of the EMU

Constrained cooperative equilibrium Now, we take into consideration the two additional constraints for cooperation:

1. *Pareto optimality constraint*: All countries must improve their welfare or should at least not be worse off than in the non-cooperative situation ($U^{Ci} \geq U^{Ni}$). Such a condition is necessary when bargaining for policy cooperation.
2. *Stability and Growth Pact constraint*: The SGP aims at a budgetary position of the EMU member states of close to balance or in surplus in the medium-run. An excess over this reference value is only allowed when it results from a severe economic downturn which is exceptional (i.e. when real GDP declines by at least 2% per annum). In our empirical analysis we only concentrate at the upper bound of the SGP budget deficit target of 3% of GDP which we use as an additional condition for the optimization procedure. The constraint on fiscal deficit is included in the form of a multiplier equation $\tilde{T} \leq C\tilde{\Gamma} + \tilde{T}^B$, where $\tilde{T}^B$ is the government budget balance to GDP ratio deviation from its target value

Table 8. Outcome of Fiscal and Monetary Policy Optimization with Cooperation: Government Budget and Gross Public Debt in the EMU, 1999–2001

	Deviations from target values[a]					
	1999		2000		2001	
	T^C	T^B	T^C	T^B	T^C	T^B
I. Government Budget						
B	**−5.81**	1.29	**−5.56**	1.70	**−6.55**	1.70
D	**−2.80**	0.84	**−2.73**	1.14	**−3.49**	1.30
E	**−4.51**	1.08	**−5.28**	1.36	**−5.60**	1.41
F	**−2.74**	0.35	**−2.98**	1.07	**−3.47**	1.33
IRL	**−4.16**	5.36	**−4.76**	5.24	**−5.61**	5.21
I	**−3.81**	0.58	**−4.07**	0.84	**−4.65**	1.00
NL	**1.17**	1.85	**−0.40**	1.85	**−2.37**	1.99
A	**−6.04**	0.82	**−6.60**	1.19	**−7.07**	1.73
P	**−5.77**	0.40	**−8.28**	0.18	**−10.87**	0.00
FIN	**−2.33**	2.99	**−3.21**	3.09	**−4.16**	3.18
ECB[b]	**−3.18**	0.87	**−3.49**	1.23	**−4.21**	1.41
II. Gross Public Debt						
B	**58.58**	55.72	**61.99**	52.24	**68.67**	48.27
D	**6.21**	5.31	**9.75**	4.96	**14.83**	4.56
E	**11.20**	10.43	**16.78**	8.42	**20.85**	6.44
F	**5.52**	5.15	**8.92**	4.34	**12.35**	3.04
IRL	**−4.76**	−9.24	**−1.89**	−15.69	**2.78**	−21.44
I	**55.80**	54.92	**56.02**	51.27	**58.08**	47.54
NL	4.29	5.40	**5.88**	4.12	**9.91**	2.86
A	**5.93**	3.13	**12.45**	2.25	**19.81**	0.96
P	**1.08**	−1.52	**8.66**	−2.03	**19.81**	−2.37
FIN	**−7.75**	−9.80	**−3.92**	−12.34	**0.71**	−14.90
ECB[b]	**17.68**	16.81	**20.76**	15.24	**24.89**	13.50

[a] Target values are as follows: government budget balance to GDP ratio, −3 percent of GDP (Stability and Growth Pact upper limit); gross public debt to GDP ratio, 60 percent of GDP.
A negative (positive) sign indicates that the budget deficit and/or the public debt target is violated (is below target) by x percent of GDP.
T^C = target values at cooperative equilibrium; T^B = target values at baseline (Nash equilibrium).

[b] The outcome for the ECB is equivalent to the GDP weighted average of those of the EMU member countries.

(−3 percent of GDP) and $\tilde{\Gamma}$ are the multipliers on government budget balance to GDP ratio. Baseline and multipliers are taken from the the OEF model in an analogous way to the values of T^B and Γ in equation (1).

These two constraints for calculating a cooperative equilibrium reduces the room for manoeuvre for an optimal fiscal and monetary policy dramatically (see Table 9). Total utility improves only slightly by 0.013% GDP. Only France and Austria can expect a small improve in their welfare from cooperation. The pattern of optimal fiscal policy varies from -0.4% in Germany to 2.3% in Ireland. The ECB would reduce short-term interest rates only by 0.3%. This implies that an optimal solution under the two constraints results in a fiscal policy pattern which allocates to some countries a fiscal expansion whereas others should restrict their fiscal policy!

Table 9. Optimal Fiscal and Monetary Policy with Cooperation and Welfare Gains from Cooperation in the EMU (Utility and SGP constrained)

	Optimal Policy C^C	Utility at Nash Equilibrium U^N	Utility at Cooperative Equilibrium U^C	Welfare gain[a] $(U^C - U^N)$
I. Fiscal Policy[b]				
Belgium (B)	0.297	−0.707	−0.707	0.000
Germany (D)	−0.419	−3.045	−3.045	0.000
Spain (E)	1.235	−8.184	−8.184	0.000
France (F)	−0.279	−3.661	−3.610	0.051
Ireland (IRL)	2.272	−5.475	−5.475	0.000
Italy (I)	−0.180	−6.287	−6.287	0.000
Netherlands (NL)	0.272	−1.725	−1.725	0.000
Austria (A)	0.754	−2.962	−2.852	0.110
Portugal (P)	−0.124	−2.206	−2.206	0.000
Finland (FIN)	0.926	−2.995	−2.995	0.000
II. Monetary policy[c]				
European Central Bank (ECB)[d]	−0.308	−3.402	−3.402	0.000
Total[e]	—	−3.985	−3.972	0.013

[a] The unit of welfare gain is equivalent to a percentage change in GDP, averaged over three years (1999–2001).

[b] The unit of fiscal policy is a sustained increase of government spending equal × percent of GDP.

[c] The unit of monetary policy is a sustained decrease of EMU's short-term interest rate of × percent.

[d] Welfare of the ECB is calculated from a welfare function with GDP weighted target variables: output and inflation.

[e] Weighted average of the national utility levels (weights according to council votes; ECB is a large country).
Weighted total utility of EMU is maximized.

Gains from Partial, only Fiscal Policy Cooperation

In case of a fiscal cooperation only among the EMU member countries with an ECB not participating – a scenario which is more compatible with EMU practice so far – , the welfare gains would be only 0.02% of GDP. The fiscal impulses would be below 1% of GDP (in Belgium the fiscal policy should even be restrictionist). Four out of 10 EMU countries would be worse off with cooperation compared to non-cooperation (see Table 10).

The advantage of this partial cooperation would be that the SGP targets would practically not be violated. Due to the small fiscal impulse the direct targets of optimization (output-gap and inflation) would only slightly be improved. If one introduces the additional constraints (Pareto optimality concerning welfare in each country; SGP targets) the cooperative welfare gains would be practically nil.

In both cases, a constrained cooperative solution (results in Table 9) and a partial cooperation scenario (results in Table 10) lead to a situation which leads the EMU countries back to the baseline or Nash equilibrium (as demonstrated in Figure 1). Only full cooperation leads to massive welfare gains, however, it violates some basic targets (each country gains and the SGP objectives are binding).

Table 10. Optimal Fiscal Policy with Cooperation and Welfare Gains from Cooperation in the EMU

	Optimal Policy C^C	Utility at Nash Equilibrium U^N	Utility at Cooperative Equilibrium U^C	Welfare gain[a] $(U^C - U^N)$
I. Fiscal Policy[b]				
Belgium (B)	−0.494	−0.707	−0.707	0.000
Germany (D)	0.398	−3.045	−3.035	0.010
Spain (E)	0.690	−8.183	−8.179	0.004
France (F)	0.384	−3.661	−3.636	0.025
Ireland (IRL)	0.199	−5.475	−5.556	−0.081
Italy (I)	0.125	−6.288	−6.246	0.042
Netherlands (NL)	0.196	−1.724	−1.785	−0.061
Austria (A)	0.393	−2.962	−2.905	0.057
Portugal (P)	0.094	−2.206	−2.267	−0.061
Finland (FIN)	0.256	−2.995	−3.034	−0.039
II. Monetary policy[c]				
European Central Bank (ECB)[d]	0.000	−3.402	−3.268	0.134
Total[e]	—	−3.985	−3.965	0.020

[a] The unit of welfare gain is equivalent to a percentage change in GDP, averaged over three years (1999–2001).
[b] The unit of fiscal policy is a sustained increase of government spending equal × percent of GDP.
[c] The unit of monetary policy is a sustained decrease of EMU's short-term interest rate of × percent.
[d] Welfare of the ECB is calculated from a welfare function with GDP weighted target variables: output and inflation.
[e] Weighted average of the national utility levels (weights according to council votes; ECB is a large country).
Weighted total utility of EMU is maximized.

V. Conclusions

With a large-scale econometric world model we calculate the multipliers for fiscal and monetary policy for 10 EMU countries and the ECB in order to identify in order to identify the degree of economic interdependencies in Euroland. The specific architecture of economic policy assign fiscal policy in the responsibility of the EMU member countries, monetary policy is conducted centrally by the ECB for Euroland. Then in a Tinbergen-like approach we link targets to policy instruments. In order to evaluate the gains from cooperation we compare a cooperative equilibrium with the non-cooperative one (by definition the baseline scenario is called the Nash equilibrium). The cooperative equilibrium is the result of the maximization of a weighted utility function with derived parameters for the targets output gap and inflation. In the case of a "full" cooperation (which is not realistic, given EMU practice so far), where the 10 EMU countries coordinate their fiscal policy with the monetary policy of the ECB the welfare gains obtained are very large for Euroland as a whole. However the strong fiscal and monetary policy impulses as a result of this optimization procedure would lead, firstly to a violation of the fiscal targets (budget deficit, public debt) of the Stability and Growth Pact (SGP) which limits the room for manoeuvre of fiscal policy of the EMU member states in stage III of

EMU. Secondly, we find that not in all countries cooperation leads to welfare gains, a result which is not Pareto efficient. Therefore, by considering these two constraints (Pareto optimality and SGP objectives) the constrained optimization leads to a solution in case of "full" cooperation which drives most countries back to the Nash position at the baseline. In addition, a "partial" cooperation in which the ECB stays aside and only the fiscal policies of the EMU member countries are active, leads to a very small welfare improvement and violates again (only to minor degree the Pareto optimality condition). The optimal fiscal policy impulses are very modest.

The policy implications are twofold: First, our results indicate that – taking realistic data over the next three years – the SGP might have a very strong limiting impact on the efforts for a positive or active cooperation in EMU which would lead to more output and employment. Second, the EMU consists of still not fully harmonized economies with different reactions to policy shocks. That means the present EMU still does not present an optimum currency area. It may well be, however, that in the medium-run the single currency leads to a stronger real convergence (convergence of the business cycle and to a comparable impact of similar policy shocks).

Notes

1. In this paper we refer to the new Articles of the Treaty establishing the European Community (TEC) à la Amsterdam, which came into power on May 1, 1999.
2. This chapter follows *Breuss* (2000a).
3. The *Stability and Growth Pact (SGP)* consists of two Council Regulations and two Resolutions of the European Council Council Regulation (EC) No 1466/97 of 7 July 1997 on the strengthening of the surveillance of budgetary positions and the surveillance and coordination of economic policies (OJ L 209, 02/08/1997 p. 1); Council Regulation (EC) No 1467/97 of 7 July 1997 on speeding up and clarifying the implementation of the excessive deficit procedure (OJ L 209, 02/08/1997, pp. 6–11); Resolution of the European Council on the Stability and Growth Pact, Amsterdam, 17 June 1997 (OJ C 236, 02/08/1997, p. 1); Resolution of the European Council on growth and employment, Amsterdam, 16 June 1997 (OJ C 236, 02/08/1997, p. 3).
4. For a survey of the different definitions of coordination and cooperation in the literature, see Mooslechner–Schürz (1999), pp. 172–173.
5. Although, in fact we calculate utility over a three-years time horizon, we still are not dealing with a full-fledged interemporal optimization problem but with a quasi-static planning environment. In a intertemporal environment, the current target variables are functions, via rational expectations, of future policy variables. Then the logic of optimizing our utility function would be called into question, as Kydland–Prescott (1977) first explained. The time incosistency problem would arise when the private sector takes action dependent on anticipations of future policies. The OEF world model used in our exercise to calculate the policy multipliers is not based on rational expectations.
6. As Oudiz–Sachs (1984, p. 64) have shown, small utility gains are equivalent to percent changes in GDP.
7. If one would choose equal weights w^i in equation (19) instead of our choice of voting power in the Council the respective values for optimal policy would be lower. For fiscal policy between 0.9% of GDP in Italy to 3.6% in Ireland, and the monetary policy impuls would only be −1.8%.
8. A comparison of the baseline forecast of the OEF world model with the stability programmes submitted by the EMU member states under the SGP rules early in 1999 shows no big differences in the budgetary position and also in the debt to GDP ratios.

References

van Aarle, B., Engwerda, J.C., Plasmans, J.E.J. and Weeren, A. 'Gestaltung der Geld- und Fiskalpolitik in der Europäischen Wirtschafts- und Währungsunion: Ein dynamischer Spielansatz', in: R. Neck and R. Holzmann (Hrsg.), Was wird aus Euroland? Makroökonomische und wirtschaftspolitische Antworten, Manzsche Verlags- und Universitätsbuchhandlung, Wien 1999, 181-198.

Breuss, F. *Flexibility, Fiscal Policy and 'Stability and Growth Pact'*, Paper presented at the Fourth ECSA-World Conference, Bruxelles, 17-18 September 1998 (forthcoming in the proceedings of the ECSA-World Conference, Brussels 2000a).

Breuss, F. *Die Wirtschafts- und Währungsunion und ihre Folgen, Vorlesung im Rahmen der Ringvorlesung 'Vom Schuman-Plan zum Vertrag von Amsterdam'*, Wirtschaftsuniversität Wien, 8. Juni 2000b.

Demertzis, M., Hughes Hallett, A. and Viegi, N. 'Can the ECB be Truly Independent? Should it Be?', *Empirica*, Vol. 26, No. 3, 1999, 217–240.

European Commission, Economic Policy in EMU, Part A: Rules and Adjustment (Economic Papers, No. 124, November 1997A), Part B: Specific Topics (Economic Papers, No. 125, November 1997B).

European Commission, Commission's Recommendation for the Broad Guidelines of the Economic Policies of the Member States and the Community, Brussels, European Commission, 13.05.1998, COM(1998) 279 final (II/144/98 – EN).

Huizinga, H. aand Nielsen, S.B. *Is Coordination of Fiscal Deficits necessary?*, CEPR Discussion Paper Series, No., 1936, London, July 1998.

Italianer, A. 'The Euro and Internal Economic Policy Coordination', Paper prepared for the VOWA workshop 'Challenges for Economic Policy Coordination within EMU', *Empirica*, Vol. 26, No. 3, 1999, 201–216.

Karner, G. 'Geld- und Fiskalpolitik in einer Währungsunion: Eine dynamische spieltheoretische Analyse', in: R. Neck and R. Holzmann (Hrsg.), *Was wird aus Euroland?* Makroökonomische und wirtschaftspolitische Antworten, Manzsche Verlags- und Universitätsbuchhandlung, Wien 1999, 199–211.

Krichel, Th., Levine, P. and Pearlman, J. 'Fiscal and Monetary Policy in a Monetary Union: Credible Inflation Targets or Monetized Debt?', Weltwirtschaftliches Archiv, Band 132, Heft 1, pp. 28–54.

Kydland, F.E. and Prescott, E.C. 'Rules Rather than Discretion: The Inconsistency of Optimla Plans', *Journal of Political Economy*, Vol. 85, June 1977, 473–491.

Levine, P. *Monetary Union: The Ins and Outs of Strategic Delegation*, European Forum, European University Institute, Florence, 20 June 1997.

McKibbin, W.J. 'Empirical Evidence on International Economic Policy Coordination', in: M.U. Fratianni, D. Salvatore, J. Von Hagen, *Handbook of Comparative Economic Policies*, No. 5: Macroeconomic Policy in Open Economics, Greenwood Press: Westport, Conn., 1997, pp. 148–176.

Mooslechner, P. and Schürz, M. 'International Macro-economic Policy Coordination: Any Lessons for EMU? A Selective Survey of the Literature', *Empirica*, Vol. 26, No. 3, 1999, 171–199.

Oudiz, G. and Sachs, J. 'Macroeconomic Policy Coordination among the Industrial Economies', Brookings Papers on Economic Activity 1/1984, pp. 1-75.

Oxford Economic Forecasting (OEF), The Emerging Market Models, Oxford, April 1999.

9. The Stability Pact and the Interdependence of Monetary and Fiscal Policy Rules*

ANDREW HUGHES HALLETT[†] and PETER McADAM[‡]
[†] *University of Strathclyde, and CEPR*
[‡] *University of Kent at Canterbury and New Scholar, CEPR*

I. Introduction

Monetary union in Europe has ushered in a new economic regime in which monetary and fiscal policies are treated separately, and will be treated separately. This follows from the decision to create a completely independent Central Bank to run monetary policy for the whole European Area. That was a deliberate choice, and was always intended to be the key feature of Europe's monetary regime. But if monetary policy is to be run independently of any of the national governments, then fiscal policies – which remain almost entirely in the hands of those national governments – will, by the same token, also become independent of monetary policy. That makes the issue of the rules by which monetary policies are chosen, and the extent to which they interact with fiscal policy (or vice versa), of crucial importance. Monetary and fiscal policies may be chosen and operated independently, but they will jointly determine the outcomes for each economy nevertheless.

With such a strong policy assignment, fiscal policy remains the only nationally held instrument of macroeconomic policy to compensate for any local shocks or asymmetric transmission mechanisms. However, under the Stability and Growth Pact, fiscal policy in the Euro Area is to be engineered towards medium-term balance or surplus with a 3% deficit ceiling imposed in all but the most adverse circumstances, Artis and Buti (2000).

Although such interactions are a common issue in the theoretical literature – for example Woodford's (1995) fiscal theory of the price level and Sargeant and Wallace's (1981) unpleasant arithmetic of fiscal and monetary dominance – this paper takes a more obviously concrete example of examining the present institutional arrangements. Using an estimated macro-model of the G7, we employ stochastic simulations[1] of the interactions between different monetary policy rules and the Stability Pact's deficit targeting framework to see how different types of monetary policy rules affect the probability of going beyond the maximum (3%) limit allowed, and what that does to the average performance and stability of the other indicators (e.g. inflation, output, deficit levels etc). We analyse this with the help of stochastic simulations, constructed over a 40 year period, using the IMF's multi-country model MULTIMOD. The idea being to examine how successful rigid deficit reduction strategies are to different monetary policy stances and policy rules.

* The authors would like to thank the Leverhulme Trust for financial support (under Grant No. F/273/W) while their research was being done.

A. H. Hallett et al. (eds), Challenges for Economic Policy Coordination with European Monetary Union, 69–182.

We find clear evidence that the choice of monetary rule, and the fiscal restrictions inherent in monetary union, do interact and affect the likely outcomes. But the question of which monetary rule is more favourable will depend on what you hope to achieve. A Taylor rule produces higher growth and inflation, but lower deficit ratios and greater stability on the real side and the expense of stability in nominal terms. Inflation targeting, by contrast, is better at restraining inflation-led booms, while Taylor rules are better at resolving (avoiding) recessions since they are more expansionary on average. This difference is significant because the Stability Pact, if it does anything, is likely to restrict the size of any fiscal interventions and therefore make the more expansionary form of monetary rule more desirable. Hence the European central bank's apparent decision to follow a *form* of Taylor rule in practice may simply be a way of compensating for the deflationary biases which it perceives to be present elsewhere in the system.

II. Our Modelling Approach

AN EMPIRICAL MULTICOUNTRY MODEL

MULTIMOD (Laxton et al., 1998) is an annual estimated econometric macro-model containing the G7 and smaller country blocks. In general, it is in the Keynesian-Classical mould (with standard balanced growth closures but nominal rigidities and error corrections in the short run) and is constructed more for its long-term insights than forecasting. Specific features include a non linear relationship between inflation and unemployment, investment determined by Tobin's q, age-earnings profiles for consumption, uncovered interest parity (UIP) as the determinant of exchange rates, a tax reaction function which precludes unsustainable fiscal accumulations and endogenous short-term nominal interest rates to observe money, inflation, exchange rate targets. The model, and its vintages, has been used extensively for policy analysis in public policy and academic circles. It contains explicit models for the four largest EU economies (Germany, France, the UK and Italy) representing nearly 80% of the European economy. These economies are linked with the US, Canada, Japan, and with the rest of the world, through trade, capital flows; there is a single currency across the European Block, but flexible exchange rates elsewhere.

MULTIMOD has a clear theoretical structure. The specification is designed to explain the main expenditure categories and production flows in each country, from which employment, investment, prices, interest rates and exchange rates are determined. Financial markets, trade flows, and capital movements (including loans and interest payments) are all represented. Trade is divided into three markets: oil, primary commodities and manufactured goods. Perfectly flexible prices clear the commodity markets, where demands are driven by activity levels and supplies by prices and a predetermined capacity. Manufactured goods are produced and traded everywhere. Aggregate demand is then built up from consumption (based on current and expected future earnings, and asset values), investment (based on market evaluations of firms' current and expected future earnings), trade and the net fiscal position. Both consumption and investment therefore adjust positively to earnings, but negatively to rising prices or interest rates. This determines output in the short run. Note that since assets incorporate the stock of capital and government bonds, as well as net foreign assets, with the result that human capital will be constrained to cover discounted future tax liabilities. That is the effect of the budget constraint. The model therefore embodies strong, but incomplete, Ricardian equivalence. That said, potential output is determined by a production function so that capacity utilisation (the ratio of actual to potential output) can vary. Domestic output prices are also subject to a Phillips curve, so there is no absolute output constraint in the short run. In fact prices change by an amount which depends both on the remaining spare capacity and on the state of the labour markets. Prices are therefore partly sticky and partly forward looking, depending on wage contracts, international competitiveness and capacity utilisation.

In the monetary sector, non-EMU exchange rates are determined by uncovered interest parities and the *expected* depreciations consistent with a complete model solution. As we shall see, the assumption of UIP for exchange rates is important in constraining long-run Euro Area monetary policy, compared to US monetary policy. Monetary policy rules in the model can take a variety of forms and targets such as monetary growth values (this is the default rule of the model and the one used in these simulations for the US), exchange rate targets, inflation targets, Taylor rules etc.

Similarly, tax rates are set to gradually eliminate the gap between actual and targeted levels for the deficit to GNP ratio, subject to an intertemporal budget constraint. Fiscal expenditures are therefore exogenous, but the revenues are endogenised. A full description of MULTIMOD's properties and simulation characteristics is given in Masson et al. (1990) or Laxton et al. (1998), and some comparisons with other models in Bryant et al. (1993) or Mitchell et al. (1998).

FISCAL POLICY REACTIONS

In the simulations reported below, that is in Tables II–VII, we use the following tax reaction function

$$\text{tax rate}_t = \text{tax rate}_{t-1} + \alpha_1(d_t - d_t^*) + \alpha_2\Delta(d_{t-1} - d_{t-1}^*) \tag{1}$$

Where $\alpha_1 = 0.9$ and $\alpha_2 = 0.25$, and d^* is the target value for the deficit to GDP ratio, d. That target value is defined separately in each simulation exercise.

Thus the tax rates rise in response to excessive deficits by an amount which is equal in every country and in proportion to the amount that the deficit/GNP ratio lies above its target value, d^*. Moreover taxes will continue to rise so long as $def > def^*$, even if the deficit ratio itself is falling.

That deals with the first term and serves to keep the fiscal deficit within acceptable limits. The second term implies that the tax rates also rise in response to worsening deficit/GNP ratios (above target). That means that tax rates rise faster, at a given deficit level, if the deficit ratio is worsening; but they increase *slower* if that deficit ratio has already started to fall. In fact tax rates could even start to decrease if the deficit ratio starts to fall fast enough. The latter feature supplies a 'soft landing' effect. Conversely you get extra penalties (in the form of higher taxes) if an adverse deficit worsens still further.

Finally, any changes in the tax rate will become dominated by changes in the excess deficit ratio as we get nearer the target ratio – that is to say, changes in the tax rate are likely to be negative as we near the target ratio, so that we glide onto our target values rather than over-shoot. This 'smooth landing' condition captures the spirit of the Maastricht Treaty and Stability and Growth Pact provisions. This ensures that any fiscal corrections are made 'such that the ratio has declined substantially and continuously, and has reached a level close to [its target]". Indeed the faster the pace of correction, the smaller the fiscal corrections need be. The ratio of α_1 to α_2 therefore determines the importance attached to these aspects of the fiscal rules.

Furthermore, to eliminate the discrepancy between the current state of a variable and its target value – z_t and z_t^*, say – a controlled state variable must follow a difference equation of at least pth order (Salmon, 1982):

$$\text{i.e.}\quad (1-L)^p = B(L)Z_{t-p}$$

where $B(L)$ is a polynomial in the lag operator and where z_t^* follows a difference equation of order $p-1$. Hence the controlled variable must follow a scheme of 1 order higher than the target path. Since the Maastricht Treaty and Stability Pact specify constant debt and deficit ratios (whatever their numerical value), we have $p=1$. But our tax reaction function has $p=2$, which implies an element of over kill. However, that is just what we need. It means that we can reach a deficit ratio, which is constant on average (at 1% of GNP, say). But by manipulating the strength of the 'overkill' term, α_2, we can also select the speed with which we achieve that goal.

MONETARY POLICY

Since we know approximately fiscal policy's Stability Pact pre-assignment, more of our concern falls on its sensitivity to different monetary arrangements. We analysed two monetary feed back rules dominant in the literature: a standard Taylor rule and an inflation-targeting rule. These can be nested as:

$$r_t = r_{t-1} + \phi_1(\pi_e - \pi_e^*) + \phi_2 y_t^{gap} \tag{2}$$

where r_t = the short run nominal interest rate, π_e is the EU-wide inflation rate (with target value π_e^*), y^{gap} is the output gap (the percentage difference between actual and capacity output, as calculated by the model). Equation (2) gives a standard Taylor rule (we set $\phi_1 = \phi_2 = 0.5$ and $\pi_e^* = 1\%$); or an inflation targeting rule if $\phi_2 \to 0$.

III. The Simulation Analysis

The results of our stochastic simulation are given in Tables 2 to 7. In these tables we give the mean and standard deviation[2] of the main economic indicators for each country as measured across the 400 replications of each of the 40 simulation periods. These indicators are GDP growth, inflation, short run interest rates, the nominal exchange rate, and the public sector debt and deficit ratios. This is done for each European country, and for the US as their outside comparator. For the purpose of this exercise, we treat all four European countries as being members of EMU and aligning their fiscal policy for compliance with the Stability and Growth Pact.

Table 1. The steady state solution used in MULTIMOD's stochastic simulations

	Germany	France	Italy	UK	USA	Units
Output growth	2.18	2.18	2.18	2.18	2.18	% pa
CPI inflation	2.70	2.70	2.70	2.70	2.70	% pa
Investment/GDP	0.11	0.10	0.10	0.11	0.10	Fraction
Short interest rate	7.01	7.01	7.01	7.01	7.01	%
Nominal exch. rate	0.55	0.55	0.55	0.55	—	$
Debt/GDP	32.73	42.25	89.33	30.32	—	%
Deficit/GDP	1.98	2.18	4.67	1.62	—	%

Note: For these exercise (as in Masson and Turtleboom, 1997), we quote the Dollar-Euro exchange rate in terms of Deutsche Marks (i.e. in the baseline 1DM = 0.55$). These rates can, if desired, be recomputed into the Euro using the known and irrevocably EMU conversion rate of 1• = DM 1.95583.
—, Not applicable.

In constructing these tables we actually ran each stochastic simulation over a 150 year time period, and then discarded the first 15 observations and the last 95 observations from each in order to remove any biases that might possibly arise from starting or finishing each simulation from particular pre-assigned equilibrium values. This is standard practice (e.g. Bryant et al., 1993). Moreover, we also started each country in each of the 400 stochastic simulations in each exercise with an initial deficit ratio of 3%, in order to ensure common initial conditions. Since the Stability Pact aims to create a broad medium-term budgetary balance, we consider countries pursuing a 1% deficit target (i.e. this is the d^* in equation 1).

That said, the technique for generating the stochastic shocks that drive each of the 400 replications in each case, is essentially the method recommended by McCarthy (1972) for reproducing the characteristics of the observed random disturbances of the historical sample period – but adapted for use with rational expectations models. It is described in more detail in the appendix.[3] Thus shocks distributed according to the sample periods distribution of equation residuals are applied to MULTIMOD's behavioural equations for Germany, France, Italy and the UK. In line with Fair (1998), we do not shock policy rules, identities or quasi-identities such as the term structure or uncovered interest parity conditions. So we do not account for the possibility that policy, measurement, or implementation errors may also have contributed to the variations in deficit ratios and the proportion of time that they have exceeded 3%. Our results, therefore, represent the best that policy makers can hope for.

Finally Table 1 reports a baseline or reference path, being a steady state solution of the model with no shocks, and with the default policy rules of money targeting and standard tax rules.

This gives the background against which all other (stochastic) simulation results need to be considered. This steady state simulation was constructed using the IMF's "World Economic Outlook" information set for 1998 and beyond, and shows that the four European countries would, if left to themselves, converge on a long run growth rate of 2.2%; a long run inflation rate of 2.7%; and debt ratios of 33%, 42%, 89% and 30% for Germany, France, Italy and the UK. The long run steady state deficit ratios would be, correspondingly, 2%, 2.2%, 4.7% and 1.6%. Thus the only

Table 2. 3% deficit targets (inflation targeting regime)

	US	GERMANY	FRANCE	ITALY	UK
			GDP GROWTH		
MEAN	2.198	1.707	1.520	1.924	2.271
STD. DEVIATION	0.582	1.128	1.117	1.224	1.350
			INFLATION		
MEAN	2.710	2.560	2.149	2.667	2.899
STD. DEVIATION	0.487	1.250	1.10	1.351	1.371
		SHORT-TERM NOMINAL INTEREST RATE			
MEAN	7.951	8.667	8.667	8.667	8.667
MIN	7.434	7.522	7.522	7.522	7.522
MAX	7.958	11.748	11.748	11.748	11.748
STD. DEVIATION	0.144	1.044	1.044	1.044	1.044
			EXCHANGE RATE		
MEAN	—	0.604	0.604	0.604	0.604
STD. DEVIATION	—	0.059	0.059	0.059	0.059
			DEBT-GDP		
MEAN	—	0.352	0.468	0.944	0.299
STD. DEVIATION	—	0.019	0.055	0.039	0.021
			DEFICIT-GDP		
MEAN	—	0.0311	0.0314	0.0307	0.0302
STD. DEVIATION	—	0.00196	0.0036	0.0048	0.0012
Pr(Deficit-GDP) · 0.03	—	0.800	0.825	0.795	0.800

Note: The probabilities in the final row of this table are calculated according to $\Pr(\cdot) = (T - n/T)$ where T is the time horizon and n the number of occasions that the deficit to GDP ratio is less than 3%. Thus if $n = 0$ ($= T$), the country always (never) violates the Stability Pact ceiling – or, in probability terms, $\Pr(\cdot) = 1(0)$.
—, Not applicable.

differences in underlying performances would be on the fiscal side; not in output, inflation or investment. Monetary conditions are, however, rather tighter than those actually experienced in the first year of EMU because the control rule is tighter; and because the external events which have led to a higher dollar/lower Euro have not been modelled. However those differences play no role in what follows since every other simulation is assessed in comparison with this one; that is with the same underlying baseline and information set, so that any such changes/omissions "wash out".

IV. The Simulation Results: General Characteristics

We now consider the stochastic simulation results reported in Tables 2–7. Each represents a different deficit target rule and/or monetary policy reaction function. Tables 2 and 3 consider 3% deficit targets for everybody (except the US), with inflation targeting or a Taylor to generate monetary policy. Tables 5 and 6 do the same with 1% deficit targets.

Table 3. 3% deficit targets (standard Taylor rule)

	US	GERMANY	FRANCE	ITALY	UK
			GDP GROWTH		
MEAN	2.203	1.719	1.522	1.931	2.289
STD. DEVIATION	0.582	1.126	1.116	1.224	1.344
			INFLATION		
MEAN	2.711	2.573	2.151	2.686	2.910
STD. DEVIATION	0.498	1.254	1.101	1.35	1.391
		SHORT-TERM NOMINAL INTEREST RATE			
MEAN	7.821	8.640	8.640	8.640	8.640
MIN	7.413	7.512	7.512	7.512	7.512
MAX	7.960	11.720	11.720	11.720	11.720
STD. DEVIATION	0.143	1.050	1.050	1.050	1.050
		NOMINAL EXCHANGE RATE			
MEAN	—	0.600	0.600	0.600	0.600
STD. DEVIATION	—	0.062	0.062	0.062	0.062
			DEBT-GDP		
MEAN	—	0.350	0.465	0.942	0.300
STD. DEVIATION	—	0.019	0.053	0.041	0.025
			DEFICIT-GDP		
MEAN	—	0.0309	0.0314	0.0307	0.0308
STD. DEVIATION	—	0.00194	0.0036	0.0049	0.0012
Pr(Deficit-GDP) · 0.03	—	0.800	0.825	0.795	0.800

—, Not applicable.

Finally the last row in each of these tables quotes the proportion of times that each country exceeded the permitted 3% deficit limit in the given set up, and hence the probability that that country would attract a Stability Pact fine if it were to adopt the associated deficit targets, and tax and monetary policy rules.

General Characteristics of the 3% Deficit Targets Regime

As far as the first two stochastic simulations are concerned (Tables 2 and 3, with 3% deficit targets for all Euro countries), there appears to be little difference between the monetary policy rules. The 3% deficit targets remain well within reach; and the stability of those outcomes (as measured by their standard deviations) is broadly similar as well. The main problem appears to be that, even with an aggressive tax reaction whenever the deficit ratio exceeds 3%, the probability of violating the stability and attracting a fine remains high at 80%. This asymmetry (a symmetric distribution would imply a 50% probability of excessive deficits) implies two things. First there is (or "was" since the shocks applied to the model are historically consistent) an underlying expansionary bias in fiscal policy to compensate the tight monetary policies and contain adverse shocks and spillovers from elsewhere. That was evident in the baseline. Second, because fiscal policies focus on current and past deficits, it is hard for the fiscal authorities to be forward looking and prevent an excessive build up of deficits in the future. If they cannot do that, they need to

Table 4. Comparisons between inflation target and Taylor rule for 3% deficit targets

	US	GERMANY	FRANCE	ITALY	UK
			GDP GROWTH		
MEAN	0.9977	0.993	0.9987	0.9964	0.9921
STD. DEVIATION	1	1.0018	1.0009	1	1.0045
			INFLATION		
MEAN	0.9996	0.9949	0.9991	0.9929	0.9962
STD. DEVIATION	0.9779	0.9968	0.9991	1.0007	0.9856
			SHORT-TERM NOMINAL INTEREST RATE		
MEAN	1.0166	1.0031	1.0031	1.0031	1.0031
STD. DEVIATION	1.007	0.9943	0.9943	0.9943	0.9943
			EXCHANGE RATE		
MEAN	—	1.0067	1.0067	1.0067	1.0067
STD. DEVIATION	—	0.9516	0.9516	0.9516	0.9516
			DEBT-GDP		
MEAN	—	1.0057	1.0065	1.0021	0.9967
STD. DEVIATION	—	1	1.0377	0.9512	0.84
			DEFICIT-GDP		
MEAN	—	1.0065	1	1	0.9805
STD. DEVIATION	—	1.0103	1	0.9796	1

—, Not applicable.

operate a "safety cushion" – in particular because most fiscal decisions are taken well in advance and do not typically possess the flexibility of monetary policy actions.

Comparisons of Inflation and Taylor rule at 3% Deficit Targets In Tables 4 and 7 we normalise on the inflation-targeting regime and employ a simple constructed metric, which compares the ratio of mean performances across Inflation Targeting and Taylor monetary rules. If $\Gamma > 1$ (< 1) the values (i.e. mean and standard deviation of some variable x) in the Inflation-Targeting rule are above (below) those of the Taylor rule:

$$\Gamma = \begin{cases} \dfrac{\bar{x}^{\text{Inflation}}}{\bar{x}^{\text{Taylor}}} \\ \dfrac{\sigma_x^{\text{Inflation}}}{\sigma_x^{\text{Taylor}}} \end{cases} \qquad \Gamma \in (0, \infty]$$

The precise comparisons between the inflation and Taylor rule can be seen in the comparison table, i.e. Table 4. Although, at first, the results are not dramatic, a clear pattern emerges.

We can see that for all countries average growth and inflation are higher under a Taylor rule than under an inflation target. This expansionary bias of the Taylor rule is driven by cheaper average monetary policy as witnessed by the lower short-term nominal interest rates and Euro (vis-à-vis the US Dollar). This is also reflected in a better performance of the fiscal ratios because output growth is higher – for all countries (except the UK) the operation of the Taylor rule implies a lower debt ratio.

Table 5. 1% deficit targets (inflation target regime)

	US	GERMANY	FRANCE	ITALY	UK
			GDP GROWTH		
MEAN	2.021	1.103	0.912	0.650	0.753
STD. DEVIATION	0.583	1.326	1.260	1.411	1.422
			INFLATION		
MEAN	2.740	1.550	1.321	1.743	1.753
STD. DEVIATION	0.502	1.410	1.820	1.513	1.653
			SHORT-TERM NOMINAL INTEREST RATE		
MEAN	7.211	7.803	7.803	7.803	7.803
MIN	6.804	7.023	7.023	7.023	7.023
MAX	7.864	8.101	8.101	8.101	8.101
STD. DEVIATION	0.140	0.621	0.621	0.621	0.621
			NOMINAL EXCHANGE RATE		
MEAN	—	0.584	0.584	0.584	0.584
STD. DEVIATION	—	0.052	0.052	0.052	0.052
			DEBT-GDP		
MEAN	—	0.281	0.371	0.804	0.241
STD. DEVIATION	—	0.020	0.053	0.050	0.035
			DEFICIT-GDP		
MEAN	—	0.0109	0.0111	0.0152	0.0148
STD. DEVIATION	—	0.0027	0.0035	0.005	0.0061
Pr(Deficit-GDP)·0.03	—	0.150	0.150	0.220	0.241

—, Not applicable.

Similarly for deficits in three out of four cases the deficit ratio is either lower under a Taylor rule or (as for France and Italy) at least just as good. However these differences are not strong enough to translate into different stability pact success probabilities for any of the Euro economies.

If we consider higher moments (i.e. performance on standard deviations) the picture changes a little. Growth is less variable under a Taylor rule but inflation is more variable when both are compared to the inflation-targeting regime. Similarly the variability of monetary policy (i.e. the interest and exchange rate) is higher under a Taylor rule than an inflation one. So Taylor rules are more interventionist. Finally the fiscal ratios are generally lower with a Taylor rule than under an inflation target.

What these results seem to suggest is that an inflation-targeting rule produces lower growth and inflation and a more aggressive monetary policy reaction. An inflation target regime also stabilises nominal variables generally better than a Taylor rule. The latter stabilises the real variables better.

1% Deficit Targets If, instead, the policy makers set their deficit targets at 1% of GDP (compared to a baseline of 3%), we get more magnified differences. Under a Taylor rule, there is a significant-monetary easing to compensate the tighter fiscal policies, compared to the inflation-targeting regime. This eases interest rates (_% point), lowers the Euro (6%) and allows slightly higher inflation. Yet, in both cases, the European freedom of monetary action is closely constrained by US interest rates.

Table 6. Deficit targets (standard Taylor rule)

	US	GERMANY	FRANCE	ITALY	UK
			GDP GROWTH		
MEAN	2.001	1.203	1.056	0.810	0.915
STD. DEVIATION	0.583	1.262	1.221	1.410	1.324
			INFLATION		
MEAN	2.703	1.712	1.516	1.854	1.912
STD. DEVIATION	0.501	1.441	1.921	1.624	1.854
			SHORT-TERM NOMINAL INTEREST RATE		
MEAN	7.203	7.215	7.215	7.215	7.215
MIN	6.776	6.400	6.400	6.400	6.400
MAX	7.855	7.950	7.950	7.950	7.950
STD. DEVIATION	0.173	0.760	0.760	0.760	0.760
			NOMINAL EXCHANGE RATE		
MEAN	—	0.553	0.553	0.553	0.553
STD. DEVIATION	—	0.069	0.069	0.069	0.069
			DEBT-GDP		
MEAN	—	0.277	0.368	0.771	0.231
STD. DEVIATION	—	0.022	0.055	0.066	0.039
			DEFICIT-GDP		
MEAN	—	0.011	0.011	0.015	0.015
STD. DEVIATION	—	0.003	0.004	0.007	0.006
Pr(Deficit-GDP) · 0.03	—	0.130	0.135	0.190	0.210

—, Not applicable.

In no case, for example, do mean Euro interest rates fall below those of the US. That imposes a long-term constraint on the Euro Area, in that they may not be able to relax monetary policy as much as they would like – much as we have seen in the first year of EMU's life. But that constraint is stronger under inflation targeting, where the inflationary consequences of a Euro depreciation acts as an effective breaking mechanism.

The Taylor rule also shows lower volatility in growth, at least for Germany and the UK, and avoids the worst of the output slumps for all four economies. But it produces slightly more variability in inflation on the upside. Thus it is more effective in avoiding deflations, but less effective for containing inflationary pressures. And the Taylor rule also uses interest rate changes more vigorously, and that slows investment. Thus there will be considerable interaction between the impacts of fiscal and monetary policies under the Stability Pact, whatever monetary rule is used.

But to reach a judgement on which policy rule is more desirable must depend on what you want (or need) to achieve. A Taylor rule outperforms inflation targeting during a slowdown or large fiscal contraction, but not otherwise. And there is an obvious trade off between deficit control- and output losses when extremely low deficit ratios (compared to baseline) are targeted. These trade offs cannot be avoided, it seems. Moreover there are relatively few country differences – at least until we come to low deficit targets, whereupon the losses in output appear to be skewed against the traditionally higher inflation countries (the UK and Italy). The main

Table 7. Comparisons between inflation target and Taylor rule for 1% deficit targets

	US	GERMANY	FRANCE	ITALY	UK
			GDP GROWTH		
MEAN	1.01	0.9169	0.8636	0.8025	0.823
STD. DEVIATION	1	1.0507	1.0319	1.0007	1.074
			INFLATION		
MEAN	1.0137	0.9054	0.8714	0.9401	0.9168
STD. DEVIATION	1.002	0.9785	0.9474	0.9317	0.8916
			SHORT-TERM NOMINAL INTEREST RATE		
MEAN	1.0011	1.0815	1.0815	1.0815	1.0815
STD. DEVIATION	0.8092	0.8171	0.8171	0.8171	0.8171
			EXCHANGE RATE		
MEAN	—	1.0561	1.0561	1.0561	1.0561
STD. DEVIATION	—	0.7536	0.7536	0.7536	0.7536
			DEBT-GDP		
MEAN	—	1.0144	1.0082	1.0428	1.0433
STD. DEVIATION	—	0.9091	0.9636	0.7576	0.8974
			DEFICIT-GDP		
MEAN	—	0.9909	1.0091	1.0133	0.9867
STD. DEVIATION	—	0.9	0.875	0.7143	1.0167

—, Not applicable.

problem however is that, despite an increase in the fiscal cushion, the probability of violating the Stability Pact has still not been reduced to a very low level. We still have single period probabilities of 15% to 24% of going beyond the 3% limit, even with these much lower deficit targets. The best that can be said is that the Taylor rule is a little less risky.

V. Conclusions

This paper has tackled a simple but important question. Do different monetary strategies matter for the achievement of Stability Pact? The answer – given the outcomes of our stochastic simulations – suggest that they do; even if enacted independently from fiscal authorities and fiscal objectives, different monetary policy rules can support Stability and Growth Pact objectives in a significant way.

In this paper, we analysed two monetary feed back rules dominant in the literature: a Taylor rule and an inflation-target. In both cases, following fiscal corrections, there is monetary easing. In the inflation target case, this reflects the less inflationary environment following the fiscal tightening. Such an outcome precludes the need for a monetary tightening. In the Taylor rule case, the relaxation is stems more directly from the real side since the output gap worsens in the fiscal contraction requiring lower interest rates to compensate.

Along with this easing comes a depreciation of the nominal exchange rate. However the degree of monetary easing differs substantially across regimes and this difference is more acute the "tougher" is the fiscal regime. In the Taylor rule the bias is always more towards looser money as the fiscal tightening constrains the real side. This regime typically leads to higher inflation, more nominal but less real variability and a largely better fiscal performance because growth profiles are better maintained. With an inflation target, the output effects of the fiscal contraction again leads to a monetary easing, but the implied fall in the exchange rate leads to inflation through the channel of higher import prices. To stop this, the monetary response would have to be more aggressive in preventing the fall in the exchange rate in the first place. As a result inflation and nominal variability is lower in an inflation target regime (compared to a Taylor rule) and interest rates (real and nominal) and the exchange rate are higher. However the performance of the real side accordingly worsens.

Nevertheless, the average of Euro interest rates (nominal and real) exceeds that of the US in all cases. It is only in the case where we have 1% deficit targets and a Taylor rule than Euro can achieve slightly lower interest rates over at least some of the horizon. This is a remarkable result since it is the Euro Area rather than the US block which is engaging in the fiscal retrenchment. In the model, this result is undoubtedly driven by the UIP closure for the exchange rate (i.e. that average nominal interest rates are bound by those of the large economy, see McAdam, 1999) but it also reflects the practical upshot of a world of perfect capital mobility where even tough stability pact arrangements cannot be systematically compensated by looser monetary policy. This only serves to make the design and accommodation of monetary policy (and our discussion of them) even more important.

Notes

1. Stochastic simulations have been a common way to analyse EMU-related issues (e.g. Hughes-Hallett, Minford and Rastogi, 1993 and European Commission, 1990). Deterministic analysis of stability pact arrangments may be found in Hughes-Hallett and McAdam (1998, 1999).
2. Fuller results are available on request.
3. Efficient stochastic simulation and control of forward-looking non-linear models is discussed extensively in Holly and Hughes Hallett (1989) and McAdam and Hughes Hallett (1999).
4. Specifically, we have the historical variance co-variance matrix for Germany, France, Italy and the UK covering the following variables: Money, Capital, Consumption, Consumption of Oil, Exports of Manufacturing, Imports, Imports of Oil, GNP Deflator, Real Human Wealth, Price of Imports, Price of Manufacturing Exports. This yields a 44 × 44 co-variance matrix.
5. We choose the model's own (World Economic Outlook) database horizon for these estimations: 1974 to 1998.
6. As is standard, we added a small factor (1e-010) to the diagonal of this matrix to preclude singularity.
7. We use the *Stacked Time* algorithms to simulate the model, see Juillard et al (1998). In practice the STACK for the stochastic simulation is set well in advance of the actual simulation horizon in order to remove the end-point problem. We stack for 150 annual periods, which is sufficient to satisfy the terminal and steady state properties of the model.

References

Artis, M. and M. Buti (2000) 'Close to Balance or in Surplus: A policy makers guide to the Implementation of the Stability and Growth Pact', Discussion Paper No. 2515, Centre for Economic Policy Research, London.

Bryant, R., P. Hooper and C. Mann (eds). (1993) *Evaluating Policy Regimes*, The Brookings Institute, Washington DC.
European Commission (1990) 'One Market. One Money'. *European Economy*. 44. Official Publications. Luxembourg.
Fair, R.C. (1998) 'Estimated Stabilisation Costs of EMU', *National Institute Economic Review*, April, 164, 90–99.
Holly, S and A.J. Hughes Hallett (1989) *Optimal control, expectations and uncertainty* Cambridge University Press.
Hughes Hallett A.J. and P. McAdam (1998) 'Fiscal Deficit Reductions in Line with the Maastricht Criteria: An Empirical Analysis.' in Jeffry Frieden, Daniel Gros and Erik Jones, (Eds.), *The New Political Economy of EMU*. Boulder: Rowman and Littlefield. pp. 83–123.
Hughes Hallett, A.J. and P. McAdam (1999) 'Implications of the Growth and Stability Pact: Why the Growth Element is Important', A.J. Hughes Hallett, M. Hutchison and S.E. Hougaard Jensen (Eds.), *Fiscal Aspects of European Monetary Integration*, Cambridge University Press.
Hughes Hallett. A.J.P. Minford and A. Rastogi (1993) 'The European Monetary System: achievements and survival'. in Bryant. R., P. Hooper and Mann (Eds.). *Evaluating Policy Regimes*. The Brookings Institute. Washington DC.
Juillard, M., D. Laxton, P. McAdam and H. Pioro (1998) 'An Algorithm Competition: First-Order Iterations versus Newton-based Techniques', *Journal of Economic Dynamics and Control*, 22, pp. 1291–1318.
Laxton, D., P. Isard, H. Faruqee, E. Prasad, and B. Turtleboom (1998) 'MULTIMOD Mark III: The Core Dynamic and Steady State Models', IMF Occasional Paper No. 164, Washington DC.
Masson, P and B. Turtleboom (1997) 'Characteristics of the Euro, the demand for reserves and policy co-ordination under EMU', IMF Working Paper No. WP/ 97/ 58, Washington D.C., May 1997.
Masson, P, S Symansky and G Meredith (1990) 'Multimod Mark II: A Revised And Extended Model', IMF Occasional Paper 71, Washinton DC.
McAdam, P. (1999), 'The long Run in Macro Models: A Guide', in *Analyses in Macroeconomic Modelling*, edited by A. J. Hughes-Hallett and Peter McAdam, Kluwer Academic Press.
McAdam, P. and A. Hughes Hallett (1999), 'Nonlinearity, Computational Complexity and Macroeconomic Modelling', *Journal of Economic Surveys*, 13, 577–618.
McCarthy, M (1972) 'Appendix' on p. 392 of B.G. Hickman (ed) 'Economic Models of Cyclical Behaviour', *NBER Studies of Income and Wealth*, vols I and II, Columbia University Press, New York, NY.
Mitchell, P., J. Sault, P.N. Smith and K.F. Wallis (1998) 'Comparing Global Economic Models', *Economic Modelling*, 15, 1–48.
Salmon, M. (1982) 'Error Correction Mechanisms', *Economic Journal*, 92, 615–29.
Sargent, T And N. Wallace (1981) 'Some Unpleasant Monetarist Arithmetic', *Federal Reserve Bank Of Minneapolis Quarterly Review*, 5, 1–17.
von Hagen, J., A. Hughes Hallett, R. Perotti and R. Strauch (2000) 'Budgetary Consolidation in EMU', report submitted to the European Commission (DG II), June 2000.
Woodford, Michael (1995) 'Price-Level Determinacy without Control of a Monetary Aggregate', *Carnegie Rochester Conference Series on Public Policy*, 43(0), December, 1–46.

Appendix

METHODOLOGY FOR PERFORMING STOCHASTIC SIMULATIONS

Given the residuals from the estimated behavioural equations of the model[4] (denoted U) we derived the shocks or innovations (denoted by v) in the residual process by performing the following filter over a historical horizon:[5]

$$U_t = \alpha_0 + \sum_{i=1}^{I} \alpha_i U_{t-i} + \alpha_{I+1} t + v_t$$

Where t is a linear time trend and I is chosen to ensure white noise error processes. These innovations (v_t) were then used to create a variance co-variance matrix, C. A Choleski decomposition was then performed on C, generating the lower-triangle matrix, L.

$$LL' = C$$

From a random number generator we generate drawings from a standard normal distribution, k, $k \sim N(0, 1)$. The actual shocks then applied to the model (v_t^*) are drawn from the pre-multiplication of the decomposition of the historical variances and the random number generated:[6]

$$v^* = Lk$$

These drawings have the same historical properties of the original historical co-variance matrix (McCarthy, 1972):

$$E\,(v^* v^{*\prime}) = C.$$

Thus, having drawn up the appropriate matrix of historical innovations, we can then set up a replication procedure with the same stochastic properties as the model exhibited in the sample period. For each vector of shocks at period t, the model is simulated from the start date to the date of the simulation period,[7] and agents form expectations of the future based on their information set at t. We then make the transition to period $t + 1$ and update the information set and repeat over the whole replication sample. So for each replication, a set shocks are drawn, the model is simulated, time is advanced and then another set of shocks drawn and so on. The agents' information set (at t) contains all data up to and including t (that is, including any expectations formed at t).

10. Unemployment, Wage Developments and the Economic Policy Mix in Europe

STEFAN COLLIGNON
Head of Directorate EUROPE, Federal Ministry of Finance, Wilhelmstraße T97, 10117 Berlin, Germany; E-mail: Stefan.Collignon@bmf.bund.de

With the start of European Monetary Union, questions about the optimal policy mix in the euro area have gained prominence, especially against the background of persistent high unemployment. Monetary policy is now centrally controlled by the independent European Central Bank (ECB), whose primary objective is to maintain price stability. Yet, most other policy responsibilities remain at the national level, notably fiscal policy and wage bargaining. Traditionally, the issue of the policy mix has focused on the interaction between monetary and budget policies.[1] But in view of Europe's high unemployment, it is necessary to bring wage developments into the picture (Welfens and Jungmittag, 1997). Most of the literature on EMU and labour markets focuses on the need for structural reforms in order to increase flexibility,[2] but little has been said on wage bargaining. At an institutional level, the European Council in Cologne in June 1999 complemented structural reform policies pursued in the labour (Luxembourg-process) and product markets (Cardiff-process) by a Macroeconomic Dialogue (Cologne-process) which involves wage bargainers, governments and the ECB. Its purpose is to increase economic growth and employment. However, the theoretical foundations for integrating wage bargaining into the policy mix are not always clear. This paper aims at contributing to such a theory, first by looking at some of the theoretical questions involved in the dominant view, followed by considerations of capital accumulation and finally some policy conclusions.

I. Wages and the Labour Market in the Short-Term Perspective

Wage developments were introduced to macroeconomics through the Phillips curve. Labour market equilibrium is determined by an upward sloping supply curve and a labour demand curve that reflects the marginal product of labour. Modern developments have shifted the focus to wage bargaining and the concept of the non-accelerating inflation rate of unemployment (NAIRU). Both theories primarily focus on labour market rigidities for the explanation of unemployment, rejecting a lasting role for monetary policy in the fight against unemployment. However, by bringing investment into a model of wage and price developments, it can be shown that money can matter also in the long run.[3]

* The author works in the German Ministry of Finance. However the views expressed in this paper are purely personal.

A. H. Hallett et al. (eds), Challenges for Economic Policy Coordination with European Monetary Union, 183–192.

THE NEOCLASSICAL SYNTHESIS

In its simplest form, the Keynesian-neoclassical-monetarist synthesis can be summarised as follows:[4]

$$y^* = F(K, L) \quad F_K, F_L < 0; \quad F_{KK}, F_{LL} < 0 \tag{1a}$$

$$y = y^D(g, M^S/P) \tag{1b}$$

$$\acute{y} = y - y^* \tag{1c}$$

$$\Delta w = \Delta p^e + \Delta h + \alpha \acute{y} \quad \alpha > 0 \tag{2}$$

$$\Delta p = \Delta w - \Delta h + \Delta c \tag{3}$$

$$u = f(\acute{y}) \quad u^* = f(0), \quad f' < 0. \tag{4}$$

The first equation (1a) represents aggregate supply (potential output) as a function of capital and labour. Equation (1b) is aggregate demand in the IS-LMequilibrium, where g stands for the budget deficit and M^S/P for real money holdings. Equation (1c) stands for excess demand or the output gap. Equation (2) is the expectations-augmented Phillips curve with Δh as productivity growth, and Equation (3) reflects mark-up pricing with Δc as the change in the average mark-up on labour cost.

Equation (4) relates (un-)employment to output. When actual output is equal to potential ($\acute{y} = 0$), unemployment is at its natural rate. It is important to note that this labour market equilibrium depends on a crucial assumption: labour demand is determined by the marginal product of labour, implying that the capital stock is constant – presumably because it is at its steady state equilibrium. When we abandon this premise, we obtain very different results. Because of Equations (2) and (3), $\acute{y} = 0$ implies that in the steady state expected equals actual inflation, so that both the rate of inflation and the size of the mark-up are constant. Real wages grow at the rate of labour productivity and the wage share is stationary. Money supply increases at the same rate as steady inflation plus potential output. Furthermore, if potential output is determined by the production function (1a), monetary policy will in the long run only determine inflation. In the short term, however, it affects aggregate demand (1b), and real wages and mark-ups may deviate from the steady state. Expected real wages will then vary procyclically ($\alpha > 0$) and the mark-up anticyclically, because wage bargainers respond to slack and tightness in the labour market. Hence, money is neutral in the long run, but not in the short run. Output effects are only temporary, while unemployment always returns to its long run "natural" level (u^*), which is defined as the labour market equilibrium where inflation does not accelerate.

THE NAIRU-MODEL

In the 1980s and 1990s unemployment remained abnormally high, and deviations of actual from the natural rate appeared to be more persistent than seemed compatible with the neoclassical synthesis. The NAIRU-model was an attempt to explain this new phenomenon through the structures and behaviour of wage bargains. The new theory also aimed at providing microfoundations to the macro-phenomenon of unemployment. It was assumed that *firms* set prices as a mark-up on wage costs (unit labour costs) and wages are set by *trade unions* as a mark-up over the reservation wage (Layard, Nickell and Jackman, 1991, 1994). If these two mark-ups are inconsistent, the rate of inflation accelerates, because this "is the mechanism that reconciles the struggle for shares of the national cake, by cheating both price-setters (capitalists) and wage setters of what they intend" (Layard, Nickell and Jackman, 1994, p. 28). Equilibrium is achieved when both actors settle for a wage share (or profit mark-up) that is consistent with their expectations. The variable that brings about this result is unemployment. The persistence of high unemployment is then due to rigidities in the labour market which prevent wage setters from lowering real wages to the "consistent" level.

The NAIRU-model can be formulated in terms of Equations (1)–(4) as:

$$p - w^e = c - h + \alpha_1 \acute{y} \quad \alpha_1 \geq 0 \tag{5a}$$

$$w - p^e = ws + h + \alpha_2 \acute{y} \quad \alpha_2 > 0. \tag{5b}$$

Equation (5b) is the wage setting equation. Trade unions are assumed to aim for a wage share $(w - p - h)$ that increases with excess demand $(\alpha_2 \acute{y})$. The average or stationary wage share (ws), which is the long term objective of trade unions, is often supposed to be determined by a generous social system (minimum wages, replacement ratio, duration of unemployment benefits etc.) and by trade union power.[5] The latter extends to "insider" power where the competition from unemployed "outsiders" does not lower wages to the level where the required profit margin can be realised. However, as Hahn and Solow (1995) have shown, the reason why wages do not come down despite excess labour supply may have to do less with labour market structures than with simple considerations of fairness.

Equation (5a) is the price setting equation. If $\alpha_1 = 0$, normal or constant mark-up pricing under perfect competition is the rule. However, usually the mark-up is derived from imperfect competition, oligopolistic models and near-rationality theories (Carlin and Soskice, 1990) and is a function of the firm's market power. It is seen as a more or less fixed add-on to marginal cost and is independent of capital cost. Again this argument is only valid in the short run when the capital stock is constant.

When $\acute{y} = 0$ and actual prices and wages equal expectations, we have the equilibrium wage share $ws = w - p - h$. The profit mark-up c is then the reciprocal of the wage share, hence $ws = -c$. Thus, in equilibrium price-setters (5a) and wage-setters (5b) agree on the distribution of national income and both price and wage expectations are realised. If, however, prices diverge from expectations, and we assume that price and wage surprises are similar, then we obtain, given $\Delta p = \pi_t$ and rational expectations $p^e - p_{t-1} = \pi_{t-1}$:

$$\Delta\pi = \frac{\alpha_1 + \alpha_2}{2}\acute{y} + \frac{c + ws}{2}. \tag{6}$$

Hence, as before, inflation is non-accelerating at the natural rate of unemployment $[u^* = f(0)]$, with $ws = -c$. But while inflation dynamics in the Phillips curve model are aggregated in α, they are now separated in product and labour market elasticities. It is clear that the higher price flexibility (α_1) and real wage flexibility (α_2), the higher is the inflationary impact of excess demand. Thus, in this simple model, real rigidities support price stability ($\alpha_1 + \alpha_2$ are low), but they also make disinflation more expensive in terms of output loss. Because it is usually assumed that $\alpha_1 < \alpha_2$, focusing on labour market reforms and real wage elasticity takes precedence over product market flexibility when addressing employment issues. If, however, the income shares resulting from wage bargainers' objectives are inconsistent, so that $c + ws \neq 0$, inflation will not remain constant, and output ($\acute{y}$) would have to adjust in order to stabilise price developments. Consequently, if labour markets are inflexible in the sense that they do not adjust flexibly to the required profit share, unemployment will remain persistently high and the NAIRU will exceed the "natural" rate. Put differently, a central bank aiming to stabilise prices has to keep money tight so that the resulting negative output gaps will slow down or stabilise inflation.

Evidence seems to support the model when comparing the economies of Europe to the USA. While the ratio of positive to negative output gaps measured by OECD (1998) over the last 20 years was 11:9 in the USA, it was only 5:15 for the euro area and 4:16 for Germany. Hence the model must conclude that labour market rigidities and the excessive welfare state in Europe should have been the cause for high and persistent unemployment in the EU. However, the explanation is one-sided. As Solow (1998, 1999) has pointed out, European unemployment has risen in shock waves that cannot be correlated with structural changes in the labour market. If anything, European markets have become *more* flexible in the 1990s, not less. Why, then, is Europe's natural unemployment so high?

II. Wages and Capital Accumulation: The Long Term Perspective

The NAIRU approach gives prominence to labour market structures and a microeconomic interpretation of the profit mark-up under the assumption of a fixed capital stock. It does not take into account the effects of stabilisation policy for investment and the development of productive capacities which are necessary to achieve full employment. If we abandon the idea of a fixed capital stock, the demand for labour not only changes with the real wage (which equals the marginal product of labour), but also with capital accumulation.

THE INVESTMENT FUNCTION

Abstracting from technological progress, we can interprete (1a) in a simple neoclassical growth model. Potential output is on the balanced growth path when actual investment equals the (net) increase of the capital stock required to keep the labour force growing at its natural rate. Hence, we must specify an investment function. We will use a simple form taken from Tobin and Brainard (1977):

$$\frac{I}{PK} = n^* + \Phi[q(i) - 1]. \tag{7}$$

Here, n^* is the rate of growth of the labour force and $q(i)$ is Tobin's q. When $q(i) = 1$, capital accumulation proceeds at its balanced growth path. However, this does not necessarily imply full employment. For if the capital stock at any point in time happens to be lower than what is required to absorb the given labour force, the resulting unemployment will become "natural" if the capital stock grows from now on at the rate n^*. Thus the natural rate of unemployment is not exogenous, but path-dependent. This is a very simple explanation for hysteresis in unemployment.

Hence, we need a theory to explain the deviations of $q(i)$ from 1.

We can start with simple national accounting identities. Total factor income is:

$$P^*Y^* = WL + rP_kK = C + S^e, \tag{8a}$$

where W is the wage rate, L employment, P_kK the value at which capital was purchased at the previous period and r the net cost of capital, equal to its normal rate of return.[6] Of course, factor income is identical to total consumption and planned savings. However, the absorption of output consists of consumption and investment:

$$PY = C + I. \tag{8b}$$

The difference between actual and factor income are aggregate excess profits, reflecting a disequilibrium between saving and investment (Keynes, 1930):

$$Q = PY - P^*Y^* = I - S^e. \tag{8c}$$

This is not the same as the output gap, because excess demand is defined in volume terms in Equation (1c) and in value terms in Equation (8c). Yet, what matters for capital accumulation are profits and they are defined in value terms. These Keynesian Q-profits can be transformed into Tobin's q.[7] The latter is defined as the ratio of the market value of the enterprise to capital replacement cost, or simply the ratio of the internal rate of return of an investment project to the risk-free money market interest rate (Bofinger et al., 1996, p. 556).[8] Thus, when entrepreneurs expect to realise a profit on productive investment above the risk-free interest rate i, they borrow money, rise aggregate investment above the level of expected savings and therefore realise in aggregate the return they expect. Formally the q-ratio is

$$q = \frac{1+i_K}{1+i} = \frac{1+i_K - E(\pi)}{(1+i-\pi_t)} \sim \frac{R}{r} \quad q_i < 0, \quad q(i^*) = 1, \tag{9}$$

where i_K is the internal rate of return, R the expected real return on investment and $r = i - \pi_t$ the real short-term interest rate. π_t is the current rate of inflation and $E^*(\pi)$ is the expected average rate over the life of the capital equipment. Entrepreneurs compare the rate of return from productive investment to alternative investment opportunities in risk-free domestic monetary assets. Hence the investor's portfolio is in equilibrium at $q = 1$.[9] In models with neo-classical production functions like Equation (1a), R is equivalent to the marginal product of capital (F_K), a technical variable dependent on the size of the capital stock.

With diminishing returns, investment will be determined by the growth of the capital stock to the point where the marginal product of capital ($F_K \equiv R$) is equal to r and $q = 1$. Hence, q represents entrepreneurial quasi-rents or excess profits which tend to disappear over time if interest rates remain unchanged. The speed of this arbitrage depends on the cost of adjustment: if these costs were zero, q would instantaneously jump to 1. Once the capital stock has adjusted, the prevailing interest is the "natural rate of interest" (i^*) and $q(i) = q(i^*) = 1$. It corresponds to the natural rate of unemployment.

MONETARY POLICY

We will now assume that the risk-free monetary interest rate (i) is set exogenously by the central bank. This simplification can be justified under ceteris paribus conditions.[10] It follows from Equation (9) that a rise in short-term interest rates (i) will lower q and inversely. Therefore a change in monetary policy will change the desired portfolio allocation of assets, and this will ultimately affect the volume of productive investment.[11] Consequently, the level of the capital stock and, at given technology, of employment is no longer independent of interest rates and ultimately of the central bank.

The question is then, what determines the interest rate policy of the central bank? The answer is, of course: the objective of price stability. Therefore we must show how interest rates affect the aggregate price level. By inserting Equation (8c) into Equation (8a) and dividing by Y^* we obtain the aggregate price equation:

$$P = W/H + rq(i)P_k K/Y^*, \tag{10}$$

with $H = Y/L$ as labour productivity. Thus the *price level* responds to excess profits resulting from interest rate deviations from the equilibrium rate $q(i^*) = 1$.

This set of the two Equations (7) and (10) form what we may call a monetary-Keynesian model. It provides us with a theory for the average profit mark-up which is only dependent on capital markets. Dividing P by unit labour cost ($W = H$), assuming $P = P_k$, and taking logs, we get the average profit mark-up:[12]

$$p - w + h = \ln(1 + rqK/Y), \tag{11}$$

which is again the inverse of the wage share.

Under neoclassical assumptions q is always unity and the mark-up c is exclusively a function of the cost of capital per unit of output. It can therefore be treated as exogenous. With a Keynesian investment function, q can deviate from unit value as a consequence of portfolio shifts in asset markets. Monetary policy will affect both, investor's portfolio decisions and capital costs. This has important implications for policy.

1. Because the average profit mark-up is determined by capital markets, the wage share is independent of labour market developments and wage bargaining. The reason is that a change in the interest rate (i) will shift the aggregate price level initially and thereby change the wage share. As investment and competition respond to excess demand, the price level returns to its steady state path where $q = 1$. If capital costs remain unaffected, the wage share and the average profit mark-up return to their original value. Otherwise they are stationary around the long term trend set by capital markets.[13]
2. The time path of the price level is determined by two factors: unit labour cost and the average profit mark-up. Given that the profit mark-up is stationary, the price level is also stationary around the trend which is determined by unit labour cost. Hence wage bargaining is important not for the determination of the wage share, but because it sets the inflationary trend.

3. Under these conditions, monetary policy must observe two developments: (a) excess profits as reflected in Tobin's q because they will shift the price level up or down; (b) the development of unit labour costs because they determine the inflation trend. In order to maintain price stability, the interaction between (a) and (b) is crucial. As long as unit labour cost do not increase faster than the price objective set by the central bank, there is room for lowering interest rates and stimulating investment and employment. But if nominal wages grow faster than productivity plus the inflation target, monetary policy needs to be tightened. In this case q falls below unit, and net investment becomes negative. Output and employment will fall.
4. However, if subsequently unit labour costs stabilise, and the central bank simply keeps (real) short term interest rates constant, the capital stock will adjust to the new, lower equilibrium level, where $q(i) = 1$. As a consequence the natural rate of unemployment has permanently increased. It will only come down again when (possibly repeated) interest rate cuts have allowed persistent excess profits without unit labour costs increasing at a rate that is incompatible with the central bank's objective for price stability.

III. Conclusions

Our analysis has shown that from a short-term perspective unemployment is a problem of inflexible labour markets. Because the capital stock is assumed fixed, the wage share can only be varied by different wage claims relative to the price level. If, however, the capital stock changes over time as a function of investment, natural unemployment also becomes variable and may exhibit hysteresis. Because investment depends on profits and the portfolio dispositions of investors, policies to improve economic growth and employment must create the perspective for high real returns (R in Equation (9)) and conditions that allow the central bank to lower (real) interest rates. The first set of measures is presently covered in Europe by product market reforms under the Cardiff process and labour market reforms under the Luxembourg process. However, for an optimal policy mix, it will be crucial that wage developments remain consistent with the price objective of the central bank. It is often argued that the United States have better succeeded on both accounts because of higher labour market flexibility. However, the more corporatist models in Europe and Japan used to produce lower unemployment until recently. It seems more likely that Europe's high real interest rates and the overvalued yen in Japan have contributed to these developments than a sudden rigidification of labour market structures. However, in this case, the mix of monetary, fiscal and wage policies will become crucial in creating a new growth dynamic in Europe. The purpose must be to stabilise unit labour costs over time, so that monetary policy can become more accommodative.[14]

More concretely we may derive the following: the ECB has declared that price stability means an inflation rate between 0 and 2%. Assuming that errors are independent and normally distributed, this implies that the actual reference target is 1% inflation with a standard deviation of 1%. Given that average labour productivity has been growing at a deterministic trend of 2%, average European wages should not increase more than 3% p.a. in nominal terms. This leaves Tobin's q an average margin of 1% in the short term without violating the ECB-norm of price stability. However, following such a policy orientation would gradually also reduce capital cost (r) and thereby improve the margin for q over time.

It seems that such a development could explain the "new economics" of the USA. It may also be that this was achieved by "flexible" labour markets as in the US. But Europe is different. Not only in the way labour markets operate, but also because the price stability objective of the ECB appears more ambitious than the Fed's. Given that regional price developments diverge sometimes quite significantly, there exists no intrinsic mechanism to ensure that regional (national) deviations could not push the average above the tolerable limits. This is in particular true for the three or four largest countries in the euro area. Thus, opening a Macroeconomic Dialogue and setting wage bargaining up as a co-operative game has a convincing logic. There is no reason why Europe's culture of social consensus and dialogue could not produce the same or even a better result than atomistically flexible labour markets in the USA.

Notes

1. See notably Hughes Hallett and Yue Ma, 1996; Thygesen, 1996; Gros and Thygesen, 1998; Collignon, 1996; Weale, 1996. For theoretical models see Sargent, 1986; Mead and Weale, 1995.
2. See for example Eichengreen (1993); Jackman (1997).
3. Blanchard (1990) reminds us that the long-run neutrality hypothesis is imposed on models out of theoretical considerations and is a matter of faith rather than empirical evidence.
4. Unless specified differently, small letters indicate logs.
5. At least this is the standard story for Europe. In the USA efficiency wage considerations may prevail. See Layard, Nickell and Jackman, 1994.
6. If the price of capital goods increases at the rate of inflation, $P = P_k(1 + \pi)$, r should be interpreted as the real interest rate at which capital purchases are financed.
7. See Collignon (1998).
8. For simplicity, this definition abstracts from time-varying term premia and default risk.
9. In reality, investment may already stop at an earlier rate, say $\bar{q} > 1$, if a minimum profit rate is required for investment, especially when firms add oligopolistic mark-ups to marginal cost. Because R and r are not easily measured, empirical studies prefer the formula where q is the ratio of the market value of an investment project to the replacement cost. Under certain assumptions the two formulations are identical, but what matters for investment is the q ratio of the margin, i.e., the increment of market valuation for the cost of the associated investment. Average q values for existing capital stock may be quite different from the supposed equilibrium value 1. But at the margin, q should be close to unity (Tobin and Golub, 1998).
10. For a more realistic description, see Goodfriend (1998).
11. At least this is the unambiguous result if we assume R independent from i. For more complex dynamics, see Collignon (1998).
12. If $P = P_k(1 + \pi)$, r should be interpreted as the real interest rate at which capital purchases are financed.
13. Blanchard (1997) has observed the increase in the capital share in Europe, and tried to explain it by shocks to labour supply and demand. As his discussant W. Nordhaus pointed out, he ignores the cost of capital but finds this reasonable in view of "the unprecedented rise in Tobin's q". Our discussion could clarify this point: Even though $q > 1$, the capital share could be fairly stable, as long as r and k/y remain stable. Evidence suggests that European real interest rates

were systematically higher than in the US during the 1990s. Hence the capital share would have risen, even though $q < 1$ over many years.

14. See also Modigliani (1997).

References

Blanchard, O. (1990) 'Why Does Money Affect Output?', in F. Friedman and F.H. Hahn (eds.), *Handbook of Monetary Economics*, Vol. 2, Elsevier Science Publisher, Amsterdam.

Blanchard, O. (1997) *The Medium Run*, Brooking Papers on Economic Activity (2).

Carlin, W. and Soskice, D. (1990) *Macroeconomics and the Wage Bargain*, Oxford University Press, Oxford.

Collignon, S. (1997) 'Unemployment and Monetary Policy in the Single Market: A Dialogue with Franco Modigliani', in S. Collignon (ed.), *European Monetary Policy*, Pinters Publishers, London.

Collignon, S. (1998) *Does the Central Bank Set the Natural Rate of Unemployment?*, Paris AMUE, www.amuel.lf.net.

Eichengreen, B. (1993) 'Labour Markets and European Monetary Unification', in P.R. Masson and M.P. Taylor (eds.), *Policy Issues in the Operation of Currency Unions*, Cambridge University Press, Cambridge.

Goodfriend, M. (1995) 'Acquiring and Maintaining Credibility for Low Inflation: The US Experience', in L. Leiderman and L. Svenson (eds.), *Inflation Target*, Centre for Economic Policy Research (CEPR), London.

Gros, D. and Thygesen, N. (1998), *European Monetary Integration. From the European Monetary System to the European Monetary Union*, 2nd edn, St. Martin's Press/Longman, London.

Hahn, F. and Solow, R. (1995) *A Critical Essay on Modern Macroeconomic Theory*, MIT Press, Cambridge, MA.

Hughes Hallett, A. and Jue Ma (1996) 'Changing Partners: The Importance of Coordinating Fiscal and Monetary Policies within a Monetary Union', *Manchester School* **64**, 115–134.

Jackman, R. (1997) 'EU Labour Market Inside and Outside the Monetary Union', in Paul J.J. Welfens (ed.), *European Monetary Union. Transition, International Impact and Policy Options*, Springer Verlag, Berlin.

Keynes, J.M. (1930) *A Treatise on Money*, Macmillan, London.

Layard, R., Nickell, S. and Jackman, R. (1991) *Unemployment – Macroeconomic Performance and the Labour Market*, Oxford University Press, New York.

Layard, R., Nickell, S. and Jackman, R. (1994) *The Unemployment Crisis*, Oxford University Press, New York.

Meade, J. and Weale, M. (1995) 'Monetary Union and the Assignment Problem', in *Scandinavian Journal of Economics* **97**(2), 201–222.

Modigliani, F. (1997) 'The Shameful Rate of Unemployment in the EMS: Causes and Cures', in S. Collignon (ed.), *European Monetary Policy*, Pinter Publishers, London.

OECD (1998) *Economic Outlook*, December, Paris.

Sargent, Th. (1986) 'Reaganomics and Credibility', in Thomas Sargent (ed.), *Rational Expectations and Inflation* (reprint), Harper and Row Publishers, New York.

Solow, R. (1998) 'How Cautious Must the Fed Be?, in Robert M. Solow and John. B. Taylor (eds.), *Inflation, Unemployment and Monetary Policy*, MIT-Press, Cambridge, MA.

Thygesen, N. (1996) *Monetary Union and the Coordination of National Budgetary Policies*, Mimeo, November.

Thygesen, N. (1996) 'Should Budgetary Policies be Coordinated Further in Economic and Monetary Union – and is that Feasible?', *Banca Nationale del Lavoro Quarterly Review*.

Tobin, J. and Brainard, W. (1977) 'Asset Markets and the Cost of Capital', in J. Tobin (ed.), *Essays in Economics: Theory and Policy*, Vol. 3, MIT Press, Cambridge, MA (1982).

Welfens, P.J.J. and Jungmittag, A. (1997) 'Political Economy of EMU and Stabilization Policy', in Paul J.J. Welfens (ed.), *European Monetary Union. Transition, International Impact and Policy Options*, Springer Verlag, Berlin.

11. Perspectives for Future Economic Policy Coordination within EMU

KURT BAYER
Austrian Ministry of Finance, Himmelpfortgasse 4, A-1015 Wien
E-mail: kurt.bayer@bmf.gv.at

I. Need for and Types of Coordination

There is widespread consensus that the Economic and Monetary Union (EMU) at its outset did not represent an optimal currency area (e.g., Breuss, 1997, 169). Markets within EMU are not perfect. The EU Treaty states that institutions at the community and member states level are called upon to handle economic problems in such a way that the objectives of Art. 2 of the Treaty will be achieved.[1] This can be read to mean that the community and member states institutions' are required to strive for a policy mix conducive to growth and employment, in order to raise the standard of living of EU citizens.[2]

This implies, in turn, that given the institutional setup of macroeconomic policy and the distribution of competences between the EU level and the member states, uncoordinated activities may cause spill-overs, in the form of negative externalities, from one level to another. This might result in undesirable effects. In addition, coordination may also have positive effects, given that the euro area is a large, relatively closed economic space in which (coordinated) policy action will be more effective than in its previously open member states.

The economic argument in favor of economic policy coordination in EMU rests on the following objectives:

- to avoid institutional spillovers
- to avoid regional spillovers
- to create additional benefits for the member countries

With respect to *institutional* spillovers it needs to be mentioned that EMU has a very specific setup of institutions dealing with macroeconomic policy: This refers to the fact that in EMU monetary policy is centralized in the European Central Bank (ECB), acting as agent of European System of Central Banks, while fiscal policy remains decentralized in the competence of the member states. Given that interactions exist between the monetary and fiscal policy areas,[3] coordination is necessary if an appropriate ("optimal") policy mix is to be achieved.

With respect to *regional spillovers* coordination might become necessary in order to avoid fiscal policy activities of one EU Member State to spill over into one or more other EU countries, or decisions taken at the community level might have negative effects on individual regions of the Union (CEPS, 1999, 49).

Conceptually, two different steps of policy coordination can be distinguished, even though in practice these steps might occur simultaneously (Bayer et al., 1998, 7):

A. H. Hallett et al. (eds), Challenges for Economic Policy Coordination with European Monetary Union, 193–200.

- Coordination of fiscal policies between Euro-11 member states, in order to prevent regional spill-overs (Allsopp and Vines, 1996, 96), and in order to determine a common Euro-11 fiscal policy stance as a pre-condition for coordinating fiscal policy at the Euro-11 level with monetary policy; this type of coordination will commonly occur in the Euro-11 meeting and in the Ecofin Council;
- Coordination between the common Euro-11 fiscal policy and the single monetary policy,[4] in order to arrive at an optimal macro-policy mix. This will in general occur in the Euro-11 meeting in the presence of the president of the ECB and/or at the ECB Council meetings when the Euro-11 president participates.[5]

An additional issue is the coordination requirement with respect to the external dimension of EMU, namely exchange rate policy. Here, according to the Treaty, the competence rests with the Council (Art. 111), which must however coordinate with the ECB and work with the Commission. Since the ECB is responsible for monetary policy (which of course has effects on the exchange rate), economic common sense already would call for coordination between these two institutions, so that counter-productive effects (spill-overs) of lone policies are avoided. In spite of the fact that the euro area is a relatively closed economy, with an export share in GDP of around 13%, financial market interlinkages and the volatility of export flows can still exert significant influence on the economic development of the euro area. Estimates by the IMF (1998) and other institutions show that a 15% appreciation of the dollar would lead to extra GDP growth in the euro area of around 1 percentage point and a similar loss in the USA. For this reason, additional coordination among the euro zone and the USA, possibly also including Japan, would be called for, in order to avoid large swings in external balances with their concomitant effects on the stability of the world economy (CEPS, 1999, 44f.)

From the above it can be concluded that coordination of macro-economic policies in EMU is a task for every day. However, most of the analytical discussion on policy coordination so far has centered on high-impact, low-frequency events, e.g., large asymmetric shocks. While there is widespread consensus that in case of such "large" events coordination is required, the case for day-to-day coordination has so far been made less clear.

II. Horizontal Equalization at EU Level

Criticism has been voiced that the EU, and EMU in particular, lack horizontal mechanisms for evening out asymmetric shocks – in contrast to most federal states where equalizing mechanisms exist as a result of burden-sharing agreements between the different levels of government. In Austria, for instance, the distribution of taxes among the three layers of government (federal, state, local level) does not depend on the cyclical situation of the individual state or community, but is defined as shares (usually fixed for a period of 4 years) for each layer of government of certain tax revenues (usually collected at the federal level). Thus, the annual federal income tax share of a given community remains the same whether the community is in depression or in a boom;[6] it depends on the federation's total tax receipts. This provides equalization across communities and states. In the same vain expenditures, e.g., unemployment compensation for unemployed workers in a depressed state do not rise or fall according to each state's cyclical situation, but are individuual entitlements paid by the federally administered unemployment insurance company. When a region is depressed and unemployment is high, this mechanism again boosts income in the region.

In this way, Austrian states and communities are sheltered to some extent from the impacts of asymmetric shocks. The EU does not have such a mechanism available. What the EU has got is the equalization mechanism provided by the Cohesion Fund and the Structural Funds, but this mechanism does not react to different cyclical stances of Member States, nor to asymmetric shocks. Proposals have been made at various times, for instance to introduce a general EU-wide unemployment insurance scheme, which would act as an automatic stabilizer at the EU level. But so far all these proposals have been rejected. On the contrary, the Amsterdam Treaty specifically prohibits the ECB or a national Central Bank to "bail out" the government or the national bank of another country (the "pre-ins" might, however, receive balance-of-payments help by member states in exceptional circumstances). Thereby the pressure on member states to conduct responsible and prudent policies is kept up and the prime objective of EU monetary policy, i.e., maintaining price stability, is not endangered.

At closer inspection it is not really true that in EMU (and in the EU as well) no horizontal equalization mechanism works to shelter member states from asymmetric cyclical downturns or shocks. This argument would only hold if one thinks rigidly in terms of all member states only: There it is clear that no EMU-wide (nor EU-wide) mechanism of that type exists. But also within EMU, in reality the effects of asymmetric shocks or cyclical conditions are in general not spread evenly over the whole area of a state. Such events do not affect one country evenly across its regions and communities. Rather, within each member state, regions and local communities will be affected to different extents by such asymmetric situations, depending on their location, their economic structure, their exposure to foreign trade, etc., thus triggering the member state‘s internal stabilizers. Thinking about this problem in this way, it becomes clear that the need for new EU-wide mechanisms can not be argued with conviction – or at least it is much less urgent than frequently perceived, because member state-specific burden-sharing agreements will mitigate the asymmetric shock or cyclical condition befalling one country.

III. High-Frequency Low Impact Events vs. Low Frequency High Impact Events

Low-frequency, high-profile asymmetric shocks on the supply or demand side dominate the economic discussion about policy coordination in EMU. Much more common, if less visible, however are high-frequency, low-profile events, such as the different cyclical positions of EMU member states, but also symmetric cyclical positions across EMU, e.g., recessions or even slow-downs in growth. Also these require coordination between member states and/or policy fields, in order to arrive at a consistent economic policy-mix. From this it follows that coordination is a daily task, not one restricted to large, rather exceptional events. While it could be argued that coordination for low-frequency, high-impact events could be done on an ad-hoc basis, in each case geared towards the specific case, high-frequency event coordination requires rules-based procedures, such that the necessary tools and procedures are available when needed.

The present cyclical situation of the EMU participants is a case in point: Beginning with the second half of 1998, the European pick-up of growth which started one year earlier has been reversed as a result of the financial turbulences in Asia which had led to contagion in Russia and then later in Latin America. Since about September 1998, annual growth rates of European exports have been negative, putting a prematurely early end to the export-led recovery. The EU Commission, OECD and IMF, as well as individual Member States, in their spring 1999 forecasts, all have revised their EMU and EU growth forecasts for 1999 down by around one percentage point (EC, 1999; OECD, 1999; IMF, 1999). There is wide-spread consensus that this slow-down in growth might just be a "blip", i.e., relatively flat and relatively short-lived. But there are considerable downside risks to these forecasts, depending both on the future development of the still strong U.S. economy and the fear that the effects of the financial market crises around the globe might still not be over. Recently, for Europe the OECD has also pointed to a further negative downside risk of the Kosovo crisis (OECD, 1999c).

At the time of writing, May 1999, there is new hope that growth might pick up again during the latter half of 1999, thus reconfirming the "blip" assumption.

This implies the following for policy coordination:

First, fiscal and monetary authorities at the EU and member states levels must come to an agreement, whether the "blip" hypothesis has high probability, or whether the EU economy is on the verge of a recession. Whatever the outcome of this debate, there seems to be consensus that Europe is dealing with an external symmetric demand shock, reinforced by a slightly positive supply shock (price levels are still falling across Europe).

One policy alternative would be to loosen the stance of monetary policy, while fiscal policy should stay on the course outlined by the member states' stability programs.

If no coordination occurred, the probability is high that the opposite policy mix results, namely that individual euro-zone member states, not being able to influence the single monetary policy to their country's advantage, attempt to alleviate the downward pressure on their economies by loosening fiscal policy, and that, in turn, the ECB then would tighten the monetary policy stance.

Thus, without coordination, the policy mix could turn out to be either overly restrictive or fiscal policy could be too expansionary because of a restrictive monetary policy position, possibly violating the rules of the Stability and Growth Pact.

IV. To Let Automatic Stabilizers Work or Not: Commitment to Stability Pact Objectives is Required

The question of whether in the face of a slow-down in growth EMU countries should let automatic stabilizers work or strictly adhere to their stability program targets was discussed in the relevant EU fora during spring 1999.

To understand this discussion, two things must be kept in mind: One, many euro-zone countries are still in a transitory phase with regard to the medium-term targets of the Stability and Growth Pact (SGP): in 1998, 5 countries (F, D, I, A, P) still had deficit ratios above 2% of GDP – among them the largest euro-zone countries; 3 countries (NL, E, B) had ratios between just below 1% and 2% of GDP, while 3 countries (EIR, L, SF) recorded surpluses.

This means that a majority of 8 countries still had deficit levels that would not shield them from possibly violating the 3% level during longer drawn-out recessions. It is clear that during this transitory phase, before the medium-term targets of the SGP have been reached, the respective countries are in a relatively vulnerable position with respect to recording an excessive deficit in case of recession.

The second issue to be kept in mind is that in 1996 a strong commitment by member governments was made, in the form of the Stability and Growth Pact, to restrain government budgets and thus create conditions favorable to sustained growth and employment. To maintain credibility vis-à-vis the financial markets, especially so shortly after the start of EMU, must be seen as a high-priority policy objective. Otherwise, the whole intricate mechanism outlining the institutional and contractual arrangements for macro-economic policy in EMU might be in jeopardy.

Basically, countries with relatively high deficits (more specifically countries with deficit ratios above around 1 1/2% of GDP) have two fiscal policy options in the face of a slow-down in growth with a high (if not overwhelming) risk of turning into a recession:

- Either to prevent automatic stabilizers from working and to stick strictly to the quantitative deficit targets outlined in the respective Stability Program, even in the face of lower-than-projected growth – and thus increasing the risk of recession by restricting effective domestic demand;
- Or to let automatic stabilizers work and maybe even add discretionary policy measures (a non-compensated tax cut or an increase in transfer payments), in order to boost demand and thus contribute towards stabilizing the cyclical position of the country – but at the risk of approaching or even surpassing the 3% deficit limit and thus risking the triggering of sanctions, since such a situation certainly does not correspond to the definition of extraordinary circumstances or heavy recession mentioned as admissible exceptions in the SGP;
- The third alternative – that the second strategy is followed by member states, the 3% limit is violated, but the SGP rules are not applied – is not considered here, since this would seriously undermine the credibility of the SGP and thus the credibility of the total EMU policy setup.[7]

From the point of view of credibility, both options 1 and 2 are equivalent: In both cases the SGP is upheld, in the first case by adjusting policy such that the sanctions are not triggered, in the second case exactly by the fact that sanctions are triggered, thus signalling to the financial markets that the rules of the SGP are taken seriously and in this way showing that option 3 is not available.

From an economic point of view, the two options have quite different effects, also with respect to the time span they have in mind: The first one gives priority to ex-ante credibility – whatever the risks to short-term growth and employment – thus showing a preference for medium-term targets over short-term ones; The latter gives priority to growth and employment in the short-term, but maintains medium-term credibility by strictly applying the ex-post rules (sanctions) of the SGP.

In both cases, coordination among actors, i.e., among countries and the ECB is preferable to non-coordination, because only with coordination can actions aiming into the same direction be pursued.

The case of non-coordination could run the type of risk that is described in the literature as the unstable equilibrium of a duopoly in which consecutive price undercutting (in pursuit of the objective to gain market shares) will eventually – if no collusion or coordination occurs – lead to bankruptcy of both duopolists. In our case, if fiscal and monetary policies are not coordinated in the face of a slow-down in growth, the consecutive reaction of fiscal and monetary authorities (each counteracting the economic effects of the other) may in turn lead to serious impairments of growth and disruption of the economy (CEPS 1999,42).

V. Streamlining of Procedures

During the run-up to EMU a large number of macroeconomic instruments and procedures has been put in place, such as the monitoring mechanisms of Art. 99,[8] which calls for coordination of economic policy (1), the annual approval by the Council of the Broad Guidelines for Economic Policy (2), the monitoring of policies with respect to the objectives of Art. 2 (3), which can lead to recommendations (4); Art. 100, which stipulates the possibility of certain supportive financial measures by the EU for a member state in trouble (2); Art. 101, which stipulates the non bail-out clause for the ECB or national central banks; Art. 104, which regulates the "excessive deficit procedure"; and based on it the Stability and Growth Pact, including all the procedures and sanctions which can be taken if a national government surpasses the benchmark value for the defict ratio and the debt ratio. Articles 105–124 regulate monetary policy issues.

A large number of instruments is already in place. In addition to macro-policy instruments, the Amsterdam Treaty added a new Title VIII on employment, requiring member states to strive for a coordinated employment strategy (Art. 125), and asking the Community to contribute to a high degree of employment by supporting cooperation between member states (Art. 127). Monitoring exercises (Art 128(4) and Employment Guidelines (128(2)) on which National Action Plans are based complete the employment coordination. The Treaty states, however, that while member states must in their employment policies contribute towards the common objectives of Art. 2, the competence for employment policy remains with the member states (Art. 127(1)).

The coming months will show in how far all these instruments, plus the other procedures put in place by various European Councils, amount to a coherent policy framework. The European Council of Helsinki in December 1999 is required to draw up an assessment of how well policy coordination in EMU is working out. It is very likely that this assessment will conclude that a major streamlining of existing procedures is necessary, that one or the other rule might not be practicable or might need to be altered. There is a strong impression that too many parallel procedures have been installed, that one instrument has been added on top of others, without due regard to the development of a coherent policy framework.

During the discussions which led to the setting up of the macroeconomic policy framework for EMU much attention was paid to the medium term (see e.g., the Stability and Growth Pact), and to large-scale events (e.g., asymmetric shocks, natural disasters, etc.).[9] Reality shows, however, that it is more the everyday management of macroeconomic policy which requires increasing attention of politicians and experts. This means that coordination mechanisms should not be set up and applied in such a way that they fit only singular, relatively rare, events. Rather, they should enable policy makers to exchange opinions, to inform each other on prospective policy actions and their effects and to coordinate policies on a day-by-day basis.

The first really visible test for the applicability of the institutional and regulatory macro-economic policy setup in EMU will come if and when the slow-down in growth will cause one or the other country to surpass the 3% deficit limit. In reality, however, the system is being put to test every day, since policy decisions are made on a day-to-day basis, at the member state level as well as at the community level. So far, the results seem to suggest that the instruments have worked well and coordination has begun to yield satisfactory results. But in the future a lot more needs to be done and more orderly procedures need to be developed, in order to make the institutional system more workable in the everyday management of economic policy and in crises situations. This revamping exercise may also lead to a different weighting of policy objectives.

Notes

1. Among these are: promotion of economic and social progress, a high level of employment, balanced and sustainable growth, strengthening of economic and social cohesion.
2. The discussion will be restricted to the case of "domestic" economic policy, i.e. macropolicy, and disregard the problems arising out of external, i.e., exchange rate policies.
3. The same argument also applies with respect to potential spill-overs from fiscal/monetary policy to employment and structural policies. These issues are not dealt with here.
4. The present discussion avoids the coordination problems arising between the European Central Bank and the European System of Central Banks, which is the topic of the CEPR ECB Monitoring Series (Begg et al., 1998, 1f.).
5. This mutual attendance right is laid down in Art. 113.
6. Unless the community in question is so large that its cyclical position would significantly influence the federal state's economic outcome. For Austria, only Vienna is large enough to yield such an effect.
7. Credibility here is defined in as restricted sense to mean credibility towards the financial market actors. This definition is interpreted to mean that during the initial phase of EMU upholding the medium-term objectives of the SGP is a top priority. This interpretation puts restrictions on the choice of policy options open to EMU member countries. However, credibility in upholding the SGP can mean to things: either to avoid violating it, or to impose the sanctions in case of violation. While for credibility purposes these alternatives may be equivalent, in economic terms they are rather different. In the medium run, once the medium-term objectives of the SGP are fulfilled, the option portfolio will be larger. In addition, after EMU has functioned successfully for a number of years, a review of the policy instruments of the EU Treaty may lead to a rearrangement of instruments.
8. All articles quoted are those of the Treaty of Amsterdam effective as of May 1, 1999.
9. The Stability and Growth Pact has also a significant short-term component, i.e., the annual

budget targets laid down in the stability programs. Part of the present discussion around the optimal policy mix centers on the fact whether – in the face of an unexpected economic downturn – the annual budget targets must be met to the point. The April 1999 acceptance of the Ecofin Council that Italy would be "allowed" a higher than envisaged deficit ratio for 1999 is a case in point. The reaction of the financial markets, as seen by a further slide in the value of the euro vis-à-vis the U.S. dollar and an increasing spread on Italian bond rates may be judged to have been excessive, but again stresses the importance of the self-imposed restrictions on the policy mix which the financial markets attribute to the SGP.

References

Allsopp, Ch. and Vines, D. (1966) 'Fiscal Policy and EMU', *National Institute Economic Review* **4**, 158.

Bayer, Kurt, Katterl, Alfred, and Wieser, Thomas (1998) 'Economic Policy in EMU: National Necessities and Coordination Requirements', Working Papers 1/1998, Federal Ministry of Finance, Vienna.

Bayoumi, T. and Eichengreen, B. (1995) 'Restraining Yourself: The Implications of Fiscal Rules for Economic Stabilization', IMF Staff Papers 42, Washington, D.C.

Begg, D., de Grauwe, P., Giavazzi, F., Uhlig, H. and Wyplosz, Ch. (1998) 'The ECB: Safe at Any Speed?', *Monitoring the European Central Bank*, Vol. 1, Center for Economic Policy Research, London.

Breuss, Fritz (1997) 'Überblick über die theoretischen Überlegungen zur "optimum currency area"', in J. Baumgartner, F. Breuss, H. Kramer, and E. Walterskirchen (eds.), *Auswirkungen der Wirtschafts- und Währungsunion, Österreichisches*, Institut für Wirtschaftsforschung, Wien.

Buti, M., Franco, D. and Ongena, Hedwig (1997) 'Budgetary Policies during Recessions – Retrospective Application of the "Stability and Growth Pact" to the Post-War Period', Economic Papers, Nr. 121, European Commission II/195/97-EN, Brussels.

CEPS (1999) 'Macroeconomic Policy in the First Year of Euroland', 1st Annual Report of the CEPS Macroeconomic Policy Group, Brussels.

European Commission (1997) 'Economic Policy in EMU: Part A: Rules and Adjustment', Economic Papers, Nr. 124, II/0452/97-EN, Brussels.

European Commission (1997b) 'Economic Policy in EMU: Part B: Specific Topics', Economic Papers, Nr. 125, II/0453/97-EN Revised, Brussels.

European Commission (1999) 'Economic Forecasts 1999–2000', Spring 1999, II/137–138/99, Brussels.

von Hagen, Jürgen (1999) 'The EMU's Stability Pact: Flexibility and Effectiveness to Assure Sustainable Public Finances', preliminary paper, Bonn.

IMF (1998) *World Economic Outlook*, International Monetary Fund, May, Washington, D.C.

IMF (1999) *World Economic Outlook*, International Monetary Fund, May, Washington, D.C.

OECD (1999a) *Macroeconomic and Structural Policies for a Successful Monetary Union: An Overview*, ECO/GEN(99)1, Paris.

OECD (1999b) *Economic Outlook 65*,May,Paris.

OECD (1999c) 'Revised Secretariat Projections for OECD Economic Outlook No. 65', Room Document for the Economic Policy Committee No. 1, May 6, Paris.

12. Challenges for International Economic Policy Coordination in EMU

Institutional Setting, Financial Market Reactions and the Importance of Systemic Risk

MARTINE DURAND
Counsellor for Macroeconomic Policies, Economics Department, Organisation for Economic and Co-operation Development (OECD), 2, André Pascal, 75775 Paris Cedex 16, France
E-mail: martine.durand@oecd.org

I. Introduction

The euro area is unique in the sense that it consists of eleven sovereign states with a single currency. Economic policy making powers at the euro-area level differ significantly from those in fully-fledged federations. In particular, while fiscal policy is formulated in the context of the Stability and Growth Pact, virtually all fiscal competencies remain at the national level according to the principle of subsidiarity. By contrast, the European Central Bank (ECB) sets monetary policy for the area as a whole. This new framework raises the issue of co-ordination of policies at the euro-area level. It also raises issues regarding the future relations of the Economic Monetary Union (EMU) with countries outside the area. In this respect, this paper addresses the following two questions:

- What are the risks that the new institutional arrangements put in place in the euro area may generate more unbalanced policies – or make it more difficult to conduct stabilisation policies – than earlier, creating negative international spillovers?
- And related to this, does the new framework imply systemic risks for the functioning of international financial markets?

II. Problems with Conducting Stabilisation Policies in EMU

Whether existing institutional frameworks are conducive to stable policies in all individual EMU countries is of course subject to debate. However, this issue is of particular interest in the case of the euro area as a whole. Because monetary union without full political union or at least some centralisation of fiscal competencies has never been implemented, there are a lot of uncertainties ahead and it is difficult to assess very precisely how effectively economic policy will be conducted in the euro area. The framework put in place in the area has in principle laid the ground for achieving medium term economic stability. In the shorter run, however, some features of this framework may pose problems for the conduct of stabilisation policies. This

A. H. Hallett et al. (eds), Challenges for Economic Policy Coordination with European Monetary Union, 201–205.

in turn is likely to have important consequences for countries outside the area, through exchange rates, trade and financial linkages.

Despite all the preparatory efforts before the start of monetary union, there are inevitably some uncharted waters ahead. A sophisticated institutional framework has been established for conducting monetary and fiscal policy in the euro area. The primary objective of monetary policy is to maintain price stability. The full independence of the European System of Central Banks (ESCB) is likely to reduce problems of time inconsistency, to foster the credibility of policy announcements and to be beneficial for inflation expectations. This is turn should make it more likely to achieve and maintain price stability. The ECB will however face a number of challenges over the coming years. An important one will be to ensure that policy is conducted with a euro-area wide perspective. Risks exist that regional conditions might have an unwarranted influence on monetary policy. Even in the United States, despite the high degree of centralisation of decision making, there is some evidence that local conditions have an influence on the votes of regional banks' presidents. Given its governing structure, the ESCB is even more vulnerable in this regard (Figure 1). The composition of the Governing Council carries the risk that heterogeneity of preferences about the output-inflation trade-off that could result in undue weight being placed on regional conditions. This, in turn, could make for inefficient choices in ECB policies.

The pressures may even intensify if the transmission mechanism has differential effects across the area. There are several potential sources of differential regional responses to a common monetary policy. These include differences in the composition of output; the degree of openness; the level of development and structure of the financial market; sectoral balance-sheet positions; and the flexibility and institutional features of product and labour markets. The exchange rate will also be an important part of the transmission mechanism, and because the euro is a new currency, there are, at this stage, uncertainties as regards the host of forces that will affect its level in international markets, in particular the potential role of the euro as an international currency. Uncertainty about the effects of monetary policy and heterogeneity of preferences could imply that monetary policy is not sufficiently pro-active when this could be needed.

Despite significant progress on budget consolidation in the run-up to EMU, establishing the full ability to pursue counter-cyclical budgetary policies will in most EMU countries require further sustained consolidation efforts in the year ahead if the constraints imposed by the Stability and Growth Pact are to be met. One of the most important problems as regards these constraints is that they focus on actual rather than structural deficits, which could tie governments' hands with regard to fiscal stabilisation policy. Not only do the rules operate to limit the scope for discretionary fiscal expansion during a slowdown, they could also require deliberate contraction, which would even prevent automatic stabilisers from operating. This implies two sorts of risks: (i) that the rules are obeyed, but at a significant cost in foregone output growth; or that (ii) the force of the rules is weakened as sanctions for violations become politicised in interpretation and application.

Elimination of these risks would require that structural deficits fall below the 3% upper limit by a wide enough margin. In view of these considerations the Stability and Growth Pact states that a "close-to-balance" or surplus budgetary stance in the medium term be required in order to provide sufficient scope for flexibility over the cycle. Based on various empirical approaches it seems that a deficit close to balance over the cycle should provide an adequate fiscal cushion necessary to comply with the Stability and Growth Pact's 3% deficit limit in the event of a non-severe recession (Figure 2). But such targets, which are based on the extrapolation of past behaviour, could be subject to greater than usual margins of uncertainty with the new EMU regime. Unless governments display greater fiscal ambition, automatic stabilisers may not be allowed to work fully over the cycle, and the current set-up does not provide incentives for fiscal prudence in good times.

Asymmetric (or country-specific shocks) could also pose a major challenge for stabilisation policy in the euro area. This is because the loss of monetary and exchange rate autonomy in currency union removes one of the main tools for macroeconomic adjustment in what will be regional economies. What is required is an endogenous adjustment in the form of flexible product and labour markets. At this stage, there is no guarantee that EMU will set forces in motion that would automatically lead to a better functioning of euro area labour and product markets. The sooner countries implement policies that foster greater labour market flexibility and strengthen competition, the more prepared they will be to absorb future shocks.

It is of course too early to say whether or not the newly created institutions will successfully meet all these challenges. They will have to be tested in the face of adverse shocks. A further important question is whether more internal EMU coordination would be useful to ensure that the euro-wide policy mix is appropriate. The ECB will be the only European institution with ready control over an area-wide macroeconomic policy instrument. As such, it could become a focus of political pressure for most economic problems that might arise. If the ECB were seen to give in to such pressures, its credibility would be damaged. Moreover policy reforms that are costly or particularly difficult, in particular in the structural area, could be put off.

The Stability and Growth Pact does not address the issue of whether macroeconomic spillovers in EMU are important enough to justify additional co-ordination of policies over the cycle, and this remains an open issue. In part, it will depend on the economic nature of the shock encountered. If the shock is country-specific (i.e. asymmetric), the appropriate instrument is national fiscal policy, and there is no clear case for co-ordination. If the shock is euro-area wide (i.e. symmetric), and has implications for price developments, the primary instrument should be monetary policy. There is a strong case for co-ordination if spillovers between monetary and fiscal policies are significant. This is more likely to be the case when large euro-area economies, or a number of small economies simultaneously adjust fiscal policy, since their actions may have an impact on euro-area wide activity and inflation prospects to prompt a monetary policy response. There is also a strong case for co-ordinating structural policies. This will enable wage and price formation to adjust more quickly to changing circumstances and significantly increase the monetary and fiscal room for manoeuvre.

In principle, the institutions and processes for co-ordinating macroeconomic and structural policy are already well in place. First, the excessive budgetary procedure brings significant peer pressure to bear on budget policies. Second, there are the Broad Economic Guidelines which allow the Council to make country-specific recommendations on both macro-economic and structural policies, and which reflect the Community's policy consensus. Third, there is the high level technical group of the Economic and Financial Committee and the high-level political Euro 11 group. Practical difficulties in co-ordinating policies exist nonetheless. One such difficulty is that the euro area is characterised by a complex decision making process that requires qualified majority voting or unanimity in order to implement common policies or act on the recommendations of the Commission. This could in some situations make it difficult to achieve an appropriate policy mix given the diverse preferences and economic sizes of EU countries. This may in the end show up in large exchange rate fluctuations between the euro and other main currencies. These fluctuations will act as a stabiliser but they may also lead to unhelpful turbulence in financial markets, as well as having adverse cyclical effects and perhaps giving rise to protectionist pressures.

III. Systemic Financial Market Risks

Another important risk of international spillover relates to the functioning of international financial markets. The ECB is not entrusted with any general responsibility related to prudential supervision of credit institutions, and the stability of the financial system lies with competent national authorities (including, in most European countries, the National Central Banks). The separation of the two functions of monetary policy and banking supervision implies a high degree of independence of monetary policy from the stability needs of the financial sector. Although no explicit reference is made in the Maastricht Treaty to the role of the ESCB as a lender of last resort, responsibility is given to the ESCB in promoting the smooth operation of payment systems, including the provision of financing facilities to credit institutions, giving it a role of lender of last resort as far as the provision of short-term liquidity through the marginal lending facility is concerned. For interventions beyond the provision of short-term liquidity, other competent national institutions are responsible.

National Central Banks (NCBs) are likely to play an important role in European banking supervision. Although recently there has been a trend towards a separation of regulatory and monetary policy responsibilities, it is always the case that at least a working relationship exists between bank supervision, the monetary authorities and policy makers. These relationships will have to adapt in the face of the changing environment. The greater integration of Europe's banking and securities markets is reflected in increased collaboration among NCBs within the Banking Supervision Committee. Regulators will have to rely increasingly on information from their counterparts in order to understand market developments. While significant progress in the areas of exchange of data and information as well as harmonization of statistics has been made, further efforts, e.g., regarding harmonization of accounting standards, would be helpful so that a Europe-wide perspective could be adopted.

Although the costs of financial institution rescues will continue to be borne by national authorities, the trend towards greater financial integration will make it increasingly difficult to establish national dividing lines. Even when a banking-sector problem can be identified as a national one, it may quickly become European in scope, warranting action by European institutions. This increases the importance of co-ordination, both among national banking supervision authorities and between them and the ESCB, with regard to policy interventions aimed at ensuring financial stability. Already there is a high degree of co-operation at the working level within committees at the ECB as well as in international fora like the BIS. In this regard it is of vital importance to ensure that there will be sufficient flexibility to react swiftly to events.

A major challenge in the years ahead will be to prevent the realisation of risks of the type mentioned above and of the associated negative external spillovers. Policy makers in the euro area have the main responsibility in this respect, but no doubt policy makers in the United States, Japan and other countries outside the euro area will express interest in discussing and perhaps influencing euro area policy orientations in order to minimise their negative external implications. Such a policy dialogue is important, and the advent of EMU raises a number of new issues as regards how best international co-ordination should be conducted.

References

Barran, F., Coudert, V. and Mojon, B. (1996) 'The Transmission of Monetary Policy in the European Countries', CEPII Working Paper, No. 96–03.

Buiter, W.H. (1998) 'Independence of the ECB Likely to be Perverted if Council Voting is Secret', Letter to the Editor of the Financial Times, September 24.

Dalsgaard, T. and De Serres, A. (1999) 'Estimating Prudent Budgetary Margins for 11 EU Countries: A Simulated SVAR Model Approach', OECD Economics Working Paper, No. 216.

Dornbusch, R., Favero, C. and Giavazzi, F. (1998) 'Immediate Challenges for the European Central Bank', in Begg et al. (eds.), *EMU Prospects and Challenges for the Euro*, Blackwell Publishers, Oxford.

European Monetary Institute (1997a) *The Single Monetary Policy in Stage Three – Specification of the Operational Framework*, Frankfurt a.M..

European Monetary Institute (1997b) *The Single Monetary Policy in Stage Three – Elements of the Monetary Policy Strategy of the ESCB*, Frankfurt a.M.

Funke, N. and Kennedy, M. (1997) 'International Implications of European Economic and Monetary Union', OECD Economics Department Working Paper, No. 174.

Gerlach, S. and Smets, F. (1995) 'The Monetary Transmission: Evidence from G-7 Countries', CEPR Discussion Paper, No. 1219.

Hagen, J. von and Eichengreen, B (1996) 'Federalism, Fiscal Restraints and European Monetary Union', *American Economic Association Papers and Proceedings* **86**(2), 134–137.

Hoeller, P., Louppe, M.-O. and Vergriete, P. (1996) 'Fiscal Relations within the European Union', OECD Economics Department Working Paper, No. 163.

OECD (1999) 'Challenges for Monetary and Fiscal Policies in the Euro Area', *OECD Economic Outlook* **64**, 137–162.

OECD (1999) *EMU Facts, Challenges and Policies*, Paris, France.

Pisani-Ferry, J., Italianer, A. and Lescure, R. (1993) 'Stabilization Properties of Budgetary Systems: A Simulation Analysis', *European Economy, Reports and Studies*.

Sachs, J. and Sala-i-Martin, X. (1992) 'Fiscal Federalism and Optimum Currency Areas: Evidence for Europe from the United States', in M.B. Canzoneri, V. Grilli and P.R. Masson (eds.), *Establishing a Central Bank: Issues in Europe and Lessons from the U.S.*, Cambridge University Press, Cambridge.

Tootel, G.M.B. (1991) 'Regional Economic Conditions and the FOMC Votes of District Presidents', *New England Economic Review*, March-April, 316.

Visco, I. (1998) 'Should Economic Policies be Co-ordinated for EMU?', *OECD Observer*, No. 215.

13. Co-ordinating Stability: Some Remarks on the Roles of Monetary and Fiscal Policy under EMU

BERNHARD WINKLER*
European Central Bank, DG Research, Kaiserstrasse 29, D-60311 Frankfurt, Germany
E-mail: bernhard.winkler@ecb.int

I. Introduction

Only a few months into Stage Three of Economic and Monetary Union in Europe (EMU) the issue of policy co-ordination looms large both on the agenda of European policy makers and in the academic debate. Calls for enhanced policy co-ordination have long been a routine ingredient of Sunday speeches and summit declarations. One possible reason why the notion of co-ordination has proved attractive is the vagueness of the concept as used in the policy context. A second reason is that the term co-ordination usually carries a positive connotation. This is also a legacy of the academic literature, where – at least for the simple two player models used initially – co-ordination is "always good", i.e. welfare improving, almost by definition. Both features, a lack of clarity of what is meant by co-ordination paired with an unreflected "pro co-ordination bias" are also present in the current European debate.

One purpose of section two of this paper is to try to redress that imbalance. In doing so the paper may admittedly err somewhat on the sceptical side. Nevertheless, economists and policymakers should not really need a reminder to be suspicious of "free lunches", including those that seem to be promised by policy co-ordination. Therefore, a meaningful discussion of policy co-ordination in practice should feature both benefits and potential costs attached to it. To this end the problem of policy co-ordination needs to be placed in the broader context of the efficient assignment of tasks and responsibilities among separate actors, and it has to be recognised that problems of information and incentives in the policy process mean that in practice policy makers have enough difficulties to implement "individually sound", let alone "optimally co-ordinated" policies.

Recognising the limits to and the preconditions for successful co-ordination does not mean that the widespread concern over policy co-ordination in EMU is misplaced. The crucial question, however, is how can co-ordinated policy *outcomes* be best achieved. The basic allocation of responsibilities under the "Maastricht assignment" and the incentive and co-ordination mechanisms currently in place – if applied properly – may already go a long way towards producing desirable macroeconomic outcomes. The paper takes the view that what is required first and foremost in a

*Submission to EMPIRICA as part of the VOWA workshop on policy co-ordination OeNB, Vienna, 22 January 1999.

A. H. Hallett et al. (eds), Challenges for Economic Policy Coordination with European Monetary Union, 207–214.

new environment such as EMU is for policymakers to fully accept and learn to live with the "Maastricht rules of the game" and embrace the "stability culture" which underlies them (Winkler, 1996). This approach should already afford a high degree of *implicit* co-ordination. By contrast, premature attempts at additional *explicit* and "discretionary" forms of policy co-ordination could in many cases undermine the incentives and the co-ordination properties inherent in the clear division of responsibilities and the primarily rules-based approach of the Treaty.

These concerns are particularly acute in the interaction of the single monetary policy with national fiscal policies discussed in section three. Calls for policy co-ordination in this dimension are based on the correct but rather diffuse perception that the new single currency binds European policymakers together and requires a common sense of responsibility in a qualitatively different way than before. However, the common purpose need not necessarily be best served by co-ordination. On the contrary, to make monetary union a success policymakers at the national level need to clearly and genuinely accept the constraint that a single and a stable currency – safeguarded by an independent central bank – represents for their behaviour and concentrate on playing their own parts within the overall Treaty framework for economic stability.

II. Co-ordination in Context

In the simplest textbook models the rationale for international policy co-ordination is clear. It appears to be always beneficial if policy makers take economic linkages which affect each others' objectives (so-called "spillovers") into account and effectively get together to maximise joint welfare. Thus policy co-ordination seems to be "always good" by definition. However, at least since the seminal paper by Rogoff (1985) even the theoretical case for co-ordination is no longer clear-cut in the presence of further distortions in the economy, such as credibility problems of monetary policy. More generally, (partial) co-ordination among a subset of players or policy areas can quite easily turn out to be counter-productive, a result which invokes a similarity to the general theorem of the second best in welfare economics. This is a first reason to be rather cautious before applying the literature to practical policy making.

The simplest co-ordination story side-steps a number of further critical issues for practical policy making, such as model uncertainty, potential inefficiencies and costs of bargaining and agreeing on co-ordinated policies (and distributing the associated gains) and, finally, the question of how any such policy bargains – once agreed – can be effectively implemented and enforced, given that incentives for unilateral deviations would normally exist. This is not the place to review the extensive literature that has started to deal with these various issues. Nevertheless, it is important to keep in mind for the purpose of this paper that all these considerations already point to the need for careful analysis of benefits *and* costs of co-ordination and to the importance of information and incentive problems in this context. Under such circumstances ambitious efforts at textbook-type policy co-ordination can indeed turn out to be ineffective, even harmful and often unnecessary.

Against this background this paper proposes to place the problem of policy co-ordination in a much broader context. The standard analysis of policy co-ordination starts with a *given* assignment of policy objectives and instruments. Instead, the problem of policy co-ordination can be regarded as embedded in and conditional on the prior question of the "assignment problem", i.e. the allocation of objectives and instruments among policy makers. Under an efficient initial policy assignment the need for additional *explicit* and "activist" co-ordination beyond the *implicit* co-ordination of behaviour induced by an appropriate and clear allocation of policy functions and incentive structures may already be rather limited. In other words, shaping the "rules of the game" appropriately may reduce spillovers and obviate the need to intervene during the course of the game itself.

A further way to think of "implicit co-ordination" is as the pre-game influences that have a bearing on equilibrium selection, i.e. help economic agents to pick out focal points among multiple equilibria. This type of co-ordination, which may be achieved by a common "culture", shared understanding and history of play (Kreps, 1990), may in fact be much more important than the standard co-ordination problem, which internalises spillovers in moving from a Nash equilibrium to a co-operative solution. A clear allocation of responsibilities, guidance from simple rules, a high degree of transparency or a shared "stability culture" should be favourable to such implicit co-ordination. This kind of co-ordination will be particularly important in the early years of EMU as economic agent and policymakers have to adapt to the new environment. Attempts at discretionary and explicit co-ordination subject to multilateral bargaining, by contrast, could render implicit co-ordination and speedy learning more difficult.

Moreover, various forms of explicit or implicit policy co-ordination can be usefully understood as "intermediate solutions" along a spectrum between the extremes of complete decentralisation of policy choices and full integration. There are two dimensions of integration. First, the degree of (vertical) centralisation within a given policy domain and, second, the degree of functional (horizontal) specialisation within a given jurisdiction. The literature on fiscal federalism is an example of the first dimension of the assignment problem, the theory of central bank independence deals with the second aspect.

In both dimensions, an "optimal" degree of centralisation would have to balance the benefits and costs from internalising policy spillovers and transforming external into internal co-ordination (and enforcement) problems. Costs of incentive provision, information aggregation and processing, complex decision making under bounded rationality and other "transaction costs" would be important determinants of the geographical and functional allocation of policy tasks to various actors.[1] On these grounds the delegation of precise, limited and well-defined tasks to separate agencies or to a level of decision making that can be easily monitored by the public would tend to be superior to diffuse or "far-removed" responsibilities. Also reflecting concerns over democratic accountability, the subsidiarity principle of the Maastricht Treaty establishes a decentralisation bias which places the burden of proof on those arguing for greater centralisation. The same set of arguments also has a bearing on the choice of the various forms of co-ordination. These can be classified according to the degree of commitment they imply (or rather presuppose) ranging from the mere informal exchange of views and information to formal sanction mechanisms of various severity. Furthermore, forms of co-ordination can also be distinguished along the spectrum of rules versus discretion (case-by-case co-ordination).[2]

It is by no means evident that intermediate forms of co-ordination would tend to be superior to the extremes of complete integration or decentralisation, perhaps complemented by a set of additional rules or constraints. Once it is realised that policy makers (and national economies) due to information and incentive problems and a host of other economic and political distortions in practice operate far away from any "Pareto-frontier" making improvements in the direction of "good" or "sound" policies will in fact be the prime concern. Thus there is a risk of sizeable adverse side effects on "sound" domestic policies from the pursuit of small, perhaps elusive, second-order gains from the co-ordination of "optimal policies" at the margin. Explicit co-ordination may then become harmful if it dilutes and undermines incentives for "sound" individual policies and induces additional transaction costs while at the same time suffering from enforcement problems – unlike stronger forms of integration.

Looking at the same problem from a slightly different angle, a complete analysis of the benefits and costs of policy co-ordination in a world characterised by a host of distortions needs to be alert to both market failure and government failure. Thus, even if markets – which can themselves be regarded as a prime co-ordination device among separate economic agents – do not function well and the inefficiencies cannot be addressed at source this does not by itself provide a sufficient case for government intervention, let along co-ordinated intervention. Moreover, efforts at policy co-ordination could in some circumstances weaken beneficial forces of competition among policy makers or work in the direction of undercutting the markets' monitoring role, both of which may be important vehicles for encouraging better individual policy performance. Thus there could sometimes be a tension between the respective merits of co-ordination and competition, where again overly ambitious co-ordination could turn out to prove counter-productive and harmful for welfare over the longer run.

III. The Roles of the Single Monetary Policy and National Fiscal Policies under EMU

With respect to the elements of a cost-benefit analysis of co-ordination sketched out in the previous section, it is clear that the European Union has developed a multi-layered complex framework for co-ordination across a wide range of policy areas and with varying degrees of intensity. As such the conditions for sustaining co-operative arrangements are certainly in general much more favourable than would be the case for international policy co-ordination elsewhere (say among the G7). Ongoing interaction over time and over multiple policy areas is conducive to developing trust and reputation, which in turn can enforce explicit or implicit forms of co-operation. A large stock of common interests and shared objectives will by itself often lead to co-ordinated behaviour and may in fact allow a more decentralised pursuit of common objectives than would otherwise be the case.

On the other hand, the complex web of policy responsibilities in Europe – as a construction *sui generis*, which is more than a loose federation of nation states but far from a unified federal entity – also creates particular challenges for accountability and appropriate incentive structures. In this context the notion of co-ordination is prone to be (ab-)used to divert and dilute individual responsibilities. Trying to enlist others in support of one's own objectives is inherent in the idea of policy co-ordination but it may be harmful if it distracts attention and shifts the blame for one's own policy mistakes elsewhere. Given concerns over information, incentives and accountability, a clear division of responsibilities and a largely decentralised allocation may indeed lead to superior results compared to explicit co-ordination or centralisation. As long as political integration remains limited and the fundamental locus of accountability remains primarily at the national level the Maastricht set-up of an isolated "double transfer of sovereignty" (Winkler, 1998) in the monetary field delegated to an independent and European institution underpinned by a set of rules and constraints on national policymakers may be superior to more ambitious forms of across-the-board co-ordination.

Before discussing the issue of potential fiscal-monetary co-ordination problems the rationale for functional and institutional separation between the two policy areas has to be recalled. The case for central bank independence is an example of the benefits of delegation and functional separation with respect to a well-defined and narrow objective, which ultimately best serves society's wider goals. The need (or otherwise) for enhanced policy co-ordination in EMU must therefore be assessed against the background of the basic division of responsibilities foreseen in the Treaty in order to achieve the shared Community objectives. In this context the Treaty has assigned the maintenance of price stability as the primary objective of monetary policy to an independent central bank precisely because in this way monetary policy can make its best contribution towards the wider Community objectives including growth and employment. In the logic of the Treaty fiscal authorities and social partners, by contrast, carry the prime responsibility for growth and employment.

One way to think about the implicit co-ordination properties of the Maastricht assignment of objectives is as a Stackelberg equilibrium in the context of strategic interaction between monetary and fiscal policy makers (Artis and Winkler, 1998). If monetary authorities can credibly pre-commit to the maintenance of price stability, this commitment will then taken as given by other policymakers who act as Stackelberg followers. This set-up, complemented by the constraints of the Stability and Growth Pact, seeks to limit policy conflicts and uncertainty, avoid "leadership battles" and ensure a favourable regime of "monetary dominance" characterised by price stability and fiscal prudence in the terminology of Canzoneri and Diba (1996), drawing on work by Woodford (1996). An independent central bank committed to the maintenance of price stability, at least in the presence of additional constraints on fiscal policy, could thus avoid the trap of the "unpleasant monetarist arithmetic" (Sargent and Wallace, 1981), which forces the central bank to monetise debt in order to guarantee the government's intertemporal solvency. In a similar way credible "monetary leadership" may be helpful in co-ordinating economic agents' responses to shocks and align expectations (especially of wage bargaining and financial markets), thereby reducing economic uncertainty and inducing a favourable "policy mix".

The Treaty therefore, for good reasons, places great emphasis on central bank independence and has assigned monetary policy the clear and limited primary objective of maintaining price stability. The ECB's stability-oriented monetary policy strategy provides a quantitative definition of price stability, which should serve as an anchor for expectations over the medium term and thus help economic agents and policymakers co-ordinate and plan their activities. The Stability and Growth Pact including the multi-annual stability programmes and in conjunction with the broad economic guidelines, if credibly adhered to, also represents a stability-oriented medium term commitment and should likewise stabilise expectations and favour implicit co-ordination among economic agents and policymakers. The single monetary policy and national fiscal policies are therefore each placed in a clearly defined stability-framework, which should reduce policy uncertainty. The (implicit) co-ordination achieved in this way is especially crucial after a regime change such as the move to Stage Three of EMU and under the conditions of a multi-country policy process.

The stark asymmetry between a single European monetary policy and continued national responsibilities for most other areas of economic policies is nevertheless often regarded as an anomaly that needed to be ameliorated through greater co-ordination. Here the case for greater co-ordination within a given policy area, such as between national fiscal policies, must be clearly distinguished from co-ordination that seeks to involve separate areas like monetary and fiscal policies (and/or wage policies). The need to limit spillovers from undisciplined fiscal policies on each other and on the aggregate outlook for price stability requires some form of co-ordination among Member States and, in particular, a commitment to adhere to the letter and the spirit of the rules and multilateral surveillance procedures enshrined in the Stability and Growth Pact. If credible, the constraints of the SGP will at the same time limit the burden on the single monetary policy and thus also contribute to implicit co-ordination between monetary and fiscal policies in EMU (Artis and Winkler, 1998).

Under the single currency monetary policy can only be geared to aggregate conditions and must always be set to safeguard the maintenance of price stability. Under the constraint of a single monetary policy it is therefore more important than ever to strengthen the operation of market mechanisms and the flexibility of remaining national policy instruments in response to local economic conditions and asymmetric shocks. If there is sufficient room for markets and automatic stabilisers to operate at the national level cross-border spillovers from fiscal policies may be rather limited and perhaps even of uncertain sign (Eichengreen, 1997) and thus render additional co-ordination largely superfluous. Worse, fiscal policy co-ordination may in fact weaken the disciplining effects of monetary union (Beetsma and Bovenberg, 1998) and could also undermine the beneficial effects of the constraints embodied in the Stability and Growth Pact (Beetsma and Uhlig, 1999).

The ECB attaches great importance to conveying to the wider public its assessment of economic developments and their impact on the outlook for price stability in line with its monetary policy strategy and to doing so in a clear, transparent and timely fashion. Establishing an additional and direct channel of communication with other policymakers for the regular exchange of views and information ("dialogue") could be helpful if this improves the mutual understanding of the respective roles in the European economic policy process. Great care must be taken, however, to ensure that such dialogue does not dilute the respective responsibilities for autonomous policy choices and does not create the impression of undue interference in the autonomous exercise of these choices. By contrast, any form of co-ordination that goes further and would seek to commit the ECB *ex ante* to any particular course of action would be incompatible with the letter and the spirit of the Treaty, since it could compromise the ECB's credibility and freedom to act in fulfilling its mandate.

If the Treaty's clear division of primary responsibilities is recognised and the ECB's commitment to price stability taken as given, other policy makers should find it in their own interest – individually or collectively – to conduct policies conducive to price stability, non-inflationary growth and a benign "policy-mix". By contrast, attempts at explicit policy co-ordination which seeks to involve monetary and fiscal policies – by mixing responsibilities – may result in additional uncertainties in the policy making environment. If the basic assignment of tasks across policymakers is sound, then – put slightly provocatively – the best form of co-ordination may indeed be "no co-ordination" over and above a regular dialogue which clarifies the respective roles and objectives in a framework of macroeconomic stability.

Notes

* I thank, without implicating, Vítor Gaspar, Alexander Jung, Klaus Masuch and Tommaso Padoa-Schioppa for helpful discussions on the topic of the paper. The paper partly draws on ideas developed more extensively in Artis and Winkler (1998). Any views expressed are the author's own and do not necessarily reflect those ofthe European Central Bank.

1. There is a clear analogy to the concerns of the literature on the economics of organisations and the theory of the firm and managerial incentives (e.g. Milgrom and Robers, 1990).
2. For a more extensive discussion of various forms of policy co-ordination in the European context see T. Padoa-Schioppa (1999).

References

Artis, M. and Winkler, B. (1998) 'The Stability Pact: Safeguarding the Credibility of the European Central Bank', *National Institute Economic Review*, January, 87–98.

Beetsma, R. and Bovenberg, L. (1998) 'Monetary Union Without Fiscal Coordination May Discipline Policymakers', *Journal of International Economics* **45**, 239–258.

Beetsma, R. and Uhlig, H. (1999) 'An Analysis of the Stability Pact', *Economic Journal*, forthcoming.

Canzoneri, M. and Diba, B.T. (1996) 'Fiscal Constraints on Central Bank Independence and Price Stability', *CEPR Discussion Paper* 1463.

Eichengreen, B. (1997) 'Saving Europe's Automatic Stabilisers', *National Institute Economic Review* **159**(1/97), 92–98.

Jensen, H. (1996) 'The Advantage of International Fiscal Cooperation under Alternative Monetary Regimes', *European Journal of Political Economy* **12**, 485–504.

Kreps, D. (1990) 'Corporate Culture and Economic Theory', in J.E. Alt and K.A. Shepsle (eds.), *Perspectives on Positive Political Economy*, MIT Press: Cambridge, Mass., 258–281.

Milgrom, P. and J. Roberts (1992) *Economics, Organization and Management*, Harvester Wheatsheaf: Hemel Hampstead.

Rogoff, K. (1985b) 'Can International Monetary Policy Coordination be Counterproductive?', *Journal of International Economics* **18**, 199–217.

Padoa-Schioppa, T. (1999) 'Europe's New Economic Policy Constitution', in *Will EMU Lead to a European Economic Government?*, Centre for European Reform, London, 15–28.

Sargent, T. and Wallace, N. (1981) 'Some Unpleasant Monetarist Arithmetic', *Quarterly Review*, Federal Reserve Bank of Minneapolis (Fall), 1–17.

Winkler, B. (1996) 'Towards a Strategic View on EMU: A Critical Survey', *Journal of Public Policy* **16**, 1–28.

Winkler, B. (1998) 'The Political Economy of European Monetary Union: Between Economic Logic and Political Imperatives', in A. Cafruny and P. Peters (eds.), *The Union and the World*, Kluwer: Dordrecht, 191–208.

Woodford, M. (1996) 'Control of the Public Debt: a Prerequisite for Price Stability?', *NBER Working Paper 5684*.

Index

MIX
Papier aus verantwortungsvollen Quellen
Paper from responsible sources
FSC® C105338

If you have any concerns about our products,
you can contact us on
ProductSafety@springernature.com

In case Publisher is established outside the EU,
the EU authorized representative is:
Springer Nature Customer Service Center GmbH
Europaplatz 3, 69115 Heidelberg, Germany

Printed by Libri Plureos GmbH
in Hamburg, Germany